THOSE PEOPLE AT THAT CHURCH

THE ST. FRANCIS LUTHERAN

COOKBOOK

To guy
with thanks for
good food &
friendship
we have about
eleven or so
recipes in the book.
Bon appetit

Morti & Jack
Larson

Recipes, reflections and prayers from a close-knit family of friends
who gather at their small, historic, red-brick neighborhood church
in the heart of San Francisco to rejoice, remember and renew—
always with laughter, love and lots of good food.

Compiled and edited by
Wayne A. Strei

ST. FRANCIS LUTHERAN CHURCH
San Francisco, California

First published in November 1994

Copyright © 1994 by St. Francis Lutheran Church

Cover photography © 1994 by Joyce Oudkerk Pool

Printed on recycled paper in the United States of America by
Waller Press, South San Francisco, California.

Library of Congress Catalog Card Number: 94-92248

ISBN 0-9642337-1-1

Cover and book design by Alice Harth Graphic Design
Technical and design assistance: Meredith Karns, M. Kathleen Kelly,
Will Clayton and Peter Chang.
Photographic assistance: Max Kirkeberg

St. Francis Lutheran Church, 152 Church Street,
San Francisco, California 94114-1111

Recycled
Paper

It is the same light that graces the dawn, blazes at noon, and bows to the evening shadows. Daily our world is enlivened by its face-to-face encounter with the sun's warmth and brilliance. Nightly our world turns away, kindling the light as a memory and a promise. Yet, we never forfeit the covenant of light to accompany and preserve us. The moon and stars woo our dreams and the cold is held at bay. In truth, the light never leaves us— even in the darkest night. So it is with the communion of God's saints.

Pastor Phyllis Zillhart

In tribute
to all the saints
of
St. Francis
Lutheran Church
San Francisco
California

*before, now
and forever …*

v

CONTENTS

Through thick and thin, hot and cold … A bowl for all seasons, from Dutch Pea and Eight Bean to Gazpacho and Cucumber-Yogurt. Suitable before the meal or as the meal. Just pass the bread!

Leaf through a field of greens. And reds. Fruits and nuts. Where the slaw is hot, the chicken curried and tradition is tossed with cracked pepper. Simple (Hot Slaw) or stoic (Classic Caesar), you'll always be well-dressed.

Who can sleep? Rise, shine and eat. Over coffee, indulge in fresh muffins, breads or biscotti. An omelet here, a pancake there. No hurry. In fact, pick a time zone—Chinese Chicken Tacos to Swiss Egg Puffs.

A time for sacrament and celebration. Spring is in the air and food is on the table. Lamb, perhaps, with fresh biscuits and vegetables. And desserts, from a Mom or from a friend. A new recipe, served with love and poppy seeds.

Almost twenty chefs have gathered for a game of culinary roulette. Right here starting on page 71 they present their favorite party dishes, secret recipes and all. It's your party, and you don't even have to clean up. Yet.

Who doesn't love a dinner party? The wine, the laughter, the lavish compliments for the host or hostess. And the food? Exceptional. One question—was it dinner for six at 8, or dinner for eight at 6?

Among the three most enticing, inviting and indulgent words in the English language: Preheat the oven. For soon emerge cookies and brownies, toffees and pralines. Serve warm. Pack in a lunchbox. And always freeze some, just in case of emergency.

PROLOGUE

Welcome to *Those People At That Church*, a collection of recipes from San Francisco's St. Francis Lutheran Church members, families and friends, as well as San Francisco Bay Area chefs, restaurants and food professionals. This urban cookbook emphasizes the cultural diversity and fascination with food for which San Francisco is famous.

ABOUT THE BOOK

The more than 200 recipes that follow are divided into chapters that reflect the lives of members and friends during a year at St. Francis Lutheran Church. We include *Soup's On* and *Salad Plates* which, although modestly titled, incorporate delicious variations on uncomplicated themes. *Weekend Brunch* includes recipes for those too busy to make breakfast during the week. *Bake Sales* and *Potluck Potpourri* are carry-overs from our past which we embrace wholeheartedly in our present. *Dinner Table* encompasses ideas for those special days when you can spend some quality time cooking for family and friends, while *Supper Dishes* includes those quick, last-minute comfort foods for quick sustenance or easy get-togethers. *Easter Celebrations* includes recipes that utilize the fresh fruits and vegetables of spring, while *Giving Thanks* contains not only suggestions for your Thanksgiving table and variations on traditional pumpkin pie, but lots of new ideas for autumn's bountiful harvest. *Merry Christmas* brings you tasty wishes for happy holidays, and *Party Flavors* offers opportunities to sample hors d'oeuvres and appetizers from around the world. *Sweet Inspirations* are truly inspired pies, tarts and cakes, while *Edible Heirlooms* chronicles family legacies and cultural gifts handed down from generation to generation, loved one to loved one.

All recipes contained in this book have been tested by members and friends of St. Francis Lutheran Church. Some were analyzed in private homes, others at potluck parties in the church parish hall or in members' homes. Sometimes a group of people gathered in marathon cooking sessions to create meals for our beloved family of friends. To test holiday recipes we even threw ourselves a Christmas party—in July! Such is the enthusiasm of *Those People At That Church*.

Because we live in California, where we have year-round access to fresh fruits, vegetables and herbs, our recipes usually list fresh ingredients first followed by frozen, canned, dried or other alternatives. However, on occasion we do recommend canned and frozen foods or even cake mixes!

The Prayer of St. Francis of Assisi, echoed line by line at the start of each chapter, has special meaning for us at St. Francis Lutheran. Not only is St. Francis the patron saint of San Francisco, but in 1964 he became the namesake of our new congregation following the merger of Ansgar Lutheran Church (Danish) and Gethsemane Lutheran Church (Finnish). The words of his well-known prayer are as relevant today as they were when they were written. Throughout the book you will also find reflections, prayers and anecdotes which introduce you to members of our congregation and ministries of our church. These comments let you know something about the variety of our lives and the issues which concern us all. By sharing our thoughts as well as our recipes we hope to reveal something of ourselves, by providing a glimpse into our hearts as well as our kitchens.

ABOUT ST. FRANCIS LUTHERAN CHURCH

Those People At That Church is more than an ordinary church cookbook because St. Francis Lutheran is an extraordinary church. St. Francis Lutheran is a small, red-brick neighborhood church which sits in the heart of San Francisco, four subway stops from the city's financial district and three blocks from Castro Street, the bustling center of America's gay and lesbian community. Our building was dedicated by Danish immigrants just twelve days before the 1906 earthquake and was honored as San Francisco Historical Landmark No. 39 in 1971. Since the turn of the century the city has grown to encompass our church, just as the surrounding community—including nearby Castro Street—embraces the church itself.

Our congregation of about 150 people is committed to caring for our neighborhood and its people. We are teachers and secretaries and nurses and lawyers. We are young and old, coupled and single, gay and lesbian and straight. We are a family of choice, a church very much of our time and place. Members of our congregation have found a strong sense of community and purpose in the work of St. Francis Lutheran Church.

Our efforts are not without controversy. In 1990, St. Francis Lutheran ordained an openly lesbian couple, Ruth Frost and Phyllis Zillhart, and another San Francisco congregation, First United Lutheran, ordained Jeff Johnson, an openly gay man. That summer the congregations were put on ecclesiastical trial and subsequently suspended by our parent denomination the Evangelical Lutheran Church in America (ELCA). We will be expelled at the end of 1995 if the church has not changed its policy regarding the ordination of openly gay and lesbian pastors or we have not rescinded the calls to Pastors Frost and Zillhart. On August 28, 1994, the congregation voted unanimously to extend a permanent full-time call to Pastor Phyllis Zillhhart and a permanent part-time call to Pastor Ruth Frost.

The suspension generated much attention. A flood of media stories led to a stream of curious visitors to St. Francis Lutheran. They came to see who we were and what the fuss was all about. Some came to confront, many came to celebrate, others to join. But to the rest of the city and the world we remain "those people at that church."

ACKNOWLEDGEMENTS

The gifts and talents of many people have made this project possible. Thank you to everyone who contributed recipes—people from our congregation, their families and friends, and the food professionals of the San Francisco Bay Area; the Cookbook Committee, a talented and dedicated group of writers, editors, recipe testers, fundraisers and friends, consisting of Erna Dennert, Paul Groth, Beverly Hines, Max Kirkeberg, Jack and Marti Lundin, Mark Pritchard and Michael Utech; the "Kitchen Cabinet" of Barbara Genay, Dale Leininger, Peter Quam and Michael Wilde, who offered encouragement, enthusiasm and support; key advisors and "master chefs," especially Kirsten Havrehed, Micheal Hiller, Alejandro Cejudo, Arthur Morris, Parker Nolen and others who just needed to be asked to come up with yet another favorite recipe; and Pastor Phyllis Zillhart, Erna Dennert, Hanna Nowakowski, Dale Johnson, Greg Egertson, Michael Hiller, Mark Scott Johnson, Mari Irvin, Bev Ovrebo, Jack Kling, Bob Crumb and Jeannine Janson for writing the community prayers used in the chapter introductions.

We also owe many thanks to Jane Tritipo for her words of encouragement and advice; Michelle Schmidt and Ann Segerstrom for their assistance in selecting and editing the recipes; Marlena Spieler for her assorted scribblings and invaluable help with recipe editing and selection; Val Robichaud for copy editing, writing the chapter introductions and for calming influence; James Lokken for proofreading the manuscript; Alice Harth for designing the book and its cover; Meredith Karns, Will Clayton, M. Kathleen Kelly, Patrick Storme and Peter Chang for all the computer and technical work on this project; Leona Lee for weeks of typing, copy editing, compiling the index and undertaking any project that landed on the desk; Peggy Fallon for helping to style all the cover photographs and her invaluable assistance with last-minute recipe editing; Joyce Oudkerk Pool for believing in the project and photographing all our cover portraits; *Cordon Bleu* for the use of equipment for our cover photographs; Jane Rubey of *Nutritiously Gourmet* for her assistance with the nutritional analyses of our recipes; the *Carnelian Room* for its donation of talent and space for our cookbook launch party; *Adobe Software* and *Digital Queers* for their gracious assistance in securing software needed to complete the project; Cynthia Traina, Julie Hamilton, Sally-Jean Shepard, Tom Walton, Mary Ann Gilderbloom and David Carriere for lending their expertise in public relations; the students, faculty and staff of the University of San Francisco School of Non-Profit Studies Development Director Certificate Program (January 1995 graduating class) for their encouragement and support; Harry Heier for his words of wisdom in negotiating with printers, paper companies and distributors; and, finally, Judith McKim and Waller Press for holding our collective hands and helping us to actually produce the book you have in front of you.

ONE STORY

Growing up on a dairy farm in northeastern Wisconsin, I have fond memories of my mother trading recipes with her sisters and friends. Any special occasion would prompt the inevitable question, "Could I have that recipe?" Since mom also collected cookbooks, especially those published by churches, it only seems natural that I would be attracted to a project such as *Those People At That Church*.

Somewhere in my teens I lost all connection with the church. I did not feel any spiritual attachment to my home congregation, even though I played the organ for two services every Sunday morning for many years. When I left high school, I went to church only for weddings, funerals, and very occasional Sunday mornings back home, but only to please my mother and father.

About the time I reached thirty, along with so many people in San Francisco and across America, I began to feel the very real tragedy of HIV and AIDS. Now, ten years later, I have lost countless friends, including two of the most important people in my life, John David Hanson and Bradley Scott DeWinde. It was John's funeral that brought me to St. Francis Lutheran Church for the first time in 1987, and although it took me two years to return, it now exists as the most important community in my life.

Finally, a note of thanks to my parents, Alfred and Clarice Strei, whose model of faith and conviction has sustained me throughout my life. I thank God daily that you are my parents and also that you are my friends. I love you.

Wayne A. Strei
Editor
November 1994

The nutritional analysis which follows each recipe is to be used as a guide only. The analysis does not include optional ingredients or garnishes unless specific amounts are given. When there is a range in the the number of servings, the larger number is used. When there is a range in the amount of an ingredient, the smaller number is used. If a recipe lists a choice of ingredients (such as butter or margarine), the first ingredient is used. Because there are variations in ingredients, all values are approximations.

Lord, make me an instrument of your peace.
Where there is hatred, let me sow love;
where there is injury, pardon;
where there is discord, union;
where there is doubt, faith;
where there is despair, hope;
where there is darkness, light;
where there is sadness, joy.
Grant that we may not so much seek
to be consoled as to console;
to be understood as to understand;
to be loved as to love.
For it is in giving that we receive;
it is in pardoning that we are pardoned; and
it is in dying that we are born to eternal life.

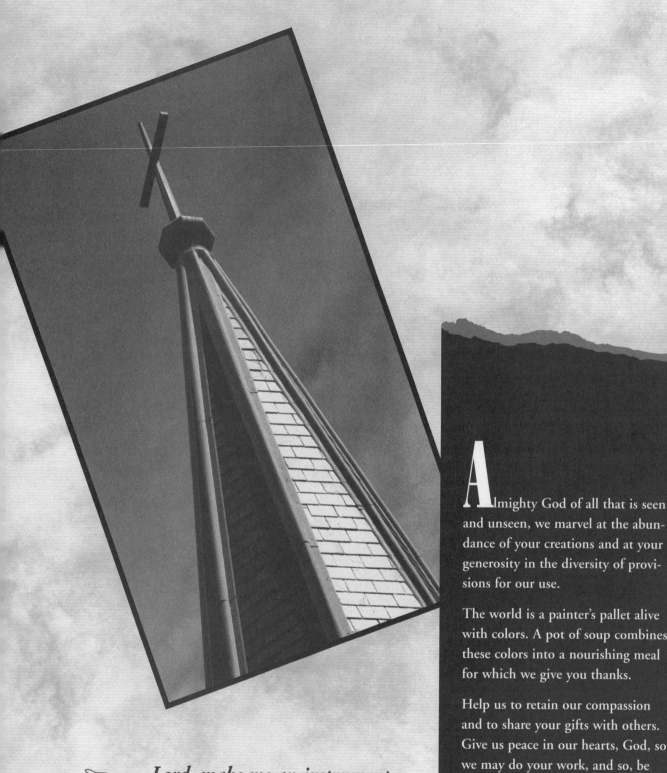

Lord, make me an instrument of your peace.

Almighty God of all that is seen and unseen, we marvel at the abundance of your creations and at your generosity in the diversity of provisions for our use.

The world is a painter's pallet alive with colors. A pot of soup combines these colors into a nourishing meal for which we give you thanks.

Help us to retain our compassion and to share your gifts with others. Give us peace in our hearts, God, so we may do your work, and so, be instruments of your peace in the world. *~Amen.*

SOUP'S ON

Making soup is the perfect project for cooks who tend to hover. A bubbling work in progress, soup invites culinary tinkering. A pinch here, a dash there. The pot accepts sudden inspirations and random experiments.

Soup can be a wonderful day-long affair—the buying and roasting of bones for stock, the chopping and cutting, the seasoning and reducing. The result is a first course or, many generous ladles and pieces of crusty bread later, a full meal. And don't forget the snack at midnight and beyond—soup invariably improves with each serving.

COLD AVOCADO SOUP
with a LITTLE SURPRISE

Serves 4-6

This is one of Marti Lundin's most popular standby summer lunch or dinner dishes. The surprise is vodka. If you want to make it fun and fancy, pour the vodka from a small crystal pitcher into the soup tureen at the table. Stir slowly and serve in chilled bowls.

1 ripe avocado, peeled and seeded

3 medium tomatoes, peeled and chopped

½ cup sour cream

4 tablespoons chopped green onions

Juice from ½ lemon or lime

2 tablespoons mild salsa (fresh preferred)

2-3 dashes Tabasco sauce

Salt and pepper to taste

1¼ cups chicken broth

1-2 drops green food coloring (optional)

1 full shot of vodka (optional)

Chopped green onion or cilantro (garnish)

✤ Place avocado, tomatoes, sour cream, green onions, lemon or lime juice, salsa and Tabasco sauce in a food processor or blender and puree until smooth. Stir in broth and adjust seasoning. Stir in food coloring, if desired, until well blended. Chill thoroughly.

✤ Just before serving, stir in vodka and pour into individual cups or bowls. Garnish with chopped green onion or cilantro.

Per serving: 125 calories; 2.35g protein; 9.58g carbohydrates; 9.78g fat (1.84g saturated fat); 1.28mg cholesterol.

Stephen is now 19, a sophomore at the University of California, Santa Barbara. When he was two, his parents brought him to our Friends of St. Francis Childcare Center. We like to think our pre-school gave him a good start in life.

Friends of St. Francis is a non-profit pre-school for families of all incomes, but the majority of our families earn very little. The church provides $12,000 a year in scholarships as well as logistical support. The Center emphasizes parent education as well as a multi-cultural experience for children and provides a support community for families of every configuration. For some, it is the only support community they have.

CUCUMBER-YOGURT SOUP

Serves 4-6

Jim Remer likes to serve this soup as the first course in a Mediterranean meal.

4 cups peeled, seeded
    and chopped cucumber
2 cups water
2 cups plain yogurt
2 cloves garlic, minced
1 tablespoon honey

1½ teaspoons salt
1 teaspoon fresh dill
    or ¼ teaspoon dried
12 fresh mint leaves
    (garnish)
2 green onions (garnish)

✤ Puree all ingredients but mint leaves and green onions in food processor or blender. Refrigerate 4-6 hours or overnight. Serve topped with the mint leaves and chopped green onions.

Per serving: 130 calories; 8.43g protein; 21.1g carbohydrates; 2.2g fat (1.29g saturated fat); 7.45mg cholesterol.

ZUCCHINI CREAMLESS SOUP

Serves 4

In this delicious soup served cold in the summer or warm in cool weather, Randy Thueme has achieved a creamy texture using oatmeal and no cream!

1 small onion, chopped
1 tablespoon corn oil
3-4 medium zucchini
    (about 1½ pounds),
    chopped
6 cups water or stock

½ cup oatmeal or
    rolled oats
½ teaspoon salt
    or to taste
2 tablespoons chopped
    parsley (garnish)

✤ Heat oil in a soup pot over medium heat and cook onion until translucent, about 5 minutes. Add zucchini and cook for 2-3 minutes. Add water or stock, oatmeal and salt. Bring to a boil, stirring constantly. Reduce heat and simmer for 15 minutes.

✤ Pour mixture into a food processor or blender and puree in batches if necessary. Strain to make a smooth texture. Serve hot or cold, garnished with parsley.

Per serving: 160 calories; 11.3g protein; 15g carbohydrates; 6.41g fat (1.19g saturated fat); 0mg cholesterol.

GAZPACHO

Serves 4-6

Marti Lundin serves this soup on hot days in California's beautiful Wine Country, where she and husband, Jack, now make their home.

3 cloves garlic, minced
1 bunch green onions (white and green parts), chopped
½ green bell pepper, seeded and sliced
1½ cups tomato juice, divided
1 medium cucumber, peeled, seeded and sliced into 1-inch pieces
2 medium tomatoes, peeled and quartered

1 teaspoon salt
¼ teaspoon white pepper
½ cup chicken broth
2-3 dashes Tabasco sauce (optional)
3 teaspoons olive oil
3 tablespoons white wine vinegar
Cucumber slices (garnish)
Croutons (garnish)

✤ Place garlic, green onions and green bell pepper in food processor or blender and puree for 30 seconds or until finely chopped. Add ½ cup of tomato juice, cucumbers, tomatoes, salt, pepper and Tabasco (optional) and process for 20 more seconds until ingredients are finely chopped but not completely smooth. Transfer mixture to mixing bowl.

✤ Stir in remaining cup of tomato juice, chicken broth, olive oil and vinegar and mix well. Cover and chill.

✤ Serve in chilled bowls garnished with cucumber slices or home-made croutons, if desired.

Per serving: 91.3 calories; 3.18g protein; 13.5g carbohydrates; 3.99g fat (.58g saturated fat); 0mg cholesterol.

CUCUMBER CREAMLESS SOUP

A delicious soup served cold in the summer or warm in colder weather. Randy Thueme is pleased that a creamy texture is achieved without any cream.

2 tablespoons corn oil	½ cup rolled oats or
¼ green pepper, chopped	oatmeal
2 ribs celery, chopped	½ teaspoon salt or to taste
1 pound cucumbers, peeled and chopped	1 tablespoon lemon juice
	2 teaspoons chopped
6 cups water or vegetable broth	fresh dill (garnish)

✤ Heat oil in a soup pot over medium heat and cook green pepper until softened but not browned, 3-4 minutes. Stir in celery and reduce heat to low. Add cucumbers, stirring constantly for 2 minutes.

✤ Add the water or stock, oats and salt. Cover and simmer 20 minutes.

✤ Transfer the soup to a food processor or blender and puree in batches if necessary. Force through a sieve placed over a large bowl. Add lemon juice and stir well. Chill for 4-6 hours if serving cold. Garnish with fresh dill before serving.

Per serving: 241 calories; 7.02g protein; 30.8g carbohydrates; 10.5g fat (1.68g saturated fat); 3.62mg cholesterol.

On Thanksgiving Day, our parish hall is filled with people from our neighborhood who come for a family-style Thanksgiving Dinner. We usually serve about 200 people. There are people who live on the streets, elderly folk and young people, even a few children. Most come alone, hoping to make a connection with someone, even if it is for just a few minutes. They often have a story to tell. The food is contributed by members of the congregation and by local merchants; all the labor is donated. We like to think we are helping others, but we are the ones who are blessed.

DUTCH PEA SOUP

Serves 8

Our resident Dutch cook, Erna Dennert, likes to serve this hearty soup with thick slices of pumpernickel bread.

1¼ pounds split peas
10 cups water
2 small celery roots, peeled and cubed
1 bunch parsley, finely chopped
2 onions, peeled and cubed

2 leeks, washed and chopped, white and green parts
2 pork chops (about 1 pound)
½ pound Kielbasa sausage
Salt and pepper to taste

✤ Check through split peas for debris and wash thoroughly. Soak overnight in water to cover.

✤ Drain split peas in colander. Place split peas in large stock pot with 10 cups of water and bring to a boil. Reduce heat and simmer for 30 minutes, stirring occasionally.

✤ Add celery root, parsley, onions and leeks. Simmer until peas are soft and fall apart, 10-15 minutes.

✤ Cook pork chops in a heavy skillet over medium heat until nicely browned and cooked through. Remove meat from pork chops and cut into ½-inch pieces and add to soup. Cut sausage into ½-inch pieces and add to soup. Season with salt and pepper to taste. Simmer until heated through. Serve hot.

Per serving: 565 calories; 34.3g protein; 25.5g carbohydrates; 36.3g fat (13.1g saturated fat); 112mg cholesterol.

BLACK-EYED PEA SOUP

Serves 4

Kathleen Prisant, former president of the San Francisco Professional Food Society, created this savory soup in her San Rafael, California home.

2 tablespoons olive oil
½ onion, chopped
2 cloves garlic, chopped
2 sage leaves
1 teaspoon curry powder
1 large carrot, chopped
1 16-ounce can chopped
   tomatoes
1 16-ounce can black-eyed
   peas, drained and rinsed

1 vegetable bouillon cube
2 cooked turkey sausages
   or 1 smoked turkey
   leg, chopped
4 tablespoons lowfat
   sour cream (garnish)
2 tablespoons minced mint
   or lemon mint (garnish)

✤ In a heavy 2-quart saucepan, cook onion and garlic in oil until onion is tender, about 2 minutes. Stir in sage, curry and carrots. Cook over medium heat, stirring occasionally, for 2 minutes. Stir in tomatoes, black-eyed peas, water and vegetable bouillon cube. Heat to boiling. Lower heat and simmer, about 10 minutes.

✤ Puree 1 to 2 cups of the soup mixture, then return to pot. Simmer until heated through. Stir in cooked sausage or smoked turkey.

✤ Top each serving with a dollop of sour cream. Sprinkle with mint. Serve hot.

Per serving: 581 calories; 33.3g protein; 38.1g carbohydrates; 33.6g fat (10.1g saturated fat); 14.8mg cholesterol.

BLACK BEAN SOUP with
TOMATO and SOUR CREAM
Serves 4

Noted Bay Area food writer Janet Fletcher gave us this recipe for a thick and hearty vegetable soup. Serve with crusty French bread for a light meal.

1 tablespoon olive oil
1 medium yellow onion, chopped
¾ cup peeled chopped tomato, fresh or canned
2 15-ounce cans black beans, rinsed and drained, or 3 cups cooked black beans

4 cups chicken stock
Salt and freshly ground black pepper
1 large clove garlic, minced
⅓ cup sour cream, whisked
2 tablespoons coarsely chopped cilantro
Salsa (optional)

✤ Heat olive oil in a large pot over moderate heat. Add onion and cook until softened, about 5 minutes. Add garlic and saute 1 minute to release its fragrance. Add chopped tomato and saute until softened, about 5 minutes, stirring and crushing tomato lightly with a wooden spoon. Add beans and stock. Bring to a simmer, then adjust heat to maintain a simmer and cook 15 minutes.

✤ With a slotted spoon, measure out 1½ cups of beans and onions. Puree in a food processor or blender until smooth. Stir the puree back into the soup.

✤ Taste and adjust seasoning with salt and pepper. If soup is not thick enough, puree a few more beans and onions; if it is too thick, thin with a little water. Reheat, stirring constantly.

✤ Ladle into warm bowls, topping each serving with a drizzle of sour cream, some cilantro and, if desired, a spoonful of salsa.

Per serving: 332 calories; 19.9g protein; 37.6g carbohydrates; 12.1g fat (5.02g saturated fat); 14.8mg cholesterol.

EIGHT BEAN SOUP

Don't be put off by the long list of ingredients. Lee Andersen says it takes longer to write out the recipe than it does to make the soup! If you want to make this soup completely vegetarian, use tomato juice in place of the chicken stock.

½ cup small dried white beans
½ cup dried pinto beans
½ cup dried garbanzo beans (chick peas)
½ cup dried red beans
½ cup dried split peas
½ cup dried lentils
6 cups chicken stock
1 large potato, peeled and diced
1 celery rib, chopped
1 medium carrot, chopped
1 large onion, chopped
½ cup frozen green beans, thawed
½ cup frozen lima beans, thawed
1 small canned green chili, rinsed, seeded and chopped
2 garlic cloves, minced
1 large tomato, diced
½ teaspoon fresh marjoram or ¼ teaspoon dried
½ teaspoon fresh rosemary or ¼ teaspoon dried
1 teaspoon fresh basil or ½ teaspoon dried
1 teaspoon curry powder
1 teaspoon dry mustard

✤ Soak white beans, pinto beans, garbanzo beans and red beans in water to cover overnight.

✤ Drain and place in a large pot with split peas, lentils and chicken stock. Bring to a boil over high heat. Reduce heat and simmer for 1 hour.

✤ Add potatoes, celery, carrot, onion, green beans, lima beans, green chili and garlic and simmer until tender, about 30 minutes.

✤ Add tomato, marjoram, rosemary, basil, curry powder and dry mustard to the soup and cook over low heat until heated through, about 10 minutes. Serve promptly.

Per serving: 301 calories; 20.6g protein; 50g carbohydrates; 2.73g fat (.518g saturated fat); 0mg cholesterol.

VEGETARIAN CHILI

Serves 4

Eugene Clark, church organist and longtime member of St. Francis Lutheran, got this recipe from a choir member at Immanuel Church in Alameda. This chili is excellent served over brown rice.

½ cup dried whole green lentils
1 tablespoon olive oil
1 onion, chopped
1 red bell pepper, seeded and chopped
1-2 garlic cloves, crushed through a press
1 14-ounce can chopped tomatoes

1 cup dried red kidney beans, soaked, cooked and drained, or 2 15-ounce cans red kidney beans
1 teaspoon paprika
1-2 tablespoons chili powder
Salt and pepper to taste
¼ teaspoon ground cumin
1 teaspoon dried oregano

✤ Simmer dried green lentils in water to cover for 40-45 minutes. Set aside.

✤ Heat oil in a large pot over medium heat and cook the onion and pepper until softened but not browned, about 10 minutes. Add garlic and cook for 1-2 minutes, then add the tomatoes.

✤ Drain the beans and lentils, reserving the liquid. Add to the tomato mixture along with the paprika and chili powder. Simmer for 15 minutes, adding the bean water until you reach the desired consistency. Stir in salt, pepper, cumin and oregano. Serve promptly.

Per serving: 327 calories; 19.5g protein; 54.6g carbohydrates; 5.24g fat (.788g saturated fat); 0mg cholesterol.

MUSHROOM SOUP with PARMESAN CHEESE

Serves 4

Growing up in the region around Lyon, France, cooking teacher Marinette Georgi offers this delightful mushroom soup from her childhood.

1 tablespoon butter
1 tablespoon olive oil
1 medium onion, grated
1 clove garlic, split
1 pound mushroom caps, thinly sliced
3 tablespoons tomato paste
3 cups chicken stock
2 tablespoons dry white Italian vermouth (optional)

Salt and pepper to taste
4 egg yolks
2 tablespoons finely chopped parsley
2½ tablespoons grated Parmesan cheese
4 1-inch thick slices of Italian bread, toasted

✤ In a heavy pot, melt the butter in olive oil over medium heat. Cook the onion and garlic until lightly browned. Discard garlic pieces. Stir in the mushrooms and cook for 5 minutes. Add the tomato paste and mix chicken stock and stir to combine. Stir in the vermouth (optional), salt and pepper. Bring to a boil. Reduce heat and simmer 10-15 minutes.

✤ In a small bowl, beat egg yolks until smooth. Add parsley and Parmesan cheese and stir to combine. Whisk about a cup of hot soup into the egg mixture and then add to the whole pot.

✤ To serve, place a slice of bread in each soup bowl. Pour soup over bread and serve at once.

Per serving: 534 calories; 21.5g protein; 69.7g carbohydrates; 18.2g fat (5.93g saturated fat); 223mg cholesterol; .

I first came to this church in about 1985 to surprise a former roommate. He wasn't there. San Francisco's gay community was in the midst of the AIDS epidemic and I was losing most of my friends. I knew I needed something badly, and after that one Sunday, I discovered I had found a church home.

My mother directed a church choir for 40 years, and the best thing she could say about my voice was that I "blended well." Nonetheless, singing in the choir has been great fun for me. I also like St. Francis Lutheran for its architecture. In its form and decoration, our sanctuary is unmistakably a small, Scandinavian Lutheran church. Yet our church is also very San Franciscan—no service passes without hearing a streetcar going by outside.

Max Kirkeberg, 61, was raised in Stanton, Iowa, and is a self-confessed grandson of Swedish and Norwegian immigrants. Since 1965, he has been a professor of geography at San Francisco State University. Max and his partner, Jim Sherman, have been together for over 24 years.

WINTER MELON SOUP

Serves 4

Well-known San Francisco food professional and cookbook author Maggie Gin gave us this uncomplicated adaptation of a traditional Chinese first course.

6 cups rich chicken stock
1 small piece dried tangerine peel, soaked to soften and minced (optional)
6 dried forest mushrooms, soaked to soften, thinly sliced
2 pounds winter melon, peeled, seeded and cut in ½-inch dice
⅓ cup finely slivered Virginia ham

✤ In a large pot, heat together stock, tangerine peel (optional) and mushrooms. Simmer 30 minutes. Raise heat and add winter melon. Bring to boil, lower heat and simmer 20 minutes. Add ham and serve promptly.

Per serving: 137 calories; 10.4g protein; 19.6g carbohydrates; 2.48g fat (.673g saturated fat); 1.1mg cholesterol; 1225mg sodium.

OYSTER, CORN and ARTICHOKE SOUP

Serves 6-8

Mike Dixon created this speciality soup at Ruby's, a popular Italian restaurant near the San Francisco Convention Center.

2 bunches green onions, chopped
½ cup butter
1 tablespoon garlic, minced
¼ cup flour
1 cup fish stock
1 cup fresh corn kernels
1 14-ounce can artichoke hearts, drained and chopped
2 bay leaves
½ teaspoon salt
½ teaspoon pepper
2 dashes Tabasco sauce
2 dozen oysters and their water
1 tablespoon lemon juice
1 tablespoon chardonnay (optional)

✤ In a heavy pot, melt butter over medium heat. Add green onions and cook until softened, about 5 minutes. Add garlic and cook until lightly browned. Add flour and cook 3 minutes.

✤ Add stock, corn, artichoke hearts, bay leaves, salt, pepper and Tabasco sauce. Bring to a simmer. Add oysters, lemon juice and chardonnay (optional) and cook until heated through. Serve promptly.

Per serving: 340 calories; 16.8g protein; 17g carbohydrates; 19.6g fat (8.68g saturated fat); 106mg cholesterol.

BROCCOLI CHEESE SOUP   Serves 12

Denise Kellett lives with her family outside of Chicago. She often serves this easy-to-make soup on chilly evenings.

1 cup chopped broccoli	3 chicken bouillon cubes
¼ cup shredded carrots	4 ounces thin noodles
1 cup chopped cauliflower florets	(such as angel hair pasta)
1 tablespoon vegetable oil	½ teaspoon salt
or butter	3 cups milk
½ cup chopped onion	½ pound Cheddar cheese,
2 cloves garlic, minced	cut into ¼-inch dice
3 cups water	Pepper to taste

✤ Steam broccoli, carrots and cauliflower in a little water over low heat until just tender, or cook vegetables in microwave on high setting for 4-5 minutes. Set aside.

✤ In a large saucepan over medium heat, heat oil or butter. Add onion and garlic and cook for 3 minutes. Add water and bouillon cubes. Bring to a boil. Gradually add noodles and salt. Stir in vegetables and boil 2-4 minutes.

✤ Reduce heat and add milk, cheese and ground pepper. Heat through until cheese melts. Serve promptly.

Per serving: 286 calories; 15.6g protein; 15g carbohydrates; 18.8g fat (11.7g saturated fat); 67.4mg cholesterol.

I tell people, "If you want to find an easy church to join, St. Francis Lutheran is not the one! However, if you want to be part of a combination family/community that shares something very powerful, then you are in the right place." At St. Francis, I am fully accepted. All of me. As a member of that community I have felt myself become stronger and more affirmed in my experience of the love of God. I cannot express the collage of feelings I experienced on my first visit to St. Francis after being away from the church for nearly 20 years. That service started a great change in my life.

God calls us to be servants and gives us faith to go out each day in good courage, not knowing where we will be going. As a congregation, St. Francis is also like that. We can't know the outcome of all that we are doing, but we are faithful in our mission, and we are not afraid. I am confident that in 25 years people will look back and say that we were significant in changing ideas in the church.

Mari Griffiths Irvin, 61, is a professor and administrator at the University of the Pacific in Stockton, California. She grew up in North Dakota, Iowa, and Oregon, and is a St. Olaf College graduate, class of 1955. Mari is currently president of the congregation.

SORREL and PARSNIP SOUP   Serves 4

Sorrel is often called sour grass and resembles spinach. Kirsten Havrehed says it grows madly in her garden every spring and is a constant part of her menus during that season.

1 pound sorrel, coarsely chopped	2 egg yolks
3 parsnips, peeled and coarsely chopped	½ cup heavy (whipping) cream
6 green onions, sliced	Ground pepper to taste
6 cups chicken stock	2 tablespoons chopped parsley (garnish)

✤ Place sorrel, parsnips and green onion in food processor or blender and puree.

✤ In a heavy pot over medium heat, heat chicken stock. Add sorrel-parsnip mixture, cover and simmer for 10 minutes. Do not let boil.

✤ In a small bowl, whisk together the egg yolks and cream. Gradually whisk 1 cup of the hot soup into egg mixture. Then pour egg mixture back into soup. Heat through, stirring constantly. Do not boil or the soup will curdle.

✤ Soup can be served hot or chilled. Garnish with chopped parsley.

Per serving: 310 calories; 13.6g protein; 28.5g carbohydrates; 16.9g fat (8.29g saturated fat); 147mg cholesterol.

PUREE of ROASTED RED PEPPER and PUMPKIN SOUP

Serves 4

This flavorful soup is from Mark Yaeger, owner-chef of Mark's Healthy Kitchen, specializing in lowfat cuisine.

1 15–ounce jar roasted red peppers, drained
1 cup canned pumpkin
1 14½–ounce can reduced sodium chicken broth or homemade chicken stock (or vegetable stock)
3 tablespoons balsamic vinegar
½ cup cooked corn kernels
2 tablespoons maple syrup

2 teaspoons dried basil
3-5 drops Tabasco sauce
1 cup plain nonfat yogurt
¼ cup Madeira, sherry or Marsala wine (optional)
1 red or yellow bell pepper seeded and cut into rings
Sprigs of fresh dill (optional)

❖ Place roasted red peppers, pumpkin, chicken stock, balsamic vinegar, corn, maple syrup, basil and Tabasco sauce into food processor or blender and puree until smooth.

❖ Transfer to large pot and cook over medium heat 15 minutes or until reduced by about one-quarter. Remove soup from heat and let cool for 10 minutes.

❖ Return soup to food processor or blender, add yogurt and puree until light and frothy. Pour soup back into pot, add wine if desired and simmer for 5-10 minutes. Do not allow soup to come to a boil. Taste and adjust seasonings. Garnish with bell pepper rings and sprig of fresh dill, if desired. Serve promptly.

Per serving: 157 calories; 8.02g protein; 28.6g carbohydrates; 1.52g fat (.414g saturated fat); 1.1mg cholesterol.

ITALIAN DUMPLING SOUP— MANTUAN STYLE

Serves 4-6

Well-known and well-loved Weezie Mott is a Bay Area cooking teacher who loves to entertain and travel. She and her husband, Howard, especially love Italy, where she learned how to make this wonderful soup.

1½ ounces pancetta
1 small garlic clove, cut into pieces
½ tablespoon soft butter
½ cup plain bread crumbs
⅔ cup grated Parmesan cheese, divided

Pinch of nutmeg
Freshly ground black pepper
1 egg
4 cups chicken or beef stock
2 green onions, sliced (garnish)

✤ To make the dumplings, place the pancetta, garlic and butter in a food processor or blender and puree to a creamy consistency.

✤ In a small bowl, mix together bread crumbs, ½ cup cheese, nutmeg and black pepper. On a workspace make a mound of the bread crumb mixture and hollow out the center (like a volcano crater). Put creamed garlic-pancetta-butter mixture into the hollow and add the egg. With a fork, beat these ingredients together, gradually incorporating the surrounding dry ingredients. Knead them well until a paste results. Shape into tiny ½-inch balls with your hands. This makes about 3 dozen.

✤ In a 1½-quart saucepan, heat 4 cups of stock to the boiling point. Lower heat, add the prepared tiny dumplings and cook at medium simmer for about 5 minutes. Divide dumplings among soup dishes, ladle broth over dumplings and garnish with sliced green onions. If desired, sprinkle lightly with remaining grated Parmesan cheese.

Per serving: 393 calories; 34.4g protein; 115.8g carbohydrates; 19.9g fat (8.23g saturated fat); 111mg cholesterol; 3718mg sodium.

FRUIT SOUP

Serves 6-8

Paul Groth tells us that this soup was the only form in which he and his sisters ever agreed to eat prunes, so their mom served it for dessert in their North Dakota home. Paul's mother, who is German-American, doesn't feel that her version (with jams and wine) is as authentically Norwegian as her mother-in-law's original recipe. Hence, Paul has included his mom's added ingredients as alternatives—and highly recommends them.

8 cups water	2 cinnamon sticks
1 cup sugar	½ lemon, sliced
1 cup prunes (pitted best, but unpitted will work)	Up to ½ cup red or white wine (optional)
½ cup raisins	About ½ cup leftover jams and jellies (optional)
½ cup sago (or tapioca)	

✚ Place the water, sugar, prunes, raisins, sago, cinnamon, wine (optional) and jams (optional) into a 3-quart saucepan. Cover and boil slowly for one hour, or until prunes are tender and well done. Just before serving, add the lemon slices. The finished soup should be fairly thick; to thin, add more water.

✚ Note: This soup can be served hot or cold. It is great served hot over vanilla ice cream, and adapts well to additions (rhubarb jam is especially good). It keeps well in the refrigerator and is easily reheated.

Per serving: 267 calories; .985g protein; 66g carbohydrates; .173g fat (1.033g saturated fat); 0mg cholesterol.

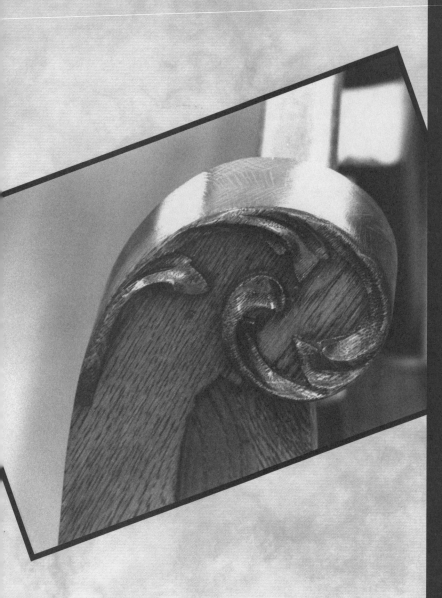

C reator God,

Endive, red cabbage, bib lettuce, arag-ula, basil, romaine, spinach; black, white, brown, yellow, old, young, poor, middle-class, child, senior citi-zen... teach us to value the diversity of your creation, each being with its own color, flavor and beauty, in this garden we call the earth.

In our hands you've placed the choice of what to sow within our-selves. Help us to choose seeds of compassion, honesty, caring and tol-erance. Lead us to water our seeds with our passion for justice and peace. When our crops mature they can change the face of our world.

And lastly, we pray for our earth, our home, our teacher. May we learn a new relationship with her. May our bodies, minds and spirits learn a new and renewing rhythm, the rhythm of the earth and of all cre-ation. We have been given so much: colors for our eyes, birds for our ears, ground for our feet, reality for our minds and work for our hands. Teach us to cherish and share the wonders of our world. ~Amen.

Where there is hatred,
let me sow love;

SALAD PLATES

Once upon a time, in a culinary world far, far away, a salad was a wedge of iceberg lettuce and a slice of hard tomato. Or so the cave drawings tell us. Today, the produce market boasts more greens than a paint store. You can find leafy greens, bitter greens and some greens that happen to be red. There are lettuces of every shape and size, even some that speak French.

The thing is, you don't even *need* lettuce anymore. The local markets abound with fresh and colorful produce, crunchy pieces of a delightful culinary puzzle. Healthy and refreshing, salad is a concept served on a cool plate. Simply toss with a little dressing and lots of imagination.

Hot Slaw

Black Bean Salad

Marinated Mushroom Salad
with Bacon

Tabouleh

Cold Vegetables
with Pistachio-Fresh Basil
Vinaigrette

Huzaren Sla

Chickpea Salad with Oil-Cured
Olives and Red Bell Pepper

Venetia's Watermelon Salad

Onion Salad

Classic Caesar Salad

Dill and Dijon Dressing

Jack's Salad Dressing

Pine Nut Butter Lettuce Salad
with Roasted Garlic-Honey
Dressing

Fresh Fruit and Greens Salad
with Raspberry Vinaigrette

Pasta Chicken Salad with Peanuts

Orzo Salad

HOT SLAW

Serves 8-10

Cabbage tossed with a boiled dressing is an easy vegetable to prepare quickly. Heidi Cusick, Mendocino food professional, says its sweet-sour flavor tastes great with fried chicken or smothered pork chops. The amount of dressing doesn't look like much, but cabbage contains a lot of moisture which is released when the salad sits for a few minutes.

1 large head cabbage	⅔ cup canola or safflower oil
1 medium yellow onion, finely chopped	1 cup white or cider vinegar
1 green bell pepper, seeded and finely chopped	½ cup sugar
1 carrot, shredded (optional)	Salt and ground black pepper

✤ Shred cabbage and place in mixing or serving bowl. Add onion, pepper and carrot (optional). Sprinkle with salt and pepper.

✤ In a small saucepan over medium heat, combine oil, vinegar and sugar and bring to a boil. Boil 1 minute and pour over cabbage mixture. Taste for seasoning. Mix and serve hot or at room temperature.

Per serving: 176 calories; .206g protein; 12.6g carbohydrates; 14.6g fat (1.33g saturated fat); 0mg cholesterol.

BLACK BEAN SALAD

Serves 6

This substantial and colorful salad from Erna Dennert features lots of fresh ingredients and a surprising citrus flavor.

3 cups cooked black beans	1½ tablespoons orange juice
1 red bell pepper, seeded and chopped	1 teaspoon olive oil
½ green bell pepper, seeded and chopped	1½ tablespoons lemon juice
¼ red onion, finely chopped	¼ teaspoon Tabasco sauce
2 green onions, sliced	¼ teaspoon salt
1 celery rib, finely chopped	½ teaspoon ground cumin, or more to taste
2 oranges	¼ teaspoon ground coriander

✤ Combine beans, bell peppers, onion, green onion and celery in large bowl. Toss well.

✤ Cut one orange in half, remove seeds. Scoop out the segments and add to beans.

✤ Squeeze juice from remaining orange into a small bowl. Whisk together remaining ingredients. Pour over salad and toss to coat thoroughly. Refrigerate until serving.

Per serving: 141 calories; 8.21g protein; 25.6g carbohydrates; 1.35g fat (.237g saturated fat); 0mg cholesterol.

MARINATED MUSHROOM
SALAD with BACON
Serves 6

This is Peggy Fallon's adaptation of a recipe that appeared in Sunset *Magazine many years ago. It's always a popular buffet item.*

¼ cup fresh lemon juice
1 teaspoon Dijon mustard
½ teaspoon Worcestershire
    sauce
½ teaspoon salt
⅛ teaspoon freshly ground
    pepper
⅔ cup olive oil
1 pound fresh mushrooms

2 green onions, thinly sliced
    (including part of the
    green tops)
½ pound thinly sliced bacon
Leaves of red leaf or
    butter lettuce
2 tablespoons chopped
    fresh parsley

✤ In a large bowl, combine lemon juice, mustard, Worcestershire, salt and pepper until well blended. Whisk in olive oil.

✤ Cut off and discard tough ends of mushrooms. Slice mushrooms thinly and add to bowl, tossing to coat with marinade. Stir in green onions. Cover and refrigerate, stirring occasionally, at least 4 hours or as long as 24 hours.

✤ Cut bacon slices crosswise into ½-inch pieces. In a large skillet or frying pan, cook bacon over medium heat until crisp and browned, 5-7 minutes. Drain on paper towels.

✤ Using a slotted spoon, remove mushrooms from marinade and mound on a lettuce-lined platter. Drizzle with some of the remaining marinade, if desired. Sprinkle with parsley and top with bacon.

Per serving: 345 calories; 7.63g protein; 5.12g carbohydrates; 33.7g fat (6.59g saturated fat); 16.1mg cholesterol.

CHICKPEA SALAD with OIL-CURED OLIVES and RED BELL PEPPER

Serves 4

This colorful salad from cookbook author Janet Hazen combines the bright flavor of sweet red bell pepper with the deep, intense flavors of oil-cured olives and nutty tasting chickpeas. Make this salad at least one day ahead so that the flavors have time to marry.

1½ cups dried chickpeas (garbanzo beans), washed and sorted (about 2½ cups cooked chickpeas)

½ cup pitted and coarsely chopped oil-cured olives

3 cloves garlic, finely chopped

5 green onions, finely chopped

1 medium red bell pepper, seeded and diced

⅓ cup fruity olive oil

3 tablespoons sherry wine vinegar

Salt and pepper to taste

✤ Soak the chickpeas in 1½ quarts of water overnight. Drain well and place in a large saucepan with 2 quarts of fresh water. Bring to a boil over high heat. Reduce the heat to moderate and cook about 1 hour, or until the chickpeas are very tender but not mushy. Drain well in a colander and place in a large bowl.

✤ Add the olives, garlic, green onions, red bell pepper, olive oil and vinegar; toss well. Season with salt and pepper. Store in a tightly sealed container in the refrigerator until ready to serve.

Per serving: 395 calories; 10.7g protein; 37.8g carbohydrates; 23.2g fat (3.02g saturated fat); 0mg cholesterol.

My wife and I joined St. Francis Lutheran in 1987. We were impressed with the friendly atmosphere and the multitude of activities sponsored by the church to serve the community. I could not help but come away from visiting this church without feeling that if Christ were walking among us, St. Francis is where he would sit down and break bread.

Paul Barker, 59, was a senior executive with the United States Forest Service. He and his wife, Nancy, have retired to Spokane, Washington.

VENETIA'S WATERMELON SALAD   Serves 12-16

Linda Utterberg was served this unusual salad during a farm stay in Bermagui, New South Wales, Australia. This recipe will serve a lot of people and can be adjusted to use less watermelon, onions and mint according to taste.

12 cups seedless watermelon, cut into chunks

1 cup chopped sweet onion
¾ to 1 cup chopped fresh mint

✢ Mix all ingredients just prior to serving.

Per serving: 42.2 calories; .86g protein; 9.49g carbohydrates; .532g fat (.078g saturated fat); 0mg cholesterol.

ONION SALAD   Serves 8-10

This simple marinated salad is from Evelyn Frank, one of the finest cooks in Gillett, Wisconsin. Evelyn passed away in 1989.

½ cup vegetable oil
½ cup white vinegar
¾ cups sugar
1 teaspoon prepared horseradish

2 teaspoons salt
1 teaspoon pepper
3 large onions, sliced ¼-inch thick

✢ In a small saucepan over medium heat, combine oil, vinegar, sugar, horseradish, salt and pepper and bring to a boil. Let cool.

✢ Add onions and toss to coat well. Cover and marinate in the refrigerator at least 4 hours before serving.

Per serving: 163 calories; .216g protein; 17.2g carbohydrates; 10.9g fat (.997g saturated fat); 0mg cholesterol.

TABOULEH

Serves 8-10

This is one of the favorite salads at French Village Delicatessen on West Portal in San Francisco. Hilda Dabai was kind enough to share it with us.

1 cup cracked bulgur wheat
½ cup lemon juice
2 cups chopped parsley
1 cup chopped mint
½ cup minced green onions
    (white and green parts)

1 cup diced tomatoes
Salt and pepper to taste
½ cup extra virgin
    olive oil
Hearts of romaine
    lettuce

✤ Soak the cracked wheat bulgur in the lemon juice for 30 minutes.

✤ In a medium bowl mix together all ingredients, folding gently to combine. Refrigerate at least 2 hours to let flavors blend. Serve using hearts of romaine lettuce as a scoop instead of a spoon.

Per serving: 195 calories; 2.97g protein; 17g carbohydrates; 14g fat (1.9g saturated fat); 0mg cholesterol.

COLD VEGETABLES with PISTACHIO-FRESH BASIL VINAIGRETTE

Makes 1 cup

Well-known food professional Stevie Bass submits this flavorful and fresh-tasting dressing. Serve over steamed and chilled fresh zucchini, green beans, broccoli, cauliflower or other seasonal vegetables.

¼ cup whole shelled
    pistachios
½ cup olive oil
¼ cup white wine vinegar
2 tablespoons chopped
    fresh basil

2 tablespoons grated
    Parmesan cheese
1 teaspoon minced garlic
4 servings chilled steamed
    fresh vegetables

✤ Combine pistachios, olive oil, vinegar, basil, Parmesan cheese and garlic in jar. Shake well and serve over vegetables.

Per serving: 321 calories; 4.4g protein; 7.24g carbohydrates; 32g fat (4.77g saturated fat); 2.46mg cholesterol.

HUZAREN SLA (Cossack salad)

Serves 4

This main-dish salad from Erna Dennert is perfect for lunch or a light supper on a hot evening. For a change, add about a cup of diced cooked beets.

6 large potatoes, peeled, boiled and cooled
3 cups diced cold meat (beef, pork or lamb)
1 small onion, finely chopped
3 small sour dill pickles, finely chopped

⅓ cup Italian dressing (without cheese)
Salt and pepper to taste
1 tart apple, diced small
Leaves of red or butter lettuce
1-2 tomatoes, sliced
1 hard-boiled egg, sliced

✤ In a large bowl mix potatoes, meat, onions and pickles with the Italian dressing, salt and pepper. Gently fold in diced apple.

✤ To serve, cover large plate with lettuce leaves. Mound salad in the middle. Decorate with sliced tomatoes and eggs.

Per serving: 388 calories; 19.3g protein; 35.1g carbohydrates; 19.2g fat (5.43g saturated fat); 78.7mg cholesterol.

I've lived in San Francisco all my life, on the same city block that my grandfather settled in the mid-1800s. We've been there for five generations. After I retired, I got involved in the church council and the Friends of St. Francis Childcare Center; I have found it very rewarding to be able to help people. Seniors are one of the widely forgotten groups in our city. Many of them live alone, and their activities are very limited. Our program at St. Francis Lutheran is only one day a week, but it means a great deal to them. I really appreciate the warmth and diversity of the people at St. Francis and that we can do something to help those people who are really in need.

Beverly, 63, is a grandmother and retired district manager for Pacific Telephone. She is also secretary of the board of the Hillsborough Bonsai Society and grows beautiful orchids.

CLASSIC CAESAR SALAD

Serves 12-15

This recipe was given to Sanford Dole by a former lover, Thomas Lukins, who enjoys French cooking. This salad is perfect for large gatherings.

6-8 slices of sourdough bread cut into ½-inch thick cubes
1 can anchovy filets
12 shakes Worcestershire sauce
4 drops Tabasco sauce
8 large cloves garlic, crushed through a press
1 large dollop Dijon mustard
Juice of 1 lemon

1 egg*
1½ cups olive oil
1-2 tablespoons white wine vinegar
3-4 heads romaine lettuce, cut crosswise into 1-inch strips
1 cup freshly grated Parmesan cheese

❖ Preheat oven to 350°. Bake bread cubes on a cookie sheet until brown, turning slices once, about 15 minutes.

❖ Combine anchovies, Worcestershire sauce, Tabasco sauce, garlic, mustard, lemon juice and egg in food processor or blender. While processor or blender is running, very slowly add olive oil in a thin steady stream. (This may take up to 5 minutes). Add vinegar to taste.

❖ Toss lettuce with dressing, add toasted bread cubes and Parmesan cheese.

❖ Note: *Because of the threat of salmonella, U.S. Government Officials recommend that the very young, the elderly, pregnant women, and people with serious illnesses or weakened immune systems not eat raw or lightly cooked eggs. Keep this in mind and consume raw or lightly cooked eggs at your own risk.

Per serving: 293 calories; 7g protein; 11.6g carbohydrates; 24.8g fat (4.46g saturated fat); 20.7mg cholesterol.

DILL AND DIJON DRESSING

Makes 3 cups

This dressing from Greg Egertson may also be used as a cold dip or as a sauce over cooked vegetables, rice or pasta. Instead of paprika and curry, try adding garlic powder and grated Parmesan cheese to taste. The tartness of the dressing contrasts nicely with apples, pears, raisins and dried cherries.

2 cups mayonnaise	1 tablespoon Dijon mustard
½ cup juice from jar of refrigerated kosher dill pickles	1 teaspoon dried dill weed
	¼ teaspoon paprika
¼ teaspoon curry powder	¼ cup milk

✚ Whisk ingredients together in a medium size mixing bowl until well blended. Refrigerate overnight to thicken.

✚ Serve over a cold lettuce salad or with chopped vegetables and/or fresh fruit.

Per serving: 134 calories; .332g protein; .708g carbohydrates; 14.8g fat (2.23g saturated fat); 11.2mg cholesterol; 114mg sodium.

JACK'S SALAD DRESSING

Makes about 4 cups

Jack Lundin, an extremely busy "retired" Lutheran minister, and his wife, Marti, are used to cooking in quantities that serve hungry hordes. This exceptional salad dressing is perfect for large gatherings.

1 cup corn oil	1 cup bottled chili sauce
1 cup apple cider vinegar	1 medium onion, finely chopped
1 cup sugar	

✚ Blend the ingredients by stirring (not shaking). Pour over cold salad greens and toss to coat.

Per serving: 176 calories; .198g protein; 14.4g carbohydrates; 13.7g fat (1.74g saturated fat); 0mg cholesterol.

PINE NUT-BUTTER LETTUCE SALAD with ROASTED GARLIC-HONEY DRESSING

Serves 4-6

This is one of Cafe for all Seasons' chef Donna Katzl's favorite salads.

DRESSING:

1 whole head garlic
¼ cup olive oil, divided
1 tablespoon Dijonnaise mustard
1½ tablespoons regular Dijon mustard

¼ cup cider vinegar
1 tablespoon honey
2 tablespoons water
Salt to taste

1 large head butter lettuce torn into bite-size pieces
3 ounces baby spinach leaves
¼ cup green onions, cut into thin coins, green part only

⅓ pound bacon, cut very thin, fried golden and drained on a paper towel, divided
½ cup pine nuts (pignoli) lightly toasted, divided

✤ Preheat oven to 350°.

✤ To roast garlic, place entire head of garlic in a small ovenproof dish. Pour 3 tablespoons olive oil over the garlic, cover and bake for 1 hour. Let cool completely. Squeeze the garlic out of the skin of each clove into a small bowl and mash. Set aside.

✤ In a small bowl, combine remaining olive oil, mustard, vinegar, honey, water and salt with garlic pulp. Mix well. Let sit for at least 2 hours in refrigerator to blend flavors.

✤ In a large salad bowl, toss together torn lettuce, baby spinach and green onions. Refrigerate.

✤ To serve, add dressing to salad ingredients and toss. Add ½ of the bacon and pine nuts and toss again lightly. Garnish each individual salad with a sprinkle of bacon and pine nuts.

Per serving: 268 calories; 9.32g protein; 7.46g carbohydrates; 23.2g fat (5.86g saturated fat); 21.5mg cholesterol.

FRESH FRUIT and GREEN SALAD
with RASPBERRY VINAIGRETTE   Serves 6-8

This beautiful salad and zesty vinaigrette from Marti Lundin makes use of both fresh greens and fresh fruit.

4-5 cups fresh greens
3 ripe nectarines or
    pears, unpeeled
4 ounces Bleu cheese or
    Gorgonzola, crumbled

½ cup chopped walnuts
Raspberry Vinaigrette
    (recipe follows)

✤ Wash and drain greens. Tear into bite-size pieces if necessary.

✤ Slice nectarines or pears into ¼-inch slices and mix with greens. Crumble cheese into salad.

✤ Toss with Raspberry Vinaigrette and sprinkle with walnuts. Serve in a large salad bowl or on individual plates.

RASPBERRY VINAIGRETTE:

½ cup avocado oil
3 tablespoons raspberry
    vinegar

¼ teaspoon garlic salt

✤ Mix well with whisk or fork just before tossing salad.

Per serving: 283 calories; 7.31g protein; 12g carbohydrates; 23.9g fat (7.32g saturated fat); 21.4mg cholesterol.

Each year at the Castro Street Fair we have a booth where we pass out literature about our church. Hundreds of people walk by and some stop to chat. They often have a church story to tell. Sometimes they are horror stories, but most of the time they are good stories that end with, "I'll come and visit your church some Sunday." Some do. One man who did was baptized on Reformation Sunday, 1993.

PASTA CHICKEN SALAD
with PEANUTS

Serves 6

This unusual dish from San Francisco food writer Stanley Eichelbaum brings an altogether novel twist to chicken salad. It may be prepared ahead, and even dressed with the vinaigrette a couple of hours before serving. But don't add the watercress garnish until the last minute.

3 whole chicken breasts
Salt and pepper
1 pound linguini, broken
      into 6-inch lengths
1 small green bell pepper,
      cut into thin strips

1 small red bell pepper,
      cut into thin strips
4 green onions, thinly sliced
1 cup chopped, salted
      roasted peanuts

VINAIGRETTE:

Juice of 1 lemon
1½ tablespoons Dijon
      mustard
1 tablespoon brown sugar
2 cloves garlic, minced
2 tablespoons finely
      chopped ginger root
1 jalapeno pepper, seeded
      and finely chopped
¼   cup red wine vinegar

2 tablespoons Asian
      sesame oil
2 tablespoons safflower or
      other light vegetable oil
3 tablespoons olive oil
Salt and pepper to taste
Cucumber, peeled, seeded
      and sliced (garnish)
Watercress sprigs (garnish)

✤ Preheat oven to 375°.

✤ Place chicken breasts in a baking dish, season with salt and pepper, and bake 25 minutes. When the chicken is cool, remove skin, pull meat from bones, and slice the meat thinly against the grain.

✤ Cook the linguini in a large pot of salted water until tender, 8-10 minutes. Drain in a colander. Place the chicken, linguini, peppers, green onions and peanuts in a large bowl.

✤ In a small bowl prepare the vinaigrette by whisking together all ingredients except cucumber and watercress. Pour dressing over the salad and toss. Garnish with cucumber slices and sprigs of watercress.

Per serving: 535 calories; 25.7g protein; 32g carbohydrates; 35.2g fat (5.64g saturated fat); 46.4mg cholesterol.

ORZO SALAD

Serves 12-16

When Michael Hiller's sister, Bonnie, married her old college boyfriend at St. Francis Lutheran Church on May 1, 1994, Michael presided at the ceremony, and their brother, Tom, pastor of Colton (Oregon) Lutheran Church, preached a very moving sermon. This recipe was served at the rehearsal dinner.

1 pound of orzo
   (rice-shaped pasta)
1 cup olive oil, or more to taste
¼ cup tarragon vinegar,
   or more to taste
2 cups frozen peas
   (keep them frozen)
¼ to ½ cup chopped
   oil-packed sun-dried
   tomatoes without herbs

½ cup pine nuts (pignoli)
¼ cup roasted red peppers,
   cut into very narrow strips
   about 2 inches long
¼ cup chopped fresh basil
2 cups broccoli florets

✤ Cook the orzo in boiling water with a little salt and some olive oil until just tender. Drain and place in a heat proof bowl.

✤ Combine the oil and vinegar in a lidded jar and shake vigorously to blend. Add the oil and vinegar mixture to the orzo. Separate the frozen peas, and toss. (Frozen peas will cool the pasta; the heat from the pasta will thaw the peas.)

✤ Toast the pine nuts in a medium skillet over medium-low heat, stirring frequently, until they are evenly brown. Be careful not to let them burn.

✤ Add the pine nuts, peppers and basil to the orzo. Toss. Taste; add salt, olive oil or vinegar to adjust the balance. Mound the orzo in a wide shallow bowl. Surround the mound with lightly steamed (or microwaved) broccoli florets. Serve at room temperature or chilled.

Per serving: 241 calories; 3.93g protein; 14.4g carbohydrates; 20.3g fat (2.87g saturated fat); 0mg cholesterol.

where there is injury, pardon;

Dear God, give us the courage to forgive our brothers and sisters when they wrong us, just as you pardon us when we wrong you.

Move us not to wait. Move us to be the first to forgive, for in forgiving we destroy resentment and bitterness that diminish, then devour us. By forgiving we do miracles. We ignite in each other a flame that warms us all. When we forgive we honor you. *~Amen.*

WEEKEND BRUNCH

It's a lazy Saturday morning, or Sunday after services. You follow the scent of fresh-baked biscuits, and the unmistakable sizzle of batter on a hot griddle, into a cozy little restaurant. A pot of coffee and the daily paper await, to be savored while lounging on an inviting couch. All the comforts of home, and no wonder. It *is* your house, and it's time for brunch.

Brunch is a quilt, a flannel shirt, an old friend. It is breakfast in the afternoon or lunch in the morning. Rules are broken, along with eggs. The pace is leisurely and self-indulgence is encouraged. The toughest decision should be choosing between marmalade or jam, cream and sugar. And please, no fights over who gets the comics!

Sangria

Bohemian Tea

Whole Wheat Banana Bread

Lemon-Glazed Pistachio Coffeecake

Lemon Bread

Pumpkin Bread

Onion Shortcake

Mostly Hall French Toast

Boundary Water Pancakes

Four-Star Muffins

Mitchell's Easy Baked Pancake

Eva's Homemade Tortillas

Great Granola

Baked Eggs Cursillo

Oven Omelet with Spinach

Swiss Egg Puffs

Flat Omelet of Red and Green Peppers, Onions and Potatoes

Tofu Scramble

Crab Quiche

Chinese Chicken Tacos

Breakfast Pasta

Meyer Lemon-Tangerine Pudding

Lowfat Mango Mousse

SANGRIA

Serves 8-10

Alejandro Cejudo and Michael Utech serve this refreshing libation on their deck overlooking San Francisco.

½ cup chopped strawberries
½ cup chopped cantaloupe
½ cup chopped apple
½ cup chopped pear
Juice of 8 limes

Juice of 2 oranges
1 cup sugar
1 bottle (750ml) red wine
4 8-ounce bottles of
  carbonated mineral water

✣ Combine all ingredients except mineral water in a large pitcher and let marinate in the refrigerator at least 2 hours or overnight if possible. To serve, stir in mineral water and pour into ice-filled glasses.

Per serving: 162 calories; .489g protein; 29.2g carbohydrates; .192g fat (.019g saturated fat); 0mg cholesterol.

BOHEMIAN TEA

Makes about 6 quarts

Meredith Karns' grandmother, Mary Wolrab, serves this refreshing tea to company during cold Iowa winters. Make this potable in a large pot on the stove and fill up pitchers as needed to serve thirsty guests.

1 teaspoon ground cinnamon
  (or 2 cinnamon sticks)
2 teaspoons whole cloves
5 tablespoons orange
  pekoe tea

24 cups boiling water
Juice of 6 oranges
Juice of 3 lemons
1½ cups sugar

✣ Place cinnamon, cloves and tea in cheesecloth and tie with string. Pour boiling water over the tea "bag." Cover and let stand 5 minutes. Remove bag and add the orange and lemon juices and sugar. Serve promptly.

Per serving: 57.2 calories; .101g protein; 14.6g carbohydrates; .067g fat (.014g saturated fat); 0mg cholesterol.

WHOLE WHEAT
BANANA BREAD

Makes 1 loaf

When those bananas get dark and "smelly," Jane Rubey suggests you bake banana bread.

2 large, overripe bananas	½ teaspoon baking soda
¼ cup nonfat plain yogurt	2 teaspoons baking powder
3 tablespoons canola oil	½ teaspoon salt
¼ cup molasses	½ cup chopped walnuts
1 egg	(optional)
1½ cups whole wheat	½ cup raisins (optional)
pastry grind flour	

✦ Preheat oven to 350°. Grease a 9x5-inch loaf pan.

✦ In a large bowl, mash bananas thoroughly. Add yogurt, oil, molasses and egg and mix well.

✦ Sift dry ingredients together. Add to wet mixture and mix only enough to blend together. Stir in nuts and raisins, if used.

✦ Turn into prepared loaf pan. Bake until toothpick inserted in center comes out clean, 45-55 minutes. Cool 5 minutes in pan before turning out onto a rack to cool.

Per serving: 215 calories; 4.77g protein; 32.6g carbohydrates; 8.89g fat (.955g saturated fat); 21.6mg cholesterol.

There are quite a number of elderly people in our neighborhood. They shop at the Safeway store across the street and we invite them to our Wednesday Neighborhood Senior Center. Most of those who attend are in their eighties, a few are in their nineties. They still live independently and have outlived most of their friends and neighbors. Our Senior Center is a place where they can make new friends, have a home-cooked lunch and hear an interesting speaker. We also offer a Bible study, exercise, and a hearty community sing-a-long. There is a core of volunteers from our church who help out every week. Everyone needs a family and we try to be family to those who have none. The Center Coordinator calls those on the list every week. Some of the seniors call each other, just to see how they are doing. One of our pastors, Phyllis Zillhart, serves as a special counselor to the seniors. She helps them get through medical forms and paperwork and, when needed, puts them in touch with community resources. In a few cases, she has had to assume power of attorney and place people in places where they can get proper care. It is difficult to give up your independence, even though you can no longer take care of yourself. We try to be a bridge of help and support.

LEMON-GLAZED PISTACHIO COFFEECAKE

Makes 16 rolls

This recipe takes a lot of words to describe, says food consultant Stevie Bass, but it is not difficult to prepare because it uses roll mix. It is also foolproof. When cutting the dough roll into spirals they tend to mash down a bit, but can be easily shaped back into rounds as you transfer them to the cake pans. The coffeecake is tender and has a tangy-sweet "sticky-bun" topping.

1 cup pistachios
1 16-ounce package hot roll mix
2 tablespoons grated lemon peel (5-6 firm lemons, medium grate)
Hot water, butter and egg as roll mix package specifies

Lemon Glaze (recipe follows)
2 tablespoons melted butter
⅓ cup light brown sugar (packed)

✤ Preheat oven to 375°.

✤ Finely chop pistachios and set aside ½ cup for the glaze. Make hot roll mix dough as package directs, but first add lemon peel to flour and yeast mixture. Mix in the warm water, butter and egg. Shape dough into ball and knead for 2 minutes (rather than 5 minutes as directed on package—more kneading is not necessary.) Set aside while making glaze.

LEMON GLAZE:

⅓ cup butter, divided
⅓ cup dark corn syrup
⅓ cup lemon juice

⅓ cup light brown sugar
½ cup chopped pistachios (reserved from above)

✤ Heat ¼ cup butter, syrup and lemon juice together in saucepan until glaze is smooth and blended.

✤ Divide glaze into bottom of 2 greased 9-inch cake pans, coating bottoms evenly. Roll or pat out dough on lightly floured surface to 16x8-inch rectangle. Melt remaining butter and spread over dough using back of a spoon. Sprinkle with brown sugar and remaining ½ cup pistachios. Roll up, starting from long side. Cut rolled dough into 16 slices and evenly space the spirals cut-side up in pans. Let rise in warm place for 30 minutes. Bake in a preheated oven until done, 25-30 minutes. Immediately invert from pans onto plates.

Per serving: 202 calories; 4.1g protein; 25g carbohydrates; 10.3g fat (3.68g saturated fat); 11.9mg cholesterol.

LEMON BREAD   Makes 1 loaf

Erna Dennert and her husband, Rudi, enjoy this breakfast treat with coffee in their San Francisco home. For best flavor be sure to glaze the bread immediately after it comes out of the oven.

⅓ cup solid vegetable shortening	½ cup milk
1⅓ cups sugar, divided	½ cup chopped nuts (optional)
2 eggs	1 lemon, grated rind and juice
1½ cups all-purpose flour	
¼ teaspoon salt	

❖ Preheat oven to 350°. Grease a 9x5-inch loaf pan.

❖ Beat together shortening and 1 cup of sugar until light and fluffy. Add eggs one at a time, beating well after each addition. Sift dry ingredients together and add alternately with milk to sugar mixture, beating well after each addition. Add nuts and lemon rind and stir to combine.

❖ Turn batter into pan and bake until a toothpick inserted in center comes out clean, about 50-60 minutes.

❖ Blend remaining ⅓ cup sugar with lemon juice. Pour over bread as soon as it comes from the oven. Let cool at least 30 minutes before removing from pan.

Per serving: 293 calories; 4.46g protein; 42.7g carbohydrates; 12.1g fat (2.65g saturated fat); 44.1mg cholesterol.

I've been a part-time pastor at St. Francis Lutheran since 1982. There are quite a few of us clergy both on staff and as members. As someone put it, "They could start their own church, but then they wouldn't have the rest of us to preach to."

Public image is crucial to a church wishing to genuinely serve a community. After all, the church is regarded by most of us as—at the least—an institution. But the institution must always keep its integrity in its theology, and at the same time be a warm and welcoming place for people. St. Francis fits that description and more. We hold fast that God is at work here, just as God is at work in the larger church. This is especially important for all of those new members who have previously been beaten down by other well-meaning churches and church people. These new members deserve better, and we must help them come to know the God of grace and the hope they have been seeking. The message of hope must be a gentle and genuine thing.

Jim Lokken, 61, is a sometime journalist and editor and a co-founder of Lutherans Concerned. He is a database-systems administrator at Barclays Law Publishers as well as a part-time pastor.

PUMPKIN BREAD

Makes 1 loaf

Parker Nolen admits this recipe was "borrowed" from the kitchen of Michael Johnson, another St. Francis member, albeit with his gracious permission. Michael passed away from AIDS in early 1994.

3 cups sugar	½ teaspoon ground cloves
4 eggs	1 teaspoon ground cinnamon
2 cups canned pumpkin	
1 cup vegetable oil	2 teaspoons salt
⅔ cup water	2 teaspoons baking soda
3½ cups all-purpose flour	1 teaspoon ground nutmeg

❖ Preheat oven to 350°. Grease and flour a 9-inch square baking pan.

❖ In a large mixing bowl, mix sugar, eggs, pumpkin, vegetable oil and water until well blended. Gradually mix in flour. Add remaining ingredients and beat until smooth.

❖ Pour mixture into prepared baking pan and bake until a toothpick inserted in the center comes out clean, about 50-55 minutes. Let cool.

Per serving: 542 calories; 5g protein; 78.6g carbohydrates; 24.2g fat (2.77g saturated fat); 84.8mg cholesterol.

ONION SHORTCAKE

Serves 8-10

This is one of Pam Blair's favorite dishes, as easy as it is tasty.

1½ cups corn muffin mix
1 egg, beaten
⅓ cup milk
1 cup cream-style corn
2 dashes Tabasco sauce
4 tablespoons (½ stick) butter
1 large sweet onion,
   chopped

1 cup sour cream
¼ teaspoon salt
¼ teaspoon dried dill weed
1 cup shredded Cheddar
   cheese, divided

✤ Preheat oven to 425°. Grease an 8-inch square baking pan.

✤ Combine corn muffin mix, egg, milk, creamed corn and Tabasco sauce. Turn into prepared pan.

✤ Melt butter in a heavy skillet or frying pan over medium heat. Add onion and cook until tender. Remove from heat. Add sour cream, salt, dill weed and ½ cup of shredded Cheddar cheese. Spread onion mixture over batter. Sprinkle evenly with remaining ½ cup shredded Cheddar cheese.

✤ Bake until a toothpick inserted in center comes out clean, 35-40 minutes. Let cool for about 10 minutes and cut into squares.

Per serving: 174 calories; 5.5g protein; 10.3g carbohydrates; 12.8g fat (7.58g saturated fat); 60.1mg cholesterol.

MOSTLY HALL FRENCH TOAST

Serves 6

Dale Johnson got this recipe from Clyde Wildes, who first tasted this unusual French toast at the East Coast resort that bears its name.

8 ounces cream cheese
¾ cup chopped walnuts
2 teaspoons vanilla,
   divided
Grated nutmeg

12 slices white or
   whole wheat bread
4 eggs
1 cup heavy (whipping)
   cream

✤ In a medium bowl, mix together the cream cheese, chopped walnuts and 1 teaspoon vanilla. Spread mixture on both sides of sliced bread.

✤ In a separate larger bowl, mix the eggs, cream, remaining vanilla and nutmeg. Dip the coated bread in the egg mixture and cook on a hot greased griddle, turning once, until nicely browned on both sides. Serve promptly.

Per serving: 572 calories; 14.9g protein; 34.3g carbohydrates; 42.3g fat (19.7g saturated fat); 239mg cholesterol.

BOUNDARY WATER PANCAKES

Serves 6-10

These very hearty pancakes made by Jim Remer have made many campers happy during wilderness trips to the Boundary Water Canoe Area of Minnesota and southern Ontario. They are just as good in your home kitchen.

1 cup plus 2 tablespoons
   all-purpose flour
2 teaspoons baking soda
2½ teaspoons baking powder
1 teaspoon salt
1 cup oatmeal

1 cup bran cereal
2 tablespoons brown sugar
2 eggs, slightly beaten
3 tablespoons vegetable oil
   plus more for cooking
3 cups buttermilk

✤ In a large bowl, mix together flour, baking soda, baking powder, salt, oatmeal, bran cereal and brown sugar. Add eggs, vegetable oil and buttermilk and stir to combine.

✤ Ladle onto greased heated griddle or frying pan about ⅛ cup at a time. Cook over medium-low heat until top is bubbly before turning to cook other side. Grease griddle as needed. Serve hot with your favorite syrup or fresh fruit.

Per serving: 188 calories; 7.5g protein; 27.7g carbohydrates; 6.49g fat (1.21g saturated fat); 45mg cholesterol.

FOUR-STAR MUFFINS   Makes 12

Flo Braker, an exceptional baker who wrote "The Simple Art of Perfect Baking" and "Sweet Miniatures" gave us this incredibly delicious recipe for fruit muffins. Experiment with different fresh fruits as they are in season.

2 cups unsifted all-purpose flour	2 teaspoons finely grated zest of lemon
½ cup sugar	1 teaspoon vanilla
1 tablespoon baking powder	¾ to 1 cup fruit (apples, blueberries or cranberries)
1 teaspoon baking soda	
½ teaspoon salt	2 tablespoons sugar mixed with ½ teaspoon cinnamon for topping
2 large eggs	
¾ cup buttermilk	
3 ounces unsalted butter, melted	

✤ Preheat oven to 400°. Grease and flour 12 muffin cups (about ½ cup capacity).

✤ In a medium bowl, sift flour, sugar, baking powder, baking soda and salt.

✤ In a separate small bowl, combine eggs, buttermilk, butter, lemon zest and vanilla. Stir into dry ingredients just until moistened. Do not beat until smooth because the muffins will bake grainy. Fold in the fruit, mixing just enough to combine.

✤ Fill muffin cups ¾ full. Top each muffin with a sprinkling of cinnamon sugar. Bake until muffins are golden and pull away from the sides of the tin, 20-25 minutes. Cool 15-20 minutes before removing.

Per serving: 195 calories; 3.85g protein; 29.6g carbohydrates; 6.97g fat (3.97g saturated fat); 51.4mg cholesterol.

MITCHELL'S EASY BAKED PANCAKE

Serves 6

Any breakfast or brunch is better with this heavenly pancake. As Nancy Barker notes, it will serve six–or one Mitchell.

4 tablespoons (½ stick) butter	1 cup all-purpose flour
6 eggs	1 teaspoon salt
1 cup milk	

✤ Preheat oven to 425°.

✤ Melt butter in a wok or large ovenproof bowl with high sides. (A 9x13-inch baking pan may also be used but pancake will rise above the sides.)

✤ In a medium bowl, whisk together eggs, milk, flour and salt. Pour the egg mixture into pan of melted butter. Bake 25 minutes. The batter will puff up unevenly as the mixture bakes to a golden brown. Cut into serving-size portions and serve promptly with butter and syrup or fresh berries and whipped cream.

Per serving: 243 calories; 9.82g protein; 18.4g carbohydrates; 14.2g fat (7.22g saturated fat); 238mg cholesterol.

EVA'S HOMEMADE FLOUR TORTILLAS

Makes 1 dozen

Debbie Côté got this recipe from her mother, Eva, who was born and raised in Mexico.

3 cups all-purpose flour	½ tablespoon salt
1 teaspoon baking powder	or to taste
1 cup solid vegetable shortening	1 cup boiling water

✤ Mix flour, baking powder, shortening and salt until smooth. Slowly add boiling water, using a fork to mix. Continue mixing by hand until dough is moist and sticks together. Let rest for 10-15 minutes.

✤ Make golf-ball size portions. Roll out tortillas on a floured work surface with a lightly floured rolling pin.

✤ Place tortillas one at a time on a lightly greased pan or griddle for 2-3 minutes over high heat. Turn over and cook until browned and cooked through. Keep warm until serving.

Per serving: 133 calories; 1.61g protein; 12g carbohydrates; 8.7g fat (2.17g saturated fat); 0mg cholesterol.

GREAT GRANOLA   Makes 12 cups

Jane Rubey, cooking teacher and owner of "Nutritiously Gourmet," says her son (aged 26) and son-in-law (aged 32) have their own granola containers which appear empty in her kitchen every month or so, hoping for refills.

7 cups rolled oats	½ cup sesame seeds
1½ cups chopped almonds	1 cup sunflower seeds
1 cup wheat bran	¼ cup canola oil
1 cup oat bran	⅔ cup honey
1 cup wheat germ	

✤ Preheat oven to 325°.

✤ In one very large or two regular baking pans, mix together all dry ingredients. Heat oil and honey briefly in microwave or over low heat and pour over mixture, stirring well to mix.

✤ Bake 20 minutes. Stir well. Continue baking and stir every 10 minutes until toasted a rich golden brown, about 1 hour. Turn off oven and allow cereal to stand another 15 minutes.

✤ Cool completely. Store in airtight containers. Refrigerate or freeze if not used within one week.

Per serving: 296 calories; 9.38g protein; 33.4g carbohydrates; 13.2g fat (1.48g saturated fat); 0mg cholesterol.

During our Sunday morning worship, a member of the congregation is invited to serve as our Living Word Storyteller. We believe the Word of God is a Living Word, that God is still being revealed through those who believe. Sometimes our Storyteller will take a lesson from the Bible and relate it to the congregation in his or her own words, often acting as the main character. Other times, the Storyteller shares with the congregation an experience which has shaped his or her life journey in faith. They make us see real Christian faith in real people. Some of them are very powerful. Through these stories, we realize that the Word of God is alive today and is revealed among us through all people of faith, past and present. Together, we are the presence of Christ in the world.

BAKED EGGS CURSILLO

Serves 8-10

Nancy Barker tells us she first used a larger version of this recipe to serve sixty people attending a "Cursillo," an intensely spiritual retreat of prayer, study and meditation It serves just eight to ten nicely, too.

½ cup (1 stick) butter
18 eggs
1⅔ cups milk

1½ teaspoons salt
8 ounces cream cheese,
    cut into ½-inch pieces

❖ Preheat oven to 350°. Melt butter and pour into a 9x13-inch baking pan, tilting pan to coat bottom evenly.

❖ In a medium bowl, beat together eggs, milk and salt. Pour the egg mixture into the pan of melted butter. Bake 20 minutes.

❖ Remove from oven and sprinkle evenly with cubed cream cheese. Gently draw a knife through the partially baked eggs to mix in the cream cheese. Return to the oven and bake an additional 10 minutes.

❖ Cut into squares. Serve with ham or sausage and fresh fruit.

Per serving: 305 calories; 13.6g protein; 2.47g carbohydrates; 26.7g fat (13.9g saturated fat); 434mg cholesterol.

OVEN OMELET with SPINACH

Serves 8

When Marti Lundin brought this dish to a Sunday brunch at St. Francis Lutheran, everybody immediately wanted the recipe. Now you have it, too!

1 10-ounce package frozen
    chopped spinach
9 eggs
2 tablespoons milk
Salt and pepper to taste
1 tablespoon chopped fresh
    basil leaves or 1 teaspoon dried

2 cloves garlic, crushed
    through a press
½ cup shredded
    mozzarella cheese
10-12 tomato slices
    (2-3 tomatoes)

❖ Preheat oven to 325°. Grease a 7x11-inch or square baking pan.

❖ Cook spinach as directed on the package. Drain well.

✤ In a large bowl, beat eggs until light and fluffy. Stir in the spinach, milk, salt, pepper, basil and garlic. Pour into prepared pan. Sprinkle with cheese. Arrange tomato slices in a single layer over the top of cheese, covering the egg mixture.

✤ Bake until egg mixture is set in the center, about 25-30 minutes. Cut into squares and serve promptly.

Per serving: 122 calories; 10.5g protein; 4.44g carbohydrates; 7.12g fat (2.62g saturated fat); 243mg cholesterol.

SWISS EGG PUFFS   Serves 4

Barbara and Jack Kling are a formidable pair in the kitchen. This is one of Barbara's favorite items to take on one of their frequent hikes and picnics.

½ cup milk
2 tablespoons butter
¼ teaspoon salt
¼ teaspoon pepper
½ cup all-purpose flour

2 eggs
½ to ¾ cup plus
   2 tablespoons shredded
   Swiss cheese, divided

✤ Preheat oven to 375°. Grease a baking sheet.

✤ In a 1½-quart saucepan over medium heat, combine milk, butter, salt and pepper and bring to a full boil.

✤ Add flour all at once. Stirring constantly, cook until the mixture pulls away from the sides of the pan and forms a ball. Remove from heat.

✤ Beat in eggs one at a time, continuing to beat until the mixture is smooth and well blended. Beat in ½ to ¾ cup cheese. (For a lighter, less cheesy taste, use less cheese. For a cheesy taste and slightly heavier puff, use more cheese.)

✤ Using two spoons, make 4 to 8 equal mounds of dough on the baking sheet at least 2 inches apart. Sprinkle 2 tablespoons of shredded cheese over all. Bake until puffs are browned and crisp, 30-40 minutes (less for smaller puffs). Serve warm or at room temperature.

Per serving: 214 calories; 9.65g protein; 14.2g carbohydrates; 13.1g fat (7.43g saturated fat); 138mg cholesterol.

FLAT OMELET of RED and GREEN PEPPERS, ONIONS and POTATOES   Serves 2-3

This appears so simple—a flat omelet of red and green peppers with diced potatoes and sweet melting onions—but respected food writer Marlena Spieler says there are two secrets that make this a really memorable dish: using enough olive oil and cooking slowly and gently to melt the potatoes and onions together.

2-4 tablespoons olive oil
1 medium to large baking
    potato, unpeeled and
    cut into small dice
½ onion, coarsely chopped
3 garlic cloves, coarsely
    chopped
½ green bell pepper, seeded
    and diced

½ red bell pepper, seeded
    and diced
1 medium to large
    tomato, sliced
3 eggs, beaten lightly and
    mixed with 1 tablespoon
    water
Salt and pepper to taste
1 teaspoon chopped fresh
    thyme (optional)

✤ In a heavy skillet over medium heat, place potato, onion, garlic and 2 tablespoons olive oil. Let cook a few minutes, then cover and let simmer for about 10 minutes, or until potatoes and onions are tender. Every so often, use a spatula to loosen pieces of potato and onion.

✤ Adding more oil if needed, add peppers and tomato, then cover again and let cook another 5-10 minutes.

✤ Pour egg over mixture, pulling up edges to let egg flow underneath and cook evenly. (Another, more traditional method is to remove sauteed vegetables from pan, mix with egg in a bowl, then pour mixture into hot pan, to which you've added a bit more olive oil.) Season with salt and pepper.

✤ Once the bottom is cooked, place under a hot broiler to brown top. Serve promptly, or later at room temperature. Sprinkle with fresh thyme, if desired.

Per serving: 289 calories; 8.6 g protein; 22.5 g carbohydrates; 18.8 g fat (3.42g saturated fat); 212 mg cholesterol.

TOFU SCRAMBLE

Serves 2-4

This colorful dish is one Randy Thueme likes to serve as an alternative to eggs for brunch or over rice in the evening for a quick, nutritious dinner. Randy usually doesn't reveal the tofu ingredient until it is eaten by the unsuspecting guests who might otherwise say they don't like (or just won't eat) tofu. Everyone is usually shocked and thinks they were eating chicken or something similar. Vary the amounts of each ingredient to your own taste.

1 finely diced carrot	½ pound fresh tofu,
1 finely diced celery rib	cut into ½-inch cubes
Kernels from 2 ears of fresh	⅓ cup water
corn or 1 cup of	1 green onion, sliced
canned or frozen corn	Salsa or Italian herbs
1 clove garlic, minced	Tamari soy sauce to taste

✤ Place carrot, celery, corn and garlic in a lightly oiled skillet. Spread tofu on top. Pour in water, bring to a boil, cover and simmer 5 minutes or more, depending on how well cooked you like your vegetables. Add green onion and salsa or herbs. Flavor with tamari soy sauce to taste, and simmer a few more minutes without a cover, until any extra water evaporates.

Per serving: 92.8 calories; 6.52g protein; 12.6g carbohydrates; 3.06g fat (.447g saturated fat); 0mg cholesterol.

I first came to St. Francis simply because it was close to where I lived. My mother needed a church she could visit without taking the bus. We were Southern Baptists from Texas, so we were surprised when Pastor DeLange first came to visit and didn't expect a free meal, as would have been the case in Galveston!

For me, my faith means that I am called to show love for my fellow man, wherever I can. Each day I pray that God will help me be a better person and a greater help for the people around me. Anybody can be nasty. We need help to be the best people we can.

For the senior group one Wednesday I read a prayer based on Romans 12, and that message has stuck with me ever since: "We are all children of God, and we all have some special talent. It takes all of us to be the body of Christ." For me, St. Francis Lutheran is just that.

Faye Robinson, 71, moved to San Francisco in 1952. She has been a housekeeper with the same family for 24 years. Faye is also the founding president of the AAL (Aid Association for Lutherans) branch at St. Francis. Her son, Clifton King, is the church sexton.

CRAB QUICHE

Serves 6

Greg Egertson, former president of the St. Francis Lutheran congregation, created this flavorful quiche especially for our cookbook. Feel free to substitute fresh crab for the canned.

1 tablespoon butter	9-inch pie crust for a
1 6-ounce can crabmeat, drained	deep dish pie
1 small sweet yellow onion, diced	½ cup (about 2 ounces) shredded pepper-jack cheese
2 medium celery ribs, diced	4 eggs
1 cup (about 4 ounces) shredded Swiss cheese, divided	1½ cup heavy (whipping) cream

❖ Preheat oven to 425°.

❖ In a medium non-stick skillet, melt butter over low heat. Add crabmeat, onions and celery and mix together until butter is fully absorbed. Cook over low heat, stirring occasionally until crabmeat is lightly browned and celery is softened. Transfer mixture to a plate and press firmly between paper towels to drain.

❖ Place pie crust in a deep 9-inch pie plate. Sprinkle ⅔ cup of the Swiss cheese over the bottom of pie crust. Add the jack-pepper cheese to the crabmeat mixture and spread over Swiss cheese. Top with the remaining ⅓ cup Swiss cheese.

❖ In a medium mixing bowl, beat eggs and cream together with a fork until blended. Pour mixture over cheese and crabmeat mixture. Bake on center oven rack for 15 minutes. Reduce heat to 300° and bake until a knife inserted in the center comes out clean and top is a golden brown, about 45 minutes. Let stand 10-15 minutes before cutting into wedges. Serve hot or at room temperature.

Per serving: 565 calories; 20.7g protein; 18.1g carbohydrates; 45.8g fat (23.6g saturated fat); 278mg cholesterol.

CHINESE CHICKEN TACOS

Serves 4

Andy Wai, chef at Harbor Village Restaurant in San Francisco's Embarcadero Center, offers this version of the popular Mexican taco.

1 whole chicken breast, skinned and boned
1 egg yolk
1 teaspoon water
½ teaspoon cornstarch
Pinch of salt
½ head romaine or iceberg lettuce
1 tablespoon cooking oil
3 tablespoons chopped Chinese sausage
3 cloves garlic, minced

1 tablespoon dark mushroom soy sauce
1 tablespoon sherry
1 teaspoon oyster sauce
¼ teaspoon powdered chicken bouillon
Pinch of sugar
¼ cup golden chives, chopped
¼ cup pine nuts (pignoli), toasted
Pickled ginger, finely minced
Hoisin sauce

✤ Mince the chicken breasts with a cleaver and place in a bowl. Mix together the egg yolk, water, cornstarch and salt. Pour over minced chicken and marinate at least 15 minutes.

✤ Separate the lettuce leaves, keeping them whole. Wash, pat dry and set aside.

✤ Heat a wok until very hot, then add the cooking oil. When the oil is hot, add the chicken. Stir fry, separating the pieces with a spatula, until the chicken is cooked. Add the Chinese sausage and garlic and stir fry for 2 minutes. Add the soy sauce, sherry, oyster sauce, chicken powdered bouillon and sugar and stir fry to combine. Add the golden chives and pine nuts and stir fry for about 2-3 minutes. Remove chicken-sausage mixture to a heated platter.

✤ Serve using a lettuce leaf as the "taco shell," spreading on it a little hoisin sauce and ginger as desired. Stuff the shell with 1-2 spoonfuls of the chicken mixture (depending on the size of the leaf), wrapping the lettuce leaf around the stuffing. Serve promptly with pickled ginger and Hoisin sauce on the side.

Per serving: 404 calories; 24.5g protein; 9.18g carbohydrates; 31.8g fat (7.11g saturated fat); 118mg cholesterol.

I believe that where the Gospel is truly preached, the Church has tremendous power to heal and liberate those who are marginalized and oppressed. For me, to be a member of St. Francis Lutheran is to join in solidarity with people who are making God real in the world through acts of justice and love.

At their best, I've always believed that Christian congregations should be places of sanctuary where people can experience that level of intimacy in which it is possible to speak the unspeakable. St. Francis is such a community. St. Francis is remarkable in many other ways, not least for its social events. One of the most memorable for me was the baby shower for our daughter, Joy Noelle, who was born on St. Francis Eve, October 3, 1993. A group of gay men threw us a shower, researched it thoroughly, invented the "Lydia Circle" to host it, and came impeccably dressed (in drag) to complete the effect. It was a totally joyous occasion.

Ruth Frost, 46, and her partner, Phyllis Zillhart, were both pastors with Lutheran Lesbian and Gay Ministry, and are now associate pastors at St. Francis Lutheran church. Ruth has studied both art and theology, and—when time permits—does stained glass design.

BREAKFAST PASTA

Serves 4

Elka Gilmore, owner-chef of Elka and Liberté in San Francisco, enjoys serving this extraordinary brunch dish.

12 ounces fresh linguine	8 eggs
2 tablespoons extra virgin olive oil	1 cup grated Parmesan cheese plus more for garnish
8 ounces sweet Italian sausage	2 tablespoons fresh basil
1 cup Spanish olives, thinly sliced	Salt and black pepper to taste
4 cloves garlic, finely chopped	Finely chopped parsley for garnish

✣ In a large pot of boiling, salted water cook pasta until tender. While boiling pasta, heat olive oil in large pan. Add sausage, onions and garlic and cook until onions are almost caramelized, about 10 minutes. Add drained pasta.

✣ In a medium bowl, whisk together eggs, Parmesan cheese, basil, salt and pepper. Add to pan and cook, stirring until eggs are scrambled.

✣ Garnish with parsley and additional Parmesan cheese. Serve promptly.

Per serving: 777 calories; 41.5g protein; 29.9g carbohydrates; 54.8g fat (16.2g saturated fat); 491mg cholesterol.

MEYER LEMON-TANGERINE PUDDING

Serves 6

Our good friend from Cafe For All Seasons, Donna Katzl, suggests that if you can't find Meyer lemons, use regular lemons—but the flavor will be distinctly different.

2 tablespoons butter, slightly softened	1½ tablespoons flour
1 cup sugar	⅓ cup Meyer lemon juice
3 eggs, separated	Finely grated zest of 1 tangerine
1 cup buttermilk	Whipped cream (optional)

✤ Preheat oven to 350°.

✤ In a large bowl, beat butter until soft. Add sugar, beating until incorporated. Beat in the egg yolks, one at a time. Add buttermilk, flour, lemon juice and zest and beat to mix well, even though the mixture may look curdled.

✤ In a separate bowl, beat the egg whites until they form soft peaks, then fold into the batter. Turn into a 1½-quart baking dish and set in a larger pan filled with about 1 inch of hot water. Bake until set, 45-50 minutes. Let cool and serve at room temperature or chilled. Top individual servings with a spoonful of whipped cream, if desired.

Per serving: 227 calories; 4.77g protein; 38.1g carbohydrates; 6.73g fat (3.4g saturated fat); 118mg cholesterol.

LOWFAT MANGO MOUSSE   Serves 2-4

This is one of Linda Carucci's stand-bys. Former dean of students at the California Culinary Academy, Linda is now a freelance food writer and consultant.

2 6-8 ounce cartons low fat or nonfat vanilla yogurt	¼ cup orange juice
	½ teaspoon rum extract
1 mango, peeled, cut into pieces and frozen	Toasted coconut (optional garnish)

✤ Process yogurt, mango, orange juice and rum extract in a food processor or blender and puree on high speed. Spoon into parfait glasses. Garnish with toasted coconut (optional). Serve promptly.

Per serving: 157 calories; 4.95g protein; 25.3g carbohydrates; 4.56g fat (3.67g saturated fat); 4.17mg cholesterol.

Gracious God, Earth-Maker, Pain-Bearer, Life-Giver, we thank you that the dawn of hope and healing rose with Christ on that first Easter morning. No more will the despair and fear of death loom over our lives. Confident in your grace, daily we move from life to fuller life, from love to deeper love, from light to brilliant light.

Redeeming Friend, as we claim your promises for everlasting life, restore us now in the resurrection's joy. Roll away stones of discord, division, and prejudice. Heal our suspicious or miserly hearts; open us to the wealth of diversity united in your call to new life and in grateful service to all in need. *~Amen.*

where there is discord, union;

EASTER CELEBRATIONS

Easter is the time when food is both sacrament and celebration. And yes, yet another grand meal of seasonal bounty.

Food is an edible metaphor, particularly when gray winter fades from the sky and the earth, warming, is once again fertile. The vegetables of spring symbolize growth and renewal. Fruits of the season signal the reemergence of the sun. This sense of rebirth is at the heart of Christian belief. But don't fill up on the symbolism, not with this incredible spread. Let others wax poetic—it's time to eat!

Macedonian Walnut Cakes

Rosemary Buttermilk Biscuits

Swedish Cardamom Braids

Artichoke and Shrimp Appetizer

Couscous Primavera

Asparagus Salad

Spring Vegetable Risotto

Leg of Lamb with Anchovies

Créme Caramel

Lemon Bavarian Cream

Fruit Cheese Flan

Lee's Deluxe Cheesecake

Simply Perfect Cake
with Citrus Glaze

Aunt Elsie's Trifle

MACEDONIAN WALNUT CAKES

Makes 4

Ed Sienkiewicz, the Northern California Bishop of the Greek Orthodox Church, offers this traditional Easter pastry.

BREAD DOUGH (make a day before):

3 ¼-ounce packages dry yeast
¼ cup warm milk (105°-115°)
½ cup plus ½ teaspoon
   sugar, divided
5 cups flour, divided

2 cups (4 sticks) chilled
   butter, divided
4 egg yolks
1 cup heavy (whipping)
   cream

FILLING:

5 egg whites at
   room temperature
1 tablespoon lemon juice
⅛ teaspoon salt

1¼ cups sugar
2 tablespoons vanilla extract
1 pound walnuts, chopped
   (about 4 cups)

GLAZE:

1 egg yolk,

3 tablespoons heavy
   (whipping) cream

✤ To make the dough, dissolve yeast and sugar in warm milk. Let rest for 10 minutes or until yeast is foamy.

✤ Place 2½ cups of the flour, ¼ cup sugar and 1 cup of butter in food processor or blender. Process until mixture resembles course meal. Transfer mixture to a large bowl and repeat with remaining flour, sugar and butter. Add to large bowl.

✤ In a small bowl, combine the egg yolks and cream with the yeast mixture. Mix into the flour mixture. Turn dough onto a lightly floured work surface and knead until smooth. (The dough will be soft and a bit sticky). Form into a ball, place in a bowl, cover with plastic wrap and refrigerate overnight.

✤ To make the filling, combine egg whites, lemon juice and salt in a large bowl and beat until soft peaks form. Mix in sugar a little at a time and beat until no sugar can be felt in the egg whites. Gently mix in vanilland fold in the walnuts.

✤ Divide chilled dough into 4 equal portions and bring to room temperature. When still cool but workable, roll each portion into a rectangle about ⅜-inch thick.

✤ Spread ¼ of the filling over the rectangle. Starting from the end nearest you, roll the dough like making a jelly roll. Place on a buttered cookie sheet, seam-side down. Repeat with the 3 remaining portions of dough. Preheat oven to 325°.

✤ Make the glaze by combining the egg yolk and cream. Brush each roll with the glaze and let rest for 10 minutes. Brush each roll again with glaze and bake until bread makes a "hollow" sound when tapped lightly, 40-50 minutes. Cool before serving.

Per serving: 355 calories; 5.65g protein; 29.5g carbohydrates; 24.6g fat (10.3g saturated fat); 76.5mg cholesterol.

ROSEMARY BUTTERMILK BISCUITS
Makes 16 biscuits

Donna Katzl, chef-owner of Cafe For All Seasons in San Francisco and San Mateo, also makes these biscuits at home for family gatherings.

2 cups all-purpose flour
½ teaspoon salt
2 teaspoons baking powder
½ teaspoon baking soda
4 teaspoons minced fresh
     rosemary or 1½
     teaspoons dried

1 tablespoon sugar
½ cup solid vegetable
     shortening
⅔ cup buttermilk

✤ Preheat the oven to 425°. Grease two 8-inch baking pans.

✤ In a large bowl, mix together flour, salt, baking powder, baking soda, rosemary and sugar. Rub the shortening into the flour mixture with a fork until mixture resembles coarse meal. Add the milk all at once and stir just until the dough forms a ball around the fork.

✤ Turn the dough onto a lightly floured board and knead 14 times. Pat until ½-inch thick. Cut into rounds with a 2-inch cookie cutter or glass. Place touching each other in the cake pan and bake until golden brown, 15-20 minutes. Serve warm with butter.

Per serving: 122 calories; 1.97g protein; 13.8g carbohydrates; 6.69g fat (1.69g saturated fat); .357mg cholesterol.

SWEDISH CARDAMOM BRAIDS   Makes 2

Ed Sienkiewicz lives in the apartment in the back of St. Francis Lutheran, part of what was once the parsonage. When he makes bread, which he does quite often, the entire congregation seems to gather outside his doors. This is one of our favorites.

4 ¼-ounce packages dry yeast	4 tablespoons cardamom seeds, finely ground
¼ cup warm milk (105°-115°)	5-6 cups all-purpose flour
½ cup plus 1 teaspoon sugar, divided	1½ pounds (6 sticks) soft butter
½ teaspoon salt	1 pound golden raisins
1 cup warm heavy (whipping) cream	1 egg, lightly beaten
1 tablespoon pure vanilla	1 tablespoon water
12 egg yolks, beaten	1 tablespoon sugar

✤ Combine yeast, milk and 1 teaspoon sugar until yeast and sugar have dissolved and foamed, about 10 minutes.

✤ Combine yeast mixture with salt, remaining sugar, cream, vanilla, egg yolks and cardamom. Add enough flour to create a medium soft dough. Knead in butter. Continue to knead until dough is shiny, elastic, and has small blisters on its surface. If dough is sticky, add flour (about 3 tablespoons at a time). Place kneaded dough into a large greased bowl. Cover with a towel and place in a warm place until it doubles in bulk, 40-50 minutes.

✤ Punch down dough. Knead in raisins. Divide into two equal portions and then divide each of these portions into three equal ropes. Braid three pieces together and form into circle, pressing ends together (like a wreath). Repeat with the remaining dough. Place braids on a buttered cookie sheet and allow to rise until almost doubled in bulk.

✤ Brush braids with a mixture of beaten egg with a tablespoon of water. Sprinkle liberally with a tablespoon of sugar. Bake at 350° for 40-50 minutes. Yeast cakes are done when a "hollow" sound is created by tapping your fingers against the bottom of the bread or cake. Cool completely. Serve with sweet butter and strong coffee.

Per serving: 342 calories; 4.64g protein; 32g carbohydrates; 22.4g fat (13.2g saturated fat); 143mg cholesterol.

ARTICHOKE and
SHRIMP APPETIZER

Serves 4

Marti Lundin recommends using a china dinner plate for each serving so that the flower effect of the artichoke is not crowded.

20-24 medium shrimp in the shell	12-16 avocado slices
4 artichokes	½ teaspoon garlic salt
½ to ¾ cup Louis dressing	Fresh rosemary sprig

½ to ¾ cup Thousand-
   Island dressing
	with flowers or small
	   edible flowers (garnish)

✤ In a large pot of boiling salted water, cook shrimp until just curled and pink, 3 to 4 minutes. Peel and devein. Refrigerate until serving.

✤ Using a sharp stainless steel knife, cut 1-inch from top of each artichoke and trim away any sharp edges from leaves. In a large pot of boiling salted water, cook artichokes until tender; a leaf should pull easily away from artichoke. Drain. When cool enough to handle, pull center leaves apart and use a melon baller or teaspoon to gently scrape hairy "choke" from center of each artichoke. Cut a slice from the bottom of each artichoke so they will stand upright.

✤ In a small bowl, mix salad dressings until well blended. Fill center of each artichoke with salad dressing mixture.

✤ Place each artichoke in the center of a plate and surround with chilled shrimp. Arrange avocado slices around the shrimp. Sprinkle with garlic salt. Garnish with sprig of rosemary or edible flowers.

Per serving: 252 calories; 12.9g protein; 21.9g carbohydrates; 14.6g fat (2.39g saturated fat); 76.1mg cholesterol.

I've always been surrounded by religion. I grew up a Catholic in the south of Ireland in a very religious region. In my home town, I served Mass for 15 years. After I moved to San Francisco, I was looking for a church that would accept me for who I am. The first day I came, I expected this experience to be the same as all the others—you go in, you pray, and then you leave. No one says anything or really knows who you are. St. Francis Lutheran was different. The minute I stepped in, two people greeted me. After the service people came over and said hello and welcomed me like they'd known me all my life. It's a group that responds and honors people. Nobody goes unnoticed and everybody is valued for what they do, no matter how little or how big it is. Everybody here is on an equal basis.

John O'Byrne, 23, a professional chef, lives and works in Mill Valley, California, just across the Golden Gate Bridge.

David Look, 49, was raised in Peoria, Illinois, and moved to San Francisco in 1980. He is a historical architect with the National Park Service.

COUSCOUS PRIMAVERA   Serves 6

Stanley Eichelbaum, a San Francisco food writer and teacher, offers this hearty, nutritious and exceptionally flavorful vegetable dish.

COUSCOUS:

2½ cups chicken stock or water
2 cups couscous

½ teaspoon salt
1 teaspoon butter

VINAIGRETTE:

2 tablespoons lemon juice
1 teaspoon balsamic vinegar

⅓ cup chopped fresh basil
3 tablespoons olive oil
Salt and pepper to taste

VEGETABLES:

1 tablespoon olive oil
1 small onion, finely diced
2 celery ribs, thinly sliced on the diagonal
2 cloves garlic, minced
2 bell peppers (red and green), peeled, seeded and cut into ¼-inch dice
1 teaspoon red pepper flakes
1 medium carrot, sliced on the diagonal and cooked to crisp-tender

¾ cup green beans, cut into 1-inch lengths and cooked to crisp-tender
1 cup broccoli florets, lightly cooked
⅔ cup snow peas, cut into 1-inch pieces
1 cup small ripe cherry tomatoes
1 teaspoon chopped fresh marjoram
1 teaspoon chopped parsley

✤ To prepare couscous, bring stock or water to a boil in a large saucepan, Remove from heat, add couscous, salt and butter. Cover and let stand 15 minutes. Uncover, fluff with a fork and set aside to cool.

✤ In a small bowl, prepare vinaigrette by whisking together lemon juice, vinegar, basil and oil. Season with salt and pepper to taste. Set aside.

✤ For vegetables, heat oil in a large skillet, add onion and cook over moderate heat until tender. Stir in celery, garlic, red and green peppers, red pepper flakes and carrot. Cook for 5 minutes. Add green beans, broccoli and snow peas, and cook 3 minutes longer stirring occasionally. Stir in cherry tomatoes. Season with salt and pepper to taste.

✛ To assemble, combine couscous, vegetables and chopped marjoram and parsley in a large bowl. Pour vinaigrette over mixture, toss and serve on greens.

Per serving: 235 calories; 6.37g protein; 27.8g carbohydrates; 11.7g fat (2.05g saturated fat); 3.79mg cholesterol; 732mg sodium.

ASPARAGUS SALAD   Serves 6

Michael Utech and Alejandro Cejudo enjoy serving this simple spring salad in their Potrero Hill home.

1 pound fresh asparagus, trimmed	1 tablespoon coarse-style Dijon mustard
2 tablespoons olive oil	¼ cup freshly grated Parmesan cheese
1 tablespoon fresh lemon juice	

✛ Cut asparagus stalks in half crosswise. Cook in a large pot of salted boiling water until crisp-tender, no more than 2-3 minutes, depending on thickness. Drain and immerse immediately in cold water to stop cooking process.

✛ In a large bowl, whisk together olive oil, lemon juice and mustard. Gently toss with asparagus and top with Parmesan cheese. Serve at room temperature.

Per serving: 78.7 calories; 3.59g protein; 3.98g carbohydrates; 6.02g fat (1.45g saturated fat); 3.29mg cholesterol.

SPRING VEGETABLE RISOTTO

Serves 4

Risotto is comfort food—loved by all, and with good reason. A successful risotto is rich, creamy and packed with flavor. This recipe from Bay Area food professional Kathleen Prisant is especially delicious. The surprise is that fat can be kept to a minimum without sacrificing any of the above attributes. Use the minimum amount of oil and butter to coat the rice and a good, flavorful cheese.

4 cups homemade chicken or vegetable stock (or 2 cups cups water and 2 cups canned chicken broth)
1 tablespoon butter
1 tablespoon olive oil
1 leek, white part only, diced
3 cloves garlic, minced
1 cup California pearl rice or Italian Arborio rice

¼ teaspoon salt
¼ teaspoon white pepper
½ cup dry white wine
2 small carrots, shredded
1 small zucchini, shredded
1 ounce (about ½ cup) aged Asiago cheese, grated
1 tablespoon chopped chives (garnish)

✤ In a medium saucepan, bring stock to a boil. Reduce heat to low; cover and simmer gently.

✤ In a large heavy pot, heat butter and oil. Add leeks and garlic. Cook over medium-low heat until softened. Add rice, salt and pepper. Cook, stirring occasionally, until rice is translucent. Increase heat to high, add wine, and cook until absorbed.

✤ Reduce heat to medium. Stirring constantly, add about ½ cup of boiling stock. Cook and stir until stock is absorbed. Continue adding stock, ½ cup at a time, stirring constantly and adding more only when previous addition of stock has been absorbed. Rice should be tender by last addition of stock. If not, stir in a small amount of hot water and cook until rice is tender yet firm. Rice will be surrounded by a creamy liquid. Stir in carrots, zucchini and cheese. Cook briefly to melt cheese. Garnish with chives. Serve promptly.

Per serving: 434 calories; 14.5g protein; 56.7g carbohydrates; 14.4g fat (5.62g saturated fat); 22.6mg cholesterol.

LEG of LAMB with ANCHOVIES

Serves 8

Marlene Levinson, noted food professional, uses this recipe in her San Francisco cooking classes.

1 leg of lamb (4½ to 5 pounds)
3 to 4 large cloves garlic,
    sliced in quarters
1 can anchovy filets
Salt and freshly ground
    black pepper to taste

½ cup olive oil
    (no substitutes)
2 cups beef stock
1 cup gin

✤ Preheat oven to 450°.

✤ Remove all fat from the lamb. Make slits in the meat and insert garlic and anchovies. Rub lamb with the olive oil, making sure all the meat is coated. This will seal in the juices. Season with salt and a generous amount of pepper.

✤ Place lamb in a large roasting pan and roast 15 minutes. Add the beef stock to pan and reduce oven temperature to 300°. Cook for 1¼ to 1½ hours for rare/medium rare (cook longer for more well done meat). Baste with some of the gin every 15 minutes or so.

✤ Let lamb rest in a warm place, out of the oven, for 10-15 minutes before slicing. To serve, slice lamb horizontally and place on a warm platter. Spoon pan juices over.

Per serving: 543 calories; 50.7g protein; 3.25g carbohydrates; 28g fat (6.83g saturated fat); 156mg cholesterol.

I am a child of God. I am also a straight, single, Caucasian female. I started attending St. Francis Lutheran regularly in about 1975, when there were only some 25 people in the congregation. For me, being in St. Francis is being in a family, and being in a congregation that practices what it preaches—that God loves all his creation and that we are all brothers and sisters.

People here really accept me for who I am. That is why I am still here. This wonderful variety of people functions because we know our common denominator. Each one of us is a child of God, working together. Thanks to St. Francis, I really do feel that the road I'm traveling—personally and spiritually—has changed tremendously for the better. I now see that individuals in a group do not need to be at the same place at the same time; we all travel at different speeds.

Leona Lee, 54, spent the first 26 years of her life in Tulare, a small town in the San Joaquin Valley of California. She works as a legal secretary and dreams of retiring early.

CRÈME CARAMEL

Serves 8

This easy and delicious dessert is one of Arni Lovitt's favorites, a perfect ending to any great meal. Once baked, the caramel forms a sauce that coats the unmolded custard.

CARAMEL SYRUP:

1½ cups sugar ⅞ cup water, divided

CUSTARD:

8 extra large eggs ½ tablespoon pure vanilla
1 quart milk extract
½ cup sugar

✤ In a small saucepan, combine sugar with ½ cup water. Cook over medium heat until mixture boils, not; occasionally washing down sides of pan with a brush dipped in water. Cook until mixture turns a light amber color. Immediately remove from heat, place saucepan in sink and slowly pour in remaining ⅜ cup water through a colander placed over the saucepan. (Sugar will make an explosive popping sound and steam will rise, so be sure to keep hands and face away from steam as it could burn.) After liquid calms, gently stir to blend water and sugar. Immediately pour warm caramel into 8 custard cups or coffee cups, turning to coat the bottom and sides evenly. Chill in refrigerator.

✤ Preheat oven to 300°.

✤ To make the custard, beat eggs at slow speed until well mixed. Slowly add milk and vanilla and mix until blended, then blend in sugar. Scrape bottom of bowl to be sure all sugar has dissolved. Pour through strainer to remove any visible egg. Pour into chilled custard cups and place cups in large pan. Fill large pan with about 1 inch of hot water. Place in preheated oven. Place a piece of parchment or waxed paper over the top and bake until a knife inserted in the center of cup comes out clean, about 2 hours. Let cool to room temperature and refrigerate until thoroughly chilled. Using a sharp knife, loosen the custards from the cups. Cut around edge of custard and invert each custard onto a small plate and shake loose, like removing jello from a mold.

Per serving: 383 calories; 11.3g protein; 63.1g carbohydrates; 9.88g fat (4.34g saturated fat); 263mg cholesterol.

LEMON BAVARIAN CREAM

Serves 8-10

Kirsten Havrehed offers this very light and popular dessert, perfect for Easter or any other festive occasion.

3 eggs, separated
1 cup sugar, divided
1 envelope unflavored
  gelatin
½ cup cold water
¾ cup fresh lemon juice
¾ cup fresh orange juice

Grated zest of 1 lemon
  (optional)
Grated zest of 1 orange
  (optional)
½ pint heavy (whipping)
  cream, whipped
  (optional)

✤ In large mixing bowl, beat the egg yolks with ½ cup of sugar until thick and lemon-colored.

✤ Combine gelatin and cold water in a small heatproof bowl. Set bowl in a small pan of simmering water, stirring until mixture is clear and has no lumps.

✤ Add gelatin mixture, lemon juice and orange juice to the egg mixture. Add the lemon and orange rind (optional) and stir until well blended. Refrigerate, stirring occasionally, until thickened, about 20 minutes.

✤ In a large bowl, beat egg whites until soft peaks form. Gradually beat in remaining ½ cup sugar. Immediately fold the stiffly beaten egg whites into the thickened gelatin mixture.

✤ Pour mixture into a serving bowl or individual sherbet glasses. If desired, top with whipped cream.

Per serving: 336 calories; 5.8g protein; 40.9g carbohydrates; 17.7g fat (10g saturated fat); 177mg cholesterol.

Going to church used to be easy. You picked up the hymnal, sang a bit, followed the liturgy, listened to a sermon and went home. At St. Francis Lutheran, you are asked to be part of the action. The prayers are new every week, composed and spoken by a member of the congregation. The hymns and liturgy are rewritten to make the language inclusive; the Eucharistic Prayer is often original. We have communion and services of healing at every service. Then you have to stay for coffee because the pastries are so good and you might miss somebody's birthday. You spend at least two hours in church on Sunday morning, three if you sing in the choir. If someone invites you to brunch, then church becomes an all-day affair.

FRUIT CHEESE FLAN

One of Arni Lovitt's beautiful desserts, this fruit-topped tart is perfect for springtime celebrations. Arrange fresh fruit in a pattern on top or just pile high with fresh berries, depending only upon your creativity and your patience!

CRUST:

4 tablespoons (½ stick) butter
   at room temperature
⅓ cup sugar

1⅓ cups cake flour
½ egg, lightly beaten
½ tablespoon milk

FILLING:

4 tablespoons (½ stick) butter
   at room temperature
8 ounces cream cheese
   at room temperature

¾ cup sugar
2 extra large eggs

TOPPING:

Fresh fruit such as blueberries, raspberries, strawberries, kiwi, peaches, apricots, etc.

✤ To make the crust, cream butter and sugar in a large bowl. Add cake flour in two stages, alternating with egg (scrape down after each addition). Add milk and mix until well blended. Chill for ½ hour.

✤ Preheat oven to 350°.

✤ Roll out dough ¼-inch thick and line a 10-inch flan or tart pan with removable bottom. Cover shell with aluminum foil and fill with beans or pie weight and bake 15 minutes. Remove aluminum foil and beans and return to oven until light brown, 5-10 minutes. Cool.

✤ To make the filling, cream butter and cream cheese. Add sugar and mix until smooth. Add eggs and mix until well blended. Fill tart shell and bake until light brown, about 30 minutes. Cool completely. Place fruit(s) on top of filling, remove side from pan and cut tart into slices to serve.

Per serving: 348 calories; 4.02g protein; 29.3g carbohydrates; 24.8g fat (14.5g saturated fat); 114mg cholesterol.

LEE'S DELUXE CHEESECAKE

Serves 10-12

Lee Allison, who now lives in Palm Springs, California, got this recipe from his aunt in New York about 20 years ago. He says it is foolproof and your guests will love it. Place Bing cherries on top and drizzle with a mixture of white chocolate and sour cream for a decadent variation.

CRUST:

2 tablespoons unsalted butter, melted

1¼ cups cinnamon graham cracker crumbs

2 tablespoons sugar

¼ teaspoon cinnamon

FILLING:

4 8-ounce packages cream cheese at room temperature

2 cups sugar

6 large eggs at room temperature

2 tablespoons vanilla

2 cups sour cream at room temperature

✣ Preheat oven to 375°. Grease only the bottom of a 9-inch spring-form pan.

✣ Mix together crust ingredients until well blended and pat evenly into bottom of springform pan.

✣ In a large bowl, beat cream cheese until light and fluffy. Gradually add the sugar, beating constantly. Add eggs, one at a time, beating well after each addition. Fold in vanilla and sour cream until well blended. Pour into prepared pan. Bake until top is lightly brown, about 45 minutes. Turn off oven and leave cake in oven 1 hour longer. Remove from oven and cool completely.

✣ Remove the side from pan and refrigerate for up to two days before serving.

Per serving: 602 calories; 11.4g protein; 49.7g carbohydrates; 40.4g fat (23.9g saturated fat); 228mg cholesterol.

SIMPLY PERFECT CAKE with CITRUS GLAZE

Serves 8

Flo Braker, author of "The Simple Art of Perfect Baking" and "Sweet Miniatures," offers this "simple" cake with a delectable citrus glaze, the perfect ending to any meal.

1½ cups sifted cake flour
1 cup sugar
2 teaspoons baking powder
⅛ teaspoon salt

2 large eggs
1 cup heavy (whipping) cream
1 teaspoon vanilla
Citrus Glaze (recipe follows)

❖ Preheat oven to 350°. Grease and flour a 9-inch springform pan.

❖ Sift together the flour, sugar, baking powder and salt. Set aside.

❖ In a small mixing bowl, beat the eggs with an electric mixer on medium speed until light and fluffy, about 1 minute. Set aside. Without washing the beaters, whip the cream in a large mixing bowl just until the cream starts to thicken but does not form soft peaks. Fold in eggs and vanilla.

❖ Add the flour mixture, stirring briskly just until the batter is smooth. Spread batter evenly in springform pan. Bake until a toothpick inserted in the center comes out clean, 30-35 minutes. Cool on wire rack 15 minutes before removing the springform's hinged band that clasps to the bottom of the cake pan. Cool completely before glazing.

CITRUS GLAZE:

1 tablespoon unsalted
   butter, melted
1 tablespoon grated zest
   of lemon and/or orange

3 tablespoons fresh
   orange juice*
1⅓ cups sifted
   powdered sugar

❖ Combine ingredients until smooth. Spread evenly over cooled cake. Sprinkle finely grated lemon and orange zest over glaze.

❖ Note: *You may substitute fresh tangerine or blood orange juice.

Per serving: 370 calories; 3.95g protein; 58.3g carbohydrates; 14.1g fat (8.21g saturated fat); 106mg cholesterol.

AUNT ELSIE'S TRIFLE

Serves 15-20

Elsie Zorn is the unofficial "trifle queen" of northeastern Wisconsin. Since her nephew, Wayne Strei, introduced her to this English dessert about ten years ago, no family gathering or church potluck is complete without one of Elsie's trifles. Vary the fruits according to season.

1 14-ounce can sweetened
    condensed milk
1½ cups cold water
2 teaspoons grated
    lemon zest
1 3.4-ounce package
    instant vanilla pudding
2 cups heavy
    (whipping) cream
2 teaspoons sugar
2 teaspoons vanilla

4 cups prepared pound cake,
    cut into ¾-inch cubes
½ cup dry sherry (optional)
2 cups halved strawberries
2 cups blueberries,
    fresh or frozen
1 cup red or golden
    raspberries
Fresh sprig of mint
    (garnish)

✤ In a large bowl, combine sweetened condensed milk, water and lemon zest and mix well. Add instant pudding and beat until well blended. Chill 5-10 minutes.

✤ In a large bowl, beat whipping cream until soft peaks form. Whip in sugar and vanilla. Fold whipped cream into pudding mixture.

✤ Spoon about 2 cups of pudding mixture into a 4-quart glass bowl. Layer with one-half of pound cake cubes. Sprinkle with ¼ cup dry sherry (optional). Spread all of strawberries over pound cake cubes. Sprinkle with remaining ¼ cup dry sherry (optional). Cover with half the remaining pudding mixture and then the blueberries. Spread the remaining pudding mixture within 1-inch of the edge of serving bowl so that blueberries show. Top with raspberries.

✤ Chill at least 4 hours or overnight before serving. Garnish with sprig of fresh mint, if desired.

Per serving: 280 calories; 3.56g protein; 33.1g carbohydrates; 15g fat (7.68g saturated fat); 53.2mg cholesterol.

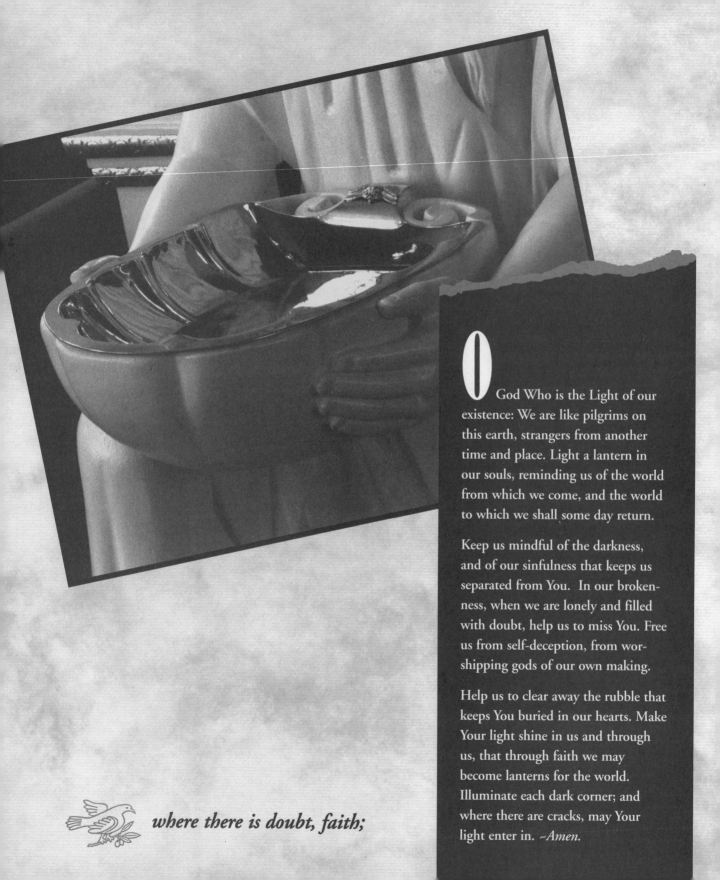

O God Who is the Light of our existence: We are like pilgrims on this earth, strangers from another time and place. Light a lantern in our souls, reminding us of the world from which we come, and the world to which we shall some day return.

Keep us mindful of the darkness, and of our sinfulness that keeps us separated from You. In our broken-ness, when we are lonely and filled with doubt, help us to miss You. Free us from self-deception, from wor-shipping gods of our own making.

Help us to clear away the rubble that keeps You buried in our hearts. Make Your light shine in us and through us, that through faith we may become lanterns for the world. Illuminate each dark corner; and where there are cracks, may Your light enter in. ~Amen.

where there is doubt, faith;

POTLUCK POTPOURRI

Love thy neighbors? How about their taco salad? Potlucks are the most democratic of meals. They allow you to cook great quantities of food—always the most efficient, affordable and fun approach—to share with others. In return you have full run of an array of stock pots, roasting pans and casseroles: a homemade buffet of exceptional treasures.

A communal affair, potluck parties are perfect for meeting people. Even if they don't talk much, the contents of their crock pot will tell you plenty. The recipes, usually personal favorites, are discussed and shared. And if the mood is right and new friendships develop, who knows—maybe a few secret ingredients will be revealed.

Aunt Jane's Mexicali Fiesta Corn Salad

Rice Salad

Napa Cabbage Salad

Jalapeno Cole Slaw

Marinated Carrots

Italian Vegetables

Calabacitas

California Scalloped Potatoes

Baked Beans

Polenta Casserole

Mom's Tamale Pie

Cheese and Macaroni with Ham

Polenta Cake

*Carrot Cake
with Cream Cheese Frosting*

Earthquake Cake

Methodist Apple Crisp

Peach-Blueberry Crisp

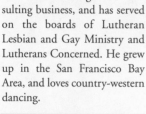

AUNT JANE'S MEXICALI FIESTA CORN SALAD

Serves 8-10

Amanda Hamilton, owner of Merry Hill Vineyards in Glen Ellen, California, serves this popular potluck dish on her terrace overlooking Sonoma County's beautiful wine region.

2 17-ounce cans whole kernel corn, white or yellow, drained
2 medium tomatoes, diced
1 red onion, chopped
1 red bell pepper, chopped
1 green bell pepper, chopped
½ pound Jarlsberg or Swiss cheese, cut into ¼-inch dice

½ cup grated Parmesan cheese
4 canned jalapenos, diced
½ cup fresh chopped cilantro or 2 tablespoons ground cumin
1 teaspoon salt
Ground pepper to taste
1 cup olive oil

✤ Combine all ingredients except olive oil until well mixed. Drizzle with olive oil and toss to a wild Latin beat!

Per serving: 387 calories; 11.5g protein; 21.5g carbohydrates; 30.4g fat (8.07g saturated fat); 24.7mg cholesterol.

RICE SALAD

Serves 10-12

John Phillip Carroll, cookbook author and food writer, suggests this as a tasty alternative to potato salad.

9 cups cooked rice (3 cups uncooked)
½ to ¾ cup olive oil
1 bunch parsley, chopped
1 bunch green onions, chopped (white and green parts)
2-3 hard-boiled eggs, chopped

2 2.2-ounce cans sliced ripe olives, drained
2 red or green apples, cored, diced, but unpeeled
½ cup chopped walnuts or pine nuts (pignoli)
½ cup red wine vinegar
Salt and pepper to taste

✤ Cook rice according to package directions. While still hot, toss with olive oil. As mixture cools, toss occasionally. Add remaining ingredients. Toss to mix. Taste and correct seasonings. You may want to season heavily with salt and pepper to bring out the flavors. Serve at room temperature.

Per serving: 413 calories; 5.93g protein; 51.1g carbohydrates; 20.9g fat (2.87g saturated fat); 35.3mg cholesterol.

NAPA CABBAGE SALAD   Serves 8-10

Jack Kling, one of the Senior Center's resident chefs, enjoys making this sensational salad. It can be transformed into a main dish by arranging cooked chopped chicken, beef or pork on top.

2 tablespoons sliced almonds	2 tablespoons sugar
2 tablespoons sesame seeds	¼ teaspoon pepper
6 green onions, thinly sliced	¼ teaspoon salt
1 head Napa cabbage, finely chopped	2 tablespoons vegetable oil
2 3-ounce packages of ramen noodles, broken into small pieces (save or discard seasoning packets)	¼ cup rice wine vinegar or distilled white vinegar

✤ Toast almonds and sesame seeds in a small non-stick pan over low heat until golden brown and fragrant.

✤ In a large bowl, combine almonds, sesame seeds, onions, cabbage and dry ramen noodles.

✤ In a small jar, combine pepper, salt, oil, vinegar. Cover and shake vigorously to blend. Pour over salad mixture, and toss to combine. Cover and refrigerate.

Per serving: 68.6 calories; 1.19g protein; 6.87g carbohydrates; 4.41g fat (.468g saturated fat); 2.67mg cholesterol

JALAPENO COLE SLAW

Serves 8-12

Werner Bachmann prepares this tangy cole slaw for church potlucks and as a side dish for dinners held in his home high on one of San Francisco's many hills. Feel free to add or decrease the amount of jalapeno peppers according to taste.

2½ to 3 pounds cabbage	2 tablespoons lemon juice
2 carrots	5 tablespoons mayonnaise
2 tablespoons sugar	½ cup wine or apple
2 teaspoons seasoning salt	cider vinegar
½ teaspoon black pepper	⅓ cup canola oil
⅓ cup diced pickled jalapeno peppers (either whole or nacho rings)	6 shakes Worcestershire sauce
	2 cloves garlic, crushed through a press

✤ Shred cabbage and carrots into a large bowl; set aside.

✤ In a small bowl, mix remaining ingredients together. Pour mixture over cabbage and carrots and toss to combine. Refrigerate until serving.

Per serving: 132 calories; 1.66g protein; 8.72g carbohydrates; 10.9g fat (1.29g saturated fat); 3.39mg cholesterol.

MARINATED CARROTS

Serves 12-16

Leona Lee, a very active member of St. Francis Lutheran, has made this tasty vegetable dish for lots of church family events. Don't be put off by the canned tomato soup.

2 pounds carrots, sliced thin	½ cup sugar
1 10¾-ounce can tomato soup, undiluted	⅔ cup vegetable oil
1 small yellow onion, finely chopped	½ cup apple cider vinegar
1 small green bell pepper, finely chopped	2 teaspoons Worcestershire sauce

✤ In a large pot, cook carrots in lightly salted water until crisp-tender. Drain well.

✦ In a large bowl, combine remaining ingredients. Add carrots, tossing to coat. Refrigerate overnight or until serving.

Per serving: 146 calories; .974g protein; 15.6g carbohydrates; 9.48g fat (.896g saturated fat); 0mg cholesterol.

ITALIAN VEGETABLES

Serves 8-12

Bill Shoaf's brother John first prepared this dish for family gatherings. While the preparation time is long, Bill says the result is spectacular—rows of red, yellow, and green with rosemary sprigs and dots of black olives plus the taste is heavenly. This dish can be prepared a day or two in advance and cooked just before serving. If you add tomatoes a lot of liquid results, but that's fine since this dish goes well with polenta, rice or foccacia.

⅛ to ¼ cup olive oil, divided
3-4 Russet potatoes, peeled and
    sliced into ¼-inch pieces
2 zucchini
2 yellow squash
2 peppers (red, yellow
    or green), seeded
1 medium eggplant
    (salted and drained)

3 garlic cloves, slivered
8 oil-cured (dry) olives,
    pitted
4 fresh rosemary sprigs
    (optional)
2 anchovy fillets
    (optional)

✦ Preheat oven to 375°. Coat the bottom of a large baking dish at least 2 inches deep with a bit of olive oil.

✦ Arrange potato slices in a single layer in baking dish.

✦ Slice vegetables into ¼-inch pieces and arrange decoratively in rows over the potatoes. (Perhaps a row of eggplant slices, then a row of red pepper slices, then a row of yellow squash slices, etc.)

✦ Scatter slivers of garlic and olives between the rows of vegetables. If you have fresh rosemary, place 4 8-inch sprigs across the top. Drizzle with olive oil. Place anchovy filets on top, if desired. Cover tightly with aluminum foil and bake until potatoes are tender, about 1½ hours. Remove the aluminum foil and bake until bubbly hot and vegetables are lightly browned, 20-30 minutes. Serve promptly or cool to room temperature.

Per serving: 109 calories; 3.28g protein; 10.5g carbohydrates; 6.75g fat (.965g saturated fat); 4.02mg cholesterol.

CALABACITAS

Serves 4-6

This is a favorite dish from Gene Clark's travels in Mexico.

1 pound zucchini (about 3-4) cut into ⅛-inch thick slices
3 tablespoons olive oil
1 8-ounce can tomato sauce
1 4-ounce can diced green chilies

1 2-ounce can sliced ripe olives
¼ cup sliced green onions
¼ teaspoon ground cumin
1 cup shredded Cheddar cheese
1 cup sour cream (optional)

✤ Preheat oven to 350°.

✤ In a large skillet, cook zucchini in olive oil until crisp-tender. Transfer to a shallow baking dish. In a small bowl, mix together tomato sauce, chilies, olives, onions and cumin and pour over zucchini. Sprinkle cheese over top. Bake until heated through and cheese is melted, about 10 minutes. Serve with sour cream on the side, if desired.

Per serving: 171 calories; 6.3g protein; 6.43g carbohydrates; 14.2g fat (5.05g saturated fat); 19.8mg cholesterol.

CALIFORNIA SCALLOPED POTATOES

Serves 8-10

Dale Johnson's friend, Patricia White, gave him this unusual recipe.

1 red bell pepper
4-5 medium red potatoes, peeled and sliced ⅛-inch thick
2 tablespoons olive oil, divided
1 onion, diced
4-5 green onions, sliced
¼ pound mushrooms, sliced
½ tablespoon butter
2 tablespoons flour

½ teaspoon salt
1 cup milk, heated
1 tablespoon chopped fresh tarragon leaves or 1 teaspoon dried
1 teaspoon Dijon mustard
4 ounces Greek kasseri cheese, crumbled

✤ Preheat oven to 350°. Lightly oil a 2-quart deep casserole.

✤ Roast red pepper over a gas flame or under a broiler until it is charred black. Cool in a paper bag. When pepper is cool, rinse off the charred skin and chop the flesh into small pieces.

✤ In a pot of salted boiling water, boil potatoes for 5 minutes. Drain in a colander.

✤ Heat 1 tablespoon olive oil in a medium skillet or frying pan. Add onions and cook until translucent, 5-7 minutes. Remove from skillet and reserve. In the same skillet, cook mushrooms over medium heat until wilted. Drain. Alternate layers of potatoes, onions, green onions and mushrooms in the casserole, ending with a top layer of potatoes.

✤ Melt butter in 1 tablespoon olive oil over low heat in the same skillet in which the mushrooms were cooked. Add the flour and salt and stir until mixture bubbles. Slowly add the hot milk and whisk until the sauce is smooth. Add the tarragon, mustard and cheese and stir until cheese is slightly melted. Pour the sauce over the potatoes. Bake uncovered until the top layer is slightly browned and mixture is bubbly hot, about 30 minutes. Serve promptly.

Per serving: 194 calories; 6.77g protein; 31.5g carbohydrates; 5.19g fat (2.92g saturated fat); 16.8mg cholesterol.

BAKED BEANS
Serves 12-16

Clarice Strei says this recipe is incredibly easy and serves a small army.

2 pounds Great Northern or Navy beans	1 onion, chopped
	½ cup molasses
	½ cup ketchup
1 cup maple syrup	Salt and pepper to taste
3 slices cooked bacon, chopped	1 tablespoon mustard

✤ Place beans in a large deep ovenproof pot. Add enough water to cover beans by 2 inches. Let soak at least 8 hours or overnight.

✤ Drain beans. Add fresh water to cover. Boil beans until tender, about 2 hours. Stir in maple syrup, bacon, onion, molasses, ketchup, salt, pepper and mustard. Preheat oven to 350°. Bake until bubbly hot, about 1 hour.

Per serving: 175 calories; 5.65g protein; 37.4g carbohydrates; 1.04g fat (.314g saturated fat); 1.08mg cholesterol.

POLENTA CASSEROLE

Serves 8-12

Ed Sienkiewicz loves to cook and this is a dish we love to eat.

I came to St. Francis Lutheran in need of spiritual peace. The congregation was friendly, and their welcome meant that I could come to services and be myself. When my partner's brother Terry was dying, Pastor Phyllis Zillhart ministered to all of us. Watching Terry die in peace (and without fear) was a real gift St. Francis gave me. It was this very peace and the feeling of God's presence that I was looking for when I came here.

When something keeps me from coming to church, I miss the sense of perspective that worship gives me. If I feel my thinking is becoming small and narrow, St. Francis helps me to open up again and see the big picture—it keeps the Gospel alive in my daily life.

Jeannine Janson, 46, is a legal secretary. She and her partner, Joyce Soules, like to entertain friends and spend time with their families. They are looking forward to Joyce's first grandchild.

POLENTA:

1 quart water
½ teaspoon salt
1 cup polenta (coarse cornmeal)
1 cup coarsely chopped oil-packed sundried tomatoes
½ pound (2 sticks) unsalted butter

1 cup grated Parmesan or Romano cheese, plus more for serving
1 cup finely chopped flat leaf (Italian) parsley
½ teaspoon white pepper
1 teaspoon fennel seeds

TOPPING

¾ cup finely shredded fresh basil or 1 tablespoon dried
4 cups meatless spaghetti sauce, plus more for serving

1 pound Greek olives, pitted and coarsely chopped
1 pound feta cheese, crumbled
¼ cup olive oil

❖ Lightly oil an 8½x17-inch or 10x15-inch pan and set aside.

❖ In a large heavy pot, bring water and salt to a rolling boil. Add polenta very slowly, stirring constantly with a wooden spoon. Reduce heat to low and continue to stir for 30 minutes. The mixture will become very thick. Remove from heat. Add the tomatoes, butter, grated cheese, parsley, white pepper and fennel seed. Return to very low heat and cook, stirring constantly, for another 10 minutes. Pour into the oiled pan. Cover with plastic wrap and let cool. Recipe can be prepared in advance through this step.

❖ Preheat oven to 350°. Bring the prepared polenta to room temperature. Sprinkle with shredded fresh basil. Spread the spaghetti sauce over the basil. Be sure that the sauce covers the entire surface of the polenta. Sprinkle the chopped olives over the sauce. Sprinkle the crumbled feta cheese over the top of the entire casserole. Drizzle surface with olive oil. Bake until heated through and lightly browned, 25-35 minutes. To serve, allow casserole to sit for about 5 minutes, then cut into squares.

Per serving: 490 calories; 12g protein; 26.6g carbohydrates; 38.9g fat (18.6g saturated fat); 81.6mg cholesterol.

MOM'S TAMALE PIE   Serves 8-12

Jack Kling's mother-in-law, Eleanor Stevenson, handed this recipe down to her children. "The best thing mom makes" is the consensus of Barbara Kling and her siblings.

1½ cups yellow cornmeal	1 teaspoon dried oregano
1½ cups milk	¼ teaspoon salt
2 eggs	1 16-ounce can chopped
¼ cup olive oil	tomatoes
1½ pounds ground beef	1 16-ounce can corn,
2 onions, coarsely chopped	drained
2 garlic cloves, chopped	1 3.5-ounce can sliced
1 tablespoon chili powder*	black olives, drained
1 teaspoon ground cumin	

✤ Preheat oven to 350°. Grease a 9x13-inch baking pan.

✤ In a large bowl mix together cornmeal, milk and eggs. Let sit for 30 minutes.

✤ In a large skillet, heat olive oil over medium heat. Add beef, onions, garlic, chili powder, cumin, oregano and salt and cook until beef is browned. Add the tomatoes, corn and black olives. Remove from heat and stir in the cornmeal mixture. Turn mixture into prepared baking pan and bake until hot and bubbly, about 1½ hours. Serve hot.

✤ Note: *As a alternative to commercial chili powder, seed and chop 3 ounces of dried New Mexico or California peppers. Bring to a boil in a cup of water, simmer 20 minutes, adding water if needed. Blend peppers and water in a blender. Add to meat mixture.

Per serving: 379 calories; 21.9g protein; 25.5g carbohydrates; 22g fat (6.3g saturated fat); 95.7mg cholesterol.

CHEESE and MACARONI with HAM

Serves 30-45

Jack Kling is one of the chefs for the Senior Center which meets every Wednesday at St. Francis Lutheran. This is one of Jack's (and the Seniors') favorite noontime meals. It is easily divided to make a smaller amount for family or friends.

3 pounds elbow macaroni	3-4 pounds cooked ham,
½ cup (1 stick) butter,	diced
cut into pieces	12 eggs
5 pounds mild Cheddar	2 quarts whole milk
cheese, shredded	1-2 teaspoons pepper

✤ Preheat oven to 400°. Butter a 10x15-inch baking pan or two 9x13-inch deep baking pans.

✤ Cook macaroni in boiling water until barely tender. Drain. Turn macaroni into prepared pan and toss with butter until melted. Add ¾ of cheese a little at a time, mixing well after each addition. Add ham cubes and mix well.

✤ In a large bowl, beat eggs until well blended. Combine with milk and pepper and mix well. Pour over macaroni. Sprinkle remaining cheese over top of casserole. Bake uncovered until milk is absorbed and top is golden brown, about 45 minutes. Serve hot.

Per serving: 412 calories; 26.3g protein; 24.3g carbohydrates; 22.9g fat (13.3g saturated fat); 136mg cholesterol.

POLENTA CAKE

Serves 12-14

Marti Lundin adapted this recipe from one that appeared in the "California Wine Country Cookbook." For a spirited alternative, substitute a tablespoon of Grand Marnier for the teaspoon of lemon extract.

1½ cups unsalted butter, softened	2 egg yolks
5 cups powdered sugar	2 cups all-purpose flour
1 teaspoon lemon extract	1 cup polenta (coarse cornmeal)
4 eggs	Fresh berries (garnish)

✤ Preheat oven to 325°. Grease and flour a 9x13-inch cake pan.

✤ In a large bowl or the bowl of an electric mixer beat the butter, sugar and lemon flavoring until creamy. Add the eggs and egg yolks one at a time, beating well after each addition. Fold in flour and polenta.

✤ Pour batter into prepared cake pan. Bake until a toothpick inserted into the center comes out clean, 1 to 1¼ hours.

✤ Cool and cut into squares. Serve with juicy fresh berries.

Per serving: 513 calories; 5.77g protein; 65.6g carbohydrates; 26.1g fat (15.2g saturated fat); 168mg cholesterol.

Soon after I was first diagnosed with HIV, I saw an ad for St. Francis Lutheran in a local paper. Although raised as a Lutheran and very active in the church through my college years, I had not been in a church in 15 years. The pastoral staff and lay members of the congregation have been essential in providing the spiritual and emotional support which I have needed during this most stressful time in my life. I cannot even conceive of what I would have done without St. Francis as a part of my life.

James Berg, from a 1990 ststement. James was a financial analyst at Stanford University and served as treasurer of the congregation. He died of AIDS at age 40 in 1992.

CARROT CAKE with
CREAM CHEESE FROSTING

Serves 12-16

Beverly Natzke of Gillett, Wisconsin, was given this wonderfully easy carrot cake recipe by her mother many years ago. It's still her family's favorite.

2 cups all-purpose flour	2 cups sugar
2 teaspoons baking soda	1½ cups oil
3 teaspoons ground cinnamon	3 cups grated carrots
½ teaspoon salt	Cream cheese frosting
4 eggs	(recipe follows)

❖ Preheat oven to 350°. Grease and flour a 9x13-inch baking pan.

❖ In a small bowl, sift together flour, baking soda, cinnamon and salt into a small bowl.

❖ In another larger bowl, beat eggs. Add sugar and oil, mixing well. Add flour mixture and mix well. Fold in carrots.

❖ Spread in prepared pan and bake until a toothpick inserted in center comes out clean, about 45 minutes.

CREAM CHEESE FROSTING:

½ cup (1 stick) butter, softened	2 cups powdered sugar
2 teaspoons vanilla	½ cup chopped nuts
1 8-ounce package cream cheese, softened	

❖ In a medium bowl, combine all ingredients and mix until well blended. Spread on cooled cake.

Per serving: 538 calories; 5.07g protein; 53.1g carbohydrates; 34.9g fat (9.2g saturated fat); 84.1mg cholesterol.

EARTHQUAKE CAKE

Serves 12-16

This delicious "self-frosting" cake reminds Ray Vickers-Traft of California's famous earthquakes.

1½ cups flaked coconut	1 8-ounce package cream
1½ cups chopped pecans	cheese
1 18-ounce German chocolate	½ cup (1 stick) butter
cake mix	1 pound powdered sugar

✤ Preheat oven to 350°. Grease and flour a 9x13-inch baking pan.

✤ Spread coconut and pecans evenly over the bottom of the pan.

✤ Prepare cake mix according to package directions. Pour batter into pan over coconut and pecans.

✤ In a large bowl, cream together the cream cheese, butter and powdered sugar until well blended. Dot mixture by teaspoonful over the cake batter. Place baking pan on foil-lined baking sheet and bake until a toothpick inserted near the center comes out clean, about 45 minutes.

Per serving: 590 calories; 4.51g protein; 76.6g carbohydrates; 32.1g fat (14.6g saturated fat); 41.5mg cholesterol.

On October 17, 1989, a 7.2 Richter scale earthquake hit San Francisco and surrounding cities. The brick veneer wall on the south side of our church ended up in a heap in the garden. Our stained glass windows twisted and everywhere there was cracked plaster. The Evangelical Lutheran Church in America (ELCA) Disaster Relief Fund gave us $9,000. It took three years and an additional $200,000 in fundraising and borrowing, but we got everything fixed, except for the yard. That is on the drawing board. Since the earthquake, there have been other disasters in Florida, Hawaii, Los Angeles and Rwanda. People at St. Francis responded generously to each of these appeals from the ELCA Disaster Relief Fund. You can understand why.

METHODIST APPLE CRISP

Serves 6-8

A dear friend of Marti Lundin brought this dish to every potluck—and there were many—at the little Methodist church in Texas where Marti grew up. It's perfect for potlucks and as a "homey" dessert for fall and winter. Equally good cold the next day or two, it can be reheated easily.

6 tart apples, peeled,
   cored and sliced
⅓ cup all-purpose flour
3 tablespoons ground
   cinnamon

¾ cup sugar ½
1 teaspoon salt

TOPPING:

1 cup instant oatmeal,
   uncooked
¾ cup all-purpose flour
¾ cup brown sugar
   (packed)   ½

½ cup (1 stick) butter,
   melted
¾ cup pecans (optional)

✤ Preheat oven to 325°.

✤ In a large bowl, toss apples with flour, cinnamon, sugar and salt until well mixed. Turn mixture into an 8-inch square baking dish.

✤ In a medium bowl, mix together oatmeal, flour and brown sugar. Add melted butter and blend until moistened.

✤ Cover apple mixture with topping. Bake until bubbly hot, apples are tender and topping is lightly browned, 30-35 minutes. Serve warm with ice cream, whipped cream or creme fraiche, if desired.

Per serving: 153 calories; .781g protein; 38.8g carbohydrates; .43g fat (.073g saturated fat); 0mg cholesterol.

PEACH-BLUEBERRY CRISP

Serves 12-16

This colorful and delicious dessert from Stanley Eichelbaum feeds a crowd.

8-10 medium-size peaches,
    ripe and firm, peeled
1 pint blueberries
2 tablespoons chopped
    crystallized ginger
¾ cup plus 3 tablespoons
    sugar, divided

1¼ cups all-purpose flour
¾ cup dark brown sugar
    (packed)
1 teaspoon ground
    cinnamon
¾ cup (1½ sticks)
    cold unsalted butter

✤ Preheat oven to 375°.

✤ Cut peaches in half and remove pits, then cut into 1-inch slices. Place in a shallow 9x13-inch baking dish. Sprinkle the blueberries over the peaches. Sprinkle with the chopped crystallized ginger and 3 tablespoons sugar.

✤ In a large bowl or in the bowl of a food processor, combine the flour, remaining sugar, brown sugar and cinnamon. Cut the butter into mixture until it resembles coarse meal. Sprinkle the topping evenly over the fruit.

✤ Bake until the topping is lightly browned and fruit is bubbling, about 40 minutes. Serve warm or at room temperature or cold from the refrigerator. This fruit crisp goes well with whipped cream or vanilla ice cream.

Per serving: 193 calories; 1.4g protein; 28.4g carbohydrates; 8.79g fat (5.41g saturated fat); 23.3mg cholesterol.

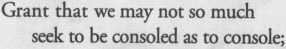
Grant that we may not so much
    seek to be consoled as to console;

Eternal God, at times our lives
are filled with turbulence and we feel
the world closing in on us. Like a
San Francisco fog, our despair hovers
close to us. Though shallow in
depth, our view of your vast creation
can become blocked by our despair.
As rays of sunlight shine through a
fog to burn it off, help us to see the
rays of hope always shining behind
the clouds in our lives.

To each of us you have given a deep
well of strength and inner power.
May we never fail to draw from
these wells of hope, whether it is
from within ourselves, from among
our community of family and
friends, or elsewhere within your creation. For in tapping these sources
we will find you have provided to us
more than we can ever use.

Breathe on us your wisdom and
inspire us so that we may trust in the
future with hope that is alive and
vibrant. From the beginning you
have been with us and your love for
us is with us until the end. ~Amen.

DINNER TABLE

Food brings people together. It lures them in from the living room, off the porch and out of the hallway. Because as anybody who has ever boiled water knows, the action at any decent dinner party is always in the kitchen.

A show of seasoning, a bit of flashy knife-play, the dramatic final whisking ... this is theater at its best, played out among friends and loved ones. The table is set and the preparation complete. Now comes an unhurried meal garnished with laughter and conversation. Candles perhaps, wine most probably. And, without doubt, a chorus of shameless flattery from the guests. If they want any dessert, that is.

Caribbean Corn Cakes

Shrimp-Avocado Relish

Shrimp with Remoulade Sauce

Caramel-Brown Potatoes

Creamed Kale

Sweet and Sour Greens

Broccoli with Toasted Walnuts
and Raspberry Vinegar

Polenta Baked with Gorgonzola,
Pine Nuts and Green Onions

Salmon with Coconut Peas

Poached Salmon
with Mustard Cream Sauce

Poached Salmon with Mussels

"Oven-Fried" Seabass with
llemon Tarragon Glaze

Mussels Steamed in Cider
with Thyme and Shallots

Stir-Fry Clams
in Black Bean Sauce

Grilled Trout with Creamed Spinach
and Raspberry/Roasted Pepper Salsa

Apricot Chicken

Chicken with Mushrooms
and Grapes

Oven-Roasted Chicken
with Preserved Lemons

Baked Chicken
with Herbs de Provence

Spiced Short Ribs

Pork Tenderloins with
Rosemary/Mustard Marinade
and Sauteed Apples

CARIBBEAN CORN CAKES

Serves 6-8

Heidi Cusick is a food writer living in beautiful Mendocino, California, on the shores of the Pacific Ocean ("Murder, She Wrote" is filmed in Mendocino—not Cabot Cove, Maine!). These delicious corn cakes were developed while Heidi was working on recipes for a book on African influences on cooking. Instead of fried fritters made from cornmeal, fresh corn kernels are combined with chilies, allspice and coconut milk into fragrant fiber-filled cakes that are complemented with Shrimp-Avocado Relish, a Caribbean version of guacamole.

Kernels from 5 ears of corn
(about 2½ cups)*
½ green or red bell
pepper, seeded and
finely chopped
1 fresh red or green
chile, seeded and
finely chopped
½ teaspoon ground allspice
1 teaspoon salt

¼ teaspoon ground black
or white pepper
½ teaspoon baking powder
1 egg, lightly beaten
½ cup coconut milk
½ to ¾ cup flour (depending
on wetness of corn)
2-3 tablespoons vegetable oil
Shrimp-Avocado Relish
(recipe follows)

✤ Puree half of the corn kernels in a food processor or blender.

✤ In a large bowl, mix together the pureed kernels, whole kernels, bell pepper, chile, allspice, salt, ground pepper, baking powder, egg and coconut milk. Add just enough of the flour to form a mixture that holds together in a thick batter like cornbread.

✤ Heat a griddle or nonstick pan over medium heat and add a tablespoon or so of oil. Ladle the batter on the griddle to make 3-inch rounds. Cook until bubbles begin to appear on the surface, about 3 minutes. Turn with a spatula and brown on the other side, 2-3 minutes longer. Repeat with remaining batter, adding oil as necessary. Serve piping hot with Shrimp-Avocado Relish (see next page).

✤ Note: *To remove kernels from shucked ears of corn, first remove cornsilk under running water. Then, in a wide, deep bowl, hold the ear of corn stem-end down and, using a sharp knife, cut off the kernels. This minimizes the amount of flying corn kernels that land all over the counter.

Per serving: 479 calories; 4.94g protein; 65.6g carbohydrates; 23.3g fat (4.07mg saturated fat); 62.1mg cholesterol.

SHRIMP-AVOCADO RELISH   Serves 6-8

You can find Trinidad Green Habanero Pepper sauce in Mexican markets or in the imported food section of supermarkets.

½ pound medium shrimp
    or rock shrimp in the shell
6 Roma tomatoes, chopped
½ red onion, finely chopped
1 clove garlic, minced
Juice of ½ lemon
1 fresh red or green chili,
    seeded and minced

1-3 teaspoons Trinidad
    Green Habanero
    Pepper sauce
½ cup fresh chopped cilantro
1 ripe yet firm avocado,
    pitted, peeled and cut
    into ¼-inch dice
Salt to taste

✤ To poach the shrimp, bring a saucepan of water to a boil, add the shrimp and boil until they turn pink and begin to curl, 3-4 minutes. Drain and let cool. Peel and devein. Cut into ½-inch pieces and place in a bowl. Add the remaining ingredients to the shrimp and gently toss until well mixed. Let stand for 1 hour to marry flavors before serving.

Per serving: 63.5 calories; 5.5g protein; 3.45g carbohydrates; 3.42g fat (.57mg saturated fat); 44.2mg cholesterol.

SHRIMP with REMOULADE SAUCE   Serves 4-6

Clayia Hamilton used to make this dish often in her New Orleans home.

1½-2 pounds shrimp
    in the shell
3 tablespoons Dijon mustard
1-2 tablespoons prepared
    horseradish
½ cup tarragon vinegar
2 tablespoons ketchup
1 tablespoon paprika

1 teaspoon salt
1 clove garlic
1 cup vegetable oil
½ cup chopped
    green onions
½ cup chopped celery
½ teaspoon cayenne

✤ Bring a saucepan of water to a boil, add shrimp and boil until they turn pink and begin to curl, about 3-4 minutes. Drain and let cool. Peel and devein. Place in a shallow dish. Combine remaining ingredients in food processor or blender and process until well blended. Pour sauce over shrimp and mix together. Cover and refrigerate at least 4 hours before serving. Serve cold.

Per serving: 748 calories; 47g protein; 8.27g carbohydrates; 58.8g fat (7.73mg saturated fat); 345mg cholesterol.

CARAMEL-BROWN POTATOES

Serves 4

Kirsten Havrehed tells us the Danes serve these on a bed of creamed kale (recipe below) surrounding a beef or pork roast. The secret to success is shaking the pan constantly to achieve a beautiful glaze on each of the potatoes.

2 pounds small red or
    white new potatoes of
    uniform size, unpeeled

½ cup sugar
½ cup (1 stick) butter

❖ In a large pot of boiling salted water, cook potatoes until just tender, before skin breaks. Cool and peel.

❖ Melt sugar in a heavy frying pan over low heat, stirring constantly so it won't burn. Add butter and continue to stir until mixture is golden. Add potatoes, shaking the pan until potatoes are golden and evenly glazed. (Use a wooden spoon, if you must!) Serve immediately.

Per serving: 479 calories; 4.94g protein; 65.6g carbohydrates; 23.3g fat(14.4mg saturated fat); 62.1mg cholesterol.

CREAMED KALE

Serves 4 -6

Kale is an unusual leafy vegetable that Kirsten Havrehed sometimes serves instead of spinach.

2 large bunches curly kale
½ cup (1 stick) butter
6 tablespoons
    all-purpose flour

2 cups milk
2 teaspoons freshly grated
    nutmeg
¼ teaspoon garlic salt

❖ Strip kale leaves off the stems and wash well.

❖ Steam kale leaves, covered, for about 2 minutes. Drain. Puree in food processor or blender. Set aside.

❖ Melt butter in a heavy saucepan. Stir in flour until well blended. Gradually add milk, stirring constantly, until mixture is smooth and thickened. Add nutmeg and garlic salt. Stir in pureed kale and bring to a boil. Remove from heat and serve immediately.

Per serving: 240 calories; 5.16g protein; 14.6g carbohydrates; 18.7g fat (11.5mg saturated fat); 52.35mg cholesterol.

SWEET and SOUR GREENS

Serves 4

In this interesting recipe, Heidi Cusick, our food writer friend from Mendocino, California writes that the onion is slowly cooked with sugar until caramelized, then hit with vinegar and cayenne pepper before adding the greens. The result combines the best of all the flavors.

2 tablespoons olive or vegetable oil	¼ teaspoon cayenne pepper
½ medium onion, chopped	1 bunch curly mustard or other greens, washed and sliced
1 tablespoon sugar	Salt to taste
¼ cup red wine or cider vinegar	

✢ In a skillet or heavy saucepan, heat oil and add onion. Sprinkle with sugar. Cook the onions over medium-low heat, stirring frequently, until very soft and beginning to brown.

✢ Carefully pour in vinegar and cayenne pepper. (Stand back so as not to inhale the potent vinegar and chile fumes.) Stir and continue cooking until onions are very brown. This gives them a tart meat-like flavor.

✢ Stir in the greens and sprinkle with salt. Add a little water if necessary. Cook until tender, 5-10 minutes. Taste for seasoning. Serve hot.

Per serving: 105 calories; 1.79g protein; 7.86g carbohydrates; 6.96g fat (.877mg saturated fat); 0mg cholesterol.

I don't know why some people are gay and other people are not. But I do believe that the most important thing in life is love in all its forms. As a straight woman, I don't say to myself, "This is a gay brother or lesbian sister in Christ." I say, "This is a person who feels the same way about God as I do." At times, I'm overwhelmed by the love expressed by the people at St. Francis. Christ was an advocate for justice and equality. He stressed that the kingdom of God was for everyone. At St. Francis, I think we are carrying out that work of Christ.

The worship services at St. Francis are wonderful, and we also know how to have fun together. I always look forward to the potluck dinner before we trim the Christmas tree. As a single person whose biological family is far away, I think of St. Francis as family, and our social events as family reunions.

Iris Vaughan, 51, moved to San Francisco in 1975 and was the first female vice president of the congregation. She often serves as a storyteller or lector for worship service. Iris has worked in public relations in the performing arts and is currently employed with the San Francisco Newspaper Agency.

BROCCOLI with TOASTED WALNUTS and RASPBERRY VINEGAR

Serves 4

Louise Fiszer, co-author of "Sweet Onions—Sour Cherries," pairs broccoli with toasted nuts and fruity vinegar for a spectacular vegetable side dish or salad.

1 large bunch broccoli,
  cut into spears,
  stems peeled
3 tablespoons walnut oil

1 cup chopped walnuts
2 tablespoons
  raspberry vinegar
Salt and pepper to taste

❖ Cook broccoli in a large pot of boiling salted water until barely tender, about 2 minutes. Drain and set aside.

❖ Heat oil in large skillet. Cook walnuts just until they start to brown and become fragrant. Add broccoli, sprinkle with vinegar and cook until heated through, about 2 minutes. Salt and pepper to taste. Serve hot or room temperature.

Per serving: 316 calories; 7.68g protein; 11.9g carbohydrates; 29.2g fat (2.67mg saturated fat); 0mg cholesterol.

POLENTA BAKED with GORGONZOLA, PINE NUTS, and GREEN ONIONS

Serves 4-6

Dale Leininger adapted this recipe from one he discovered in another San Francisco community cookbook. Feel free to vary the cheese for a different flavor.

3 cups chicken broth
8 cloves garlic, minced
1 cup polenta
  (coarse cornmeal)
½ cup milk
4 tablespoons (½ stick) butter
½ teaspoon white pepper

¼ cup grated Parmesan
  cheese
¼ cup crumbled
  Gorgonzola cheese
6 green onions, chopped
  (green and white parts)
¼ cup toasted pine nuts
  (pignoli)

❖ Preheat oven to 325°.

❖ Boil the broth with the garlic and gradually stir in polenta. After polenta begins to thicken, stir in milk and transfer mixture to the top of a double boiler. Cover and cook 20-25 minutes. Add butter, pepper, and Parmesan cheese and cook for another 25-30 minutes, until smooth. Pour into a shallow ovenproof serving bowl and sprinkle with Gorgonzola, green onions and toasted pine nuts. Bake until cheese is melted and casserole is heated through, about 10 minutes. Serve promptly.

Per serving: 479 calories; 13.5g protein; 25.1g carbohydrates; 38.3g fat (19.3mg saturated fat); 86.8mg cholesterol.

SALMON with COCONUT PEAS   Serves 4

Elka Gilmore has two restaurants in San Francisco, Liberté and her namesake venue, Elka. If you have never tried coconut milk, this is an excellent introduction to its incredible flavor. Coconut milk and Schichimi 7-pepper spice can be found at Asian markets and in the imported section of many supermarkets.

4 6-ounce salmon steaks	1 cup Morel or other wild mushrooms
1-2 tablespoons vegetable oil	
2 tablespoons unsalted butter	3 cups shelled peas (3-4 pounds unshelled)
3 tablespoons chopped green onions, divided	2 tablespoons chopped fresh basil
1 cup unsweetened coconut milk	2 tablespoons chopped fresh mint
1 tablespoon ginger juice*	Juice of 1 lime
1 teaspoon 7-pepper spice (Schichimi pepper spice)	

✤   In a large skillet, cook salmon in oil, turning once until nicely browned on both sides and just translucent in the center. Set aside.

✤   Heat butter in a large skillet. Add 1 tablespoon green onions and cook until softened but not browned. Add coconut milk, ginger juice, 7-pepper spice and mushrooms. Cook over medium heat, stirring occasionally, until mixture thickens slightly. Add peas, herbs and lime juice. Cook for about 2 minutes longer, until peas are tender. Adjust seasoning to taste. To serve, put pea mixture on plates and top with salmon. Garnish with remaining green onion.

✤   Note: *To make ginger juice, coarsely chop peeled fresh ginger and force through a juice extractor or fine sieve.

Per serving: 538 calories; 42.4g protein; 23.3g carbohydrates; 31.5g fat (18.1mg saturated fat); 109mg cholesterol.

For me, membership in St. Francis Lutheran means that no matter where I go in the world, there will be a place where people remember me, care about me, and will welcome me back with open arms. I really appreciate that I have been able to be active at St. Francis; people have allowed for the fact that my work often takes me out of town.

The St. Francis membership is few in number, but we do the work of a 500-member congregation. St. Francis is a little like frozen orange juice: when you first look at the little container, you can't believe it will really make two liters of juice. With the ordination of Jeff, Ruth and Phyllis, we set a 5.2 million member national church on its ear—and prompted it to think of change. Even if we don't succeed, we will have had an important effect.

Parker Nolen, 30, is a graduate student in business administration studying in Montreal. He is also a flight attendant with USAir. Parker lived in San Francisco from 1987 to 1994, and still considers St. Francis Lutheran his church home.

POACHED SALMON with
MUSTARD CREAM SAUCE

Serves 4

This started out as Arthur Morris' recipe for a quick meal—it takes less time than cooking rice. The original sauce was just wine and mustard, but his partner, Michael Hiller, thought it would be much better with cream. This recipe proves it is therefore possible to get home, cook, eat well and do dishes before a 7:30 p.m. meeting at St. Francis Lutheran.

1½ pounds skinned salmon fillets	2 teaspoons Dijon mustard
1 cup dry white wine	¼ cup heavy (whipping) cream
2 teaspoons chopped fresh tarragon or ¾ teaspoon dried	Fresh sprigs of tarragon (garnish)

❖ Select two large salmon fillets or four smaller fillets, enough to serve 4 people. If you can feel any bones, remove them.

❖ Pour the wine into a large non-reactive skillet and bring it to a boil over high heat. Add the tarragon and then the salmon fillets. Lower heat, cover and simmer for 2-4 minutes, depending on the thickness of the fillets. Do not turn over. Gently transfer the salmon to a serving plate and keep in a warm oven (150°-200°).

❖ Whisk into mustard the wine and cook until liquid is reduced by about half. Add the cream and continue to boil, whisking occasionally, until the sauce thickens. If it gets too thick, add a little more wine.

❖ Pour some sauce over each piece of salmon. Garnish with fresh tarragon sprigs. Serve remaining sauce at the table.

Per serving: 334 calories; 347.2g protein; .942g carbohydrates; 16.5g fat (5.09mg saturated fat); 114mg cholesterol.

POACHED SALMON with MUSSELS

Serves 4

In this entree, the sweet-briny essence of mussels combines beautifully with the rich taste of salmon. Jay Harlow, who writes the "Fishmonger" column in the San Francisco Chronicle, suggests you use halibut or seabass if salmon is unavailable.

24 - 32 small mussels
   (about 1 pound)
¾ cup dry white wine, divided
1 tablespoon chopped
   green onions (white part)
2 tablespoons butter
Handful of green onion tops
   (green part)

Sprig of fresh tarragon
   or chervil or
   ½ teaspoon dried
1 pound salmon filet, cut
   into 4 diagonal slices
Salt and pepper to taste

✤ Scrub and debeard the mussels, discarding any open ones that do not close when handled. Place in a small saucepan with ¼ cup of the wine and the shallots. Cover, bring to a boil and steam just until the shells open. Remove immediately, let cool, and shuck the mussels. Reserve the steaming liquid. (May be done several hours ahead of time.)

✤ Mix together with the remaining ½ cup wine, green onion tops, tarragon or chevil and enough water to fill a 10-inch skillet to a depth of at least 1 inch. Bring almost to a boil, simmer 15 minutes, strain, and return to the skillet.

✤ Slide the salmon slices into the simmering wine mixture and poach until a skewer easily enters the thickest part, 3-5 minutes depending on thickness. Meanwhile, bring the reserved mussel broth to a boil and reduce by half. Transfer the salmon pieces when done to a warmed platter or individual warm serving plates and set in a low oven to keep warm.

✤ When the mussel broth is reduced, add the butter and cook, swirling or stirring the pan, until the butter melts. Return the mussels to the sauce, taste for seasoning and adjust if necessary. Blot away any accumulated liquid from the salmon plates and spoon the mussel sauce over the fish.

Per serving: 345 calories; 36.4g protein; 5.57g carbohydrates; 15.6g fat (5.2mg saturated fat); 110mg cholesterol.

"OVEN-FRIED" SEABASS with LEMON-TARRAGON GLAZE

Serves 4

This recipe from Mark Yaeger, owner of Mark's Healthy Kitchen, expertly combines lowfat cooking with great taste.

1 pound sea bass, halibut or other firm-fleshed white fish
½ teaspoon freshly grated nutmeg, divided
1½ tablespoons fresh thyme or 1½ teaspoons dried, divided
Salt and pepper to taste
7 large handsful of cornflakes to make 1 cup crumbs

1 tablespoon pure maple syrup or honey
½ cup plain nonfat yogurt
2 teaspoons whole-grain mustard
Lemon wedges (optional garnish)

LEMON-TARRAGON GLAZE:

1 tablespoon cornstarch
½ cup reduced sodium chicken broth
½ cup Riesling or other fruity white wine

Juice of 1 lemon
1½ tablespoons chopped fresh tarragon or 2 teaspoons dried

✤ Cut fish into eight 1½ x 2½-inch pieces. Season with salt, pepper, ¼ teaspoon nutmeg and ¼ tablespoon fresh thyme or ½ teaspoon dried.

✤ In a medium bowl, mix cornflake crumbs with remaining ¼ teaspoon nutmeg and 1 tablespoon fresh thyme or 1 teaspoon dried.

✤ In a second medium bowl, blend together yogurt, mustard and maple syrup. Using tongs or your fingers, dip piece of fish in yogurt-mustard mixture, letting excess drain back into bowl. Then, using a second set of tongs or your other hand, dip fish into cornflake crumbs until evenly coated. Place coated fish on a large clean plate. Repeat procedure until all pieces of fish have been coated. Refrigerate at least 15 minutes or up to 8 hours to firm the coating. (Recipe can be completed to this point the night before.)

✤ Preheat oven to 425°. Spray an ovenproof rectangular wire rack with non-stick spray. Line a cookie sheet with heavy-duty foil and place rack on top. Arrange fish pieces on rack and bake in center of oven until coating is golden brown and fish is cooked through, 20-25 minutes.

✤ To prepare glaze, dissolve cornstarch in cold chicken stock, wine and lemon juice. Place mixture in a small saucepan over medium heat, stirring frequently until reduced by about one-half and is the consistency of thick syrup. Add tarragon and adjust seasonings to taste. To serve, place two pieces of fish on each plate, and drizzle with glaze. Garnish with lemon wedges, if desired.

Per serving: 238 calories; 29.2g protein; 15.3g carbohydrates; 4.02g fat (.921mg saturated fat); 117mg cholesterol.

MUSSELS STEAMED in CIDER with THYME and SHALLOTS   Serves 4

Benjamin Davis presides over the kitchen of Cypress Club, a wonderfully designed San Francisco restaurant just a stone's throw from the Transamerica Pyramid. This is one of the most popular dishes they serve.

48 black mussels	2 cups unfiltered
2 tart green apples	apple cider
4 green onions (shallots)	½ cup heavy (whipping)
(white and green parts)	cream
4 sprigs fresh thyme	Salt and pepper to taste

✤ Scrub mussels with a brush or nylon scouring pad and pull out the "beard" with your fingers. Rinse under cold running water and refrigerate until ready to use.

✤ Wash and core the apples. Cut into quarters and slice thinly. Set aside. Peel the green onions and slice thinly. Set aside. Pick the thyme leaves from the stems and set aside.

✤ In a large stainless steel pan, place the cider, green onions, apple slices and thyme and bring to a boil. Add the mussels all at once and cover with a tight-fitting lid. Cook over high heat, shaking frequently for 1-2 minutes or until all the mussels have opened completely. Using a slotted spoon, remove the mussels and divide into 4 bowls. Add the cream to the pan and return to heat. Reduce slightly, 2-3 minutes over high heat. Season with salt and freshly ground black pepper to taste. Pour sauce over the mussels and serve immediately with crusty French or Italian bread.

Per serving: 501 calories; 41.7g protein; 40.1g carbohydrates; 19g fat (8.35mg saturated fat); 136mg cholesterol.

STIR-FRIED CLAMS in BLACK BEAN SAUCE

Serves 2-4

The chef at Harbor Village Restaurant in San Francisco, Andy Wai, was born and raised in Hong Kong, where he received his training. This is an excellent main dish or serve with other dishes as part of a large banquet.

4 pounds fresh Manila or Cherrystone clams in shells	1½ teaspoons oyster sauce
	1 teaspoon sugar
	1 teaspoon dark soy sauce
2 ounces Chinese preserved black beans, minced	1 teaspoon sherry
	1 teaspoon Asian sesame oil
	Pinch white pepper
3 cloves garlic, minced	½ cup chicken stock
2 green onions, minced	¼ cup vegetable oil
1 chili pepper, minced (optional)	2 teaspoons corn starch
	2 tablespoons water

✤ Immerse clams in salted water, cover and place in the refrigerator overnight to extract sand trapped in the shells.

✤ Mix together the minced black beans, garlic, shallots, chili pepper, oyster sauce, sugar, soy sauce, sherry, sesame oil, white pepper and chicken stock in a small bowl and set aside.

✤ Drain clams and cook in a large saucepan of boiling water just until the shells open. Discard all shells that do not open. Do not overcook.

✤ Heat the vegetable oil in a wok or large saucepan over high heat. Add the black bean mixture, stir well and cook for one minute. Gently fold in clams and cook without stirring until mixture boils.

✤ Quickly dissolve the corn starch in the water. Add to the clams and stir just until sauce thickens (do not overstir). Serve immediately.

Per serving: 1044 calories; 121g protein; 41.1g carbohydrates; 41g fat (5.14mg saturated fat); 311mg cholesterol.

It is very important to me to belong to a church that accepts me. I was looking at other Lutheran churches in the San Francisco area and I always felt like I was an outsider, a victim of that whole Lutheran standoffishness that said if you're a stranger, you're not welcome. That wasn't how it was at St. Francis; here it was just real easy. I knew they accepted me because they wanted me to work. I'm involved in the Outreach Committee, trying to get the word out to the community that we're here and what we're about. There are no judgments about your personal life or anything like that. I appreciate that.

Dale Leininger, 40, is a medical technologist at San Francisco General Hospital.

GRILLED TROUT with CREAMED SPINACH and RASPBERRY/ ROASTED PEPPER SALSA

Serves 2

Michael Hiller is one of the associate pastors of St. Francis Lutheran Church. As a variation, Michael sometimes prepares the spinach with lemon and olive oil rather than a cream sauce, making a less rich dish.

2 bunches fresh spinach
2 tablespoons unsalted
   butter
2 tablespoons all-purpose flour
Salt and white pepper to taste
⅛ teaspoon freshly
   ground nutmeg
1 cup hot milk
2 teaspoons olive oil, divided

1 clove garlic, minced
1 very ripe tomato,
   finely diced
1 red pepper, roasted, peeled,
   and finely diced
1 tablespoon raspberry
   vinegar (or to taste)
2 small trout (bone
   in or out)

✢ To make creamed spinach, wash spinach and place in a large pot with enough water (about ⅔ cup) to steam. Sprinkle one teaspoon of salt over the leaves. Cover and set over high heat and cook until tender, about 10 minutes. Drain.

✢ Prepare a white sauce by melting butter in a small saucepan. Stir in flour, salt, white pepper and nutmeg. Cook for 2 minutes, stirring occasionally, until well blended. Add hot milk and whisk until thickened. Correct seasonings. Place drained spinach and white sauce in a food processor or blender and puree. Keep creamed spinach warm.

✢ To make the salsa, heat 1 tablespoon olive oil in a skillet over medium heat. Add the minced garlic and cook until just fragrant, about 1 minute. Stir in the tomato and roasted red pepper and saute for 2 minutes. Add the vinegar and cook for another minute, stirring constantly.

✢ Brush trout with the remaining tablespoon of olive oil and season with salt and pepper. Grill the trout until nicely browned on both sides, about 10 minutes for each inch of thickness. Remove trout heads and skin. Bone the filets, being careful to keep the filet intact. Spread half of creamed spinach over the bottom of each of 2 warm dinner plates. Place 1 filet over spinach and top with salsa. Top with remaining fillets, placing them at an angle to partially cover the salsa.

Per serving: 627 calories; 58.8g protein; 35.9g carbohydrates; 30.7g fat (13mg saturated fat); 246mg cholesterol.

APRICOT CHICKEN

Serves 4

This was the first meal Parker Nolen cooked for his father, Bill, after his heart bypass surgery. It was such a hit that later that year three aunts served it for Christmas dinner!

½ cup dried apricots, chopped
¼ cup cider vinegar
2 tablespoons honey
¼ teaspoon salt
½ cup water
4 skinless, boneless
    chicken breast halves

½ cup grated shredded
    Monterey jack cheese*
½ cup chopped macadamia
    nuts (optional)*
3 green onions, sliced
Parsley sprigs (garnish)

✤ Preheat oven to 325°. Grease a 9x13-inch shallow baking pan.

✤ In a small saucepan combine apricots, vinegar, honey, salt and water. Bring mixture to a boil, reduce heat and simmer until apricots are softened, 15-20 minutes. Transfer everything to a food processor or blender and puree until smooth. If the sauce is too thick, thin with a bit more water. Set the sauce aside.

✤ In a small bowl, combine the cheese, nuts and green onions. Place cheese mixture on one-half of a chicken breast and fold the other half over to cover. Arrange the chicken in the baking dish and top with apricot sauce. Cover with foil and bake 30 minutes. Uncover and bake for 15 minutes longer. Serve warm garnished with parsley.

✤ Note: *You may substitute any cheese or nuts—or leave the nuts out altogether.

Per serving: 505 calories; 36.4g protein; 26.3g carbohydrates; 29.6g fat (8.11mg saturated fat); 105mg cholesterol.

I was a preacher's kid; my father was a pastor here in San Francisco for 45 years. I was very much involved in the parish and in church work, with the synod and the Walther League. Then I got married and moved to Valparaiso, Indiana. I came back to San Francisco when my husband, O.P. Kretzmann, died. It was difficult to find a church because I had been so active in my parish, and I didn't intend to be that active anymore. I became very judgmental. Then I found— no, heard—Pastor DeLange. His words are special and meaningful, and they make sense. This congregation is really not my way of living—I'm more formal, more old-fashioned. But I see a purpose for this church in serving everybody. I'm ready for removing the boundaries that the church puts upon itself.

Betty Kretzmann, 79, managed the Western U. S. office of Scribners for many years and was active on the Congregation's Worship Committee. Between Sundays she keeps an eye on St. Francis from her hilltop house south of the church.

CHICKEN with MUSHROOMS and GRAPES

Serves 8

This especially pretty dish comes from Michael Utech.

1 tablespoon flour
½ teaspoon salt
½ teaspoon pepper
4 tablespoons (½ stick) butter
2 pounds boneless, skinless chicken breast, cut into bite-size pieces
1 small onion, minced
½ pound fresh mushrooms, sliced

½ cup white wine
¾ cup chicken stock
½ cup lowfat milk
1 tablespoon corn starch
1 tablespoon water
1 cup seedless grapes, halved
½ cup toasted slivered almonds, toasted

✤ Preheat oven to 325°. Grease a 9x13-inch shallow baking pan.

✤ Measure flour, salt and pepper into a plastic bag and shake to combine. Place chicken pieces in the plastic bag and shake to coat. Melt butter in a large skillet and cook chicken, stirring occasionally, until lightly browned. Transfer chicken to baking dish and set aside.

✤ Add onion to skillet and cook until softened but not browned, 3-5 minutes. If necessary, some chicken stock can be added to the skillet to prevent sticking. Add mushrooms and cook over low heat about 3 minutes. Remove onions and mushrooms with slotted spoon and add to baking dish.

✤ Add wine and stock to skillet and bring mixture to a boil. Add milk and simmer about 5 minutes. Mix corn starch and water together and add to the simmering sauce, whisking constantly. As soon as sauce begins to thicken, remove from heat.

✤ Pour sauce over chicken, mushrooms and onion. Bake, covered, for 20 minutes. Add grapes and bake, uncovered, until heated through, about 10 minutes. Remove from oven and top with toasted almonds. Serve promptly.

Per serving: 284 calories; 29.9g protein; 11.1g carbohydrates; 12.5g fat (4.71mg saturated fat); 82.9mg cholesterol.

OVEN-ROASTED CHICKEN with PRESERVED LEMONS

Serves 4

Michael Hiller and his friend, Barton, were sleuthing the San Francisco restaurant scene. They had this wonderful dish at an Italian restaurant on Powell Street. They asked for the recipe, but, alas, it was not to be. So Michael just recreated it himself! This recipe is easily multiplied for larger groups.

1 chicken fryer, cut up
Salt and pepper to taste
2 cloves garlic, minced
1 cup preserved lemons*
½ pound tiny new
   potatoes, halved

3 tablespoons fresh rosemary
1-2 tablespoons olive oil
½ cup dry white wine
½ cup pitted Kalamata
   olives

❖ Preheat oven to 325°.

❖ Place a rack in a large metal baking pan. Place the chicken parts on the rack, season with salt and pepper, and sprinkle with minced garlic. Scatter lemons and potatoes over the chicken and sprinkle with rosemary. Drizzle olive oil and white wine over all and bake until chicken is nicely brown and cooked through, 1-1½ hours.

❖ Scatter olives over the chicken and bake for 5 minutes longer. Serve hot or at room temperature.

❖ Note: *Preserved lemons are made by slicing lemons crosswise or cutting them into eighths, salt with coarse (kosher) salt and let desiccate at least 12 hours. Pour off the liquid, place into jars and cover with olive oil. Store in a dark place until ready to use. The lemons are quite edible and take on an even different character after baking.

Per serving: 631 calories; 44.4g protein; 13.6g carbohydrates; 41.8g fat (10.9mg saturated fat); 173mg cholesterol.

BAKED CHICKEN with
HERBS de PROVENCE

Serves 4-6

Author of numerous cookbooks, including "Hot, Hotter, Hottest" and "Baked, Rolled and Stuffed," Janet Hazen is also a restaurant reviewer for the "Bay Guardian." Here she offers a wonderful baked chicken with fresh herbs, served either hot from the oven or at room temperature.

4 chicken thighs
4 chicken drumsticks
2 chicken breast halves
3 tablespoons olive oil
3 cloves garlic, minced
1½ tablespoons minced fresh thyme
1½ tablespoons minced fresh rosemary

1½ tablespoons minced fresh sage
1½ tablespoons minced fresh marjoram
1½ tablespoons minced fresh lavender
1½ tablespoons minced fresh basil
Salt and pepper to taste

✤ Preheat oven to 400°.

✤ Pat chicken pieces dry with a towel and place in a single layer in a large, lightly oiled baking dish.

✤ In a small bowl combine olive oil, garlic and herbs. Mix well.

✤ Using your finger, gently lift the skin from the meat, separating it but not removing it from the chicken. Place about 1 tablespoon of the herb mixture between the meat and the skin of each piece of chicken. Cover the pan tightly with aluminum foil.

✤ Bake for 35 minutes. Remove the foil and bake until the skin is light golden brown and the chicken is cooked through, 20-25 minutes.

✤ Serve promptly or, if chicken is prepared ahead of serving time, wrap tightly in foil and refrigerate until ready to serve.

Per serving: 355 calories; 30.4g protein; .496g carbohydrates; 25g fat (6.08mg saturated fat); 123mg cholesterol.

Lutheran Lesbian and Gay Ministry (LLGM) came into being in the summer of 1989. A group of pastors and lay leaders in the San Francisco Bay Area decided to do something positive in response to the Evangelical Lutheran Church in America's ruling that kept openly gay and lesbian seminary graduates from serving as pastors. In the midst of the AIDS epidemic, the founders of LLGM believed there was a pressing need for an affirming ministry among gay and lesbian people who had been alienated by the church's homophobic teachings and practices. We knew that if gay and lesbian pastors were to have any credibility with this community, these pastors had to be public about their sexual orientation. However, we also knew if they went public they would be in violation of the church's policies and could not be pastors. It would require these pastors to be men and women of courage. LLGM decided the time had come to challenge the church's policies. They asked St. Francis and First United Lutheran Churches to hire Ruth Frost and Phyllis Zillhart, an openly lesbian couple, and Jeff Johnson, an openly gay man. All three were recent graduates of Lutheran seminaries.

The two congregations voted "Yes!" and on January 20, 1990, the three were ordained in a two-hour worship service that attracted international media attention. The following July, St. Francis and First

SPICED SHORT RIBS

Serves 6-8

Bob Janssen likes to cook these ribs the day before and skim off the excess fat before serving. Add a little water before reheating, if necessary.

2-2½ pounds short ribs, preferably the less fatty "English cut"	1 teaspoon salt
	8 whole cloves
½ cup bottled chili sauce	1 medium onion, sliced
⅔ cup sweet pickle juice	

❖ In a large ovenproof skillet or frying pan over medium-high heat, cook short ribs until nicely browned, in batches if necessary. Reduce heat to low, cover, and cook for 1 hour. Pour off drippings.

❖ Add remaining ingredients to pan. Cover and simmer over low heat until meat is tender, about 2½ hours.

Per serving: 684 calories; 70.2g protein; 3.73g carbohydrates; 41.3g fat (17.6mg saturated fat); 211mg cholesterol.

PORK TENDERLOINS with ROSEMARY/MUSTARD MARINADE and SAUTEED APPLES

Serves 4

This recipe grew out of a free-form cooking session with Michael Hiller and his friend, Barton. They wandered through a grocery store buying whatever was fresh and interesting, and then prepared this dish for their partners, Arthur and Billy. It has turned into a standard in each of their homes.

Juice of 1 lemon
2 teaspoons Dijon mustard
2 tablespoons fresh
   rosemary
1 clove garlic, chopped
½ cup olive oil
Salt and pepper to taste

2 pork tenderloins
2 or 3 red or green apples,
   peeled or unpeeled, sliced
2 tablespoons unsalted butter
2 teaspoons sugar
1 tablespoon whiskey
   (optional)

✤ In a food processor or blender combine lemon juice, mustard, rosemary, garlic, olive oil, salt and pepper. Process until marinade is smooth.

✤ Pour half the marinade into a rectangular glass baking dish. Add the tenderloins. Pour remaining marinade over meat and let stand 1 hour. Grill for 10-15 minutes per side, depending on the heat of your grill (the pork will be slightly pink; grill longer for more well done pork).

✤ Slice the apples and hold in water with a little lemon juice added to retard browning. Melt butter in a large skillet. Add sugar and cook for 1 minute. Add drained apples and cook, turning often, until done to taste, about 5 minutes until tender. At the last minute, add whiskey and cook until liquid is evaporated (optional).

✤ To serve, slice each tenderloin into medallions about ¼-inch thick and place on a warm plate. Place sauteed apples on the side.

Per serving: 712 calories; 64.2g protein; 16.6g carbohydrates; 40.3g fat (8.67mg saturated fat); 184mg cholesterol.

Lutheran congregations were put on trial before an ELCA Discipline Panel of eleven people. The panel supported our ministries and commended St. Francis for our outreach to the gay and lesbian community. They called upon the ELCA to re-examine its policies and to consider a change in how the larger church dealt with seminarians and pastors who are lesbian and gay.

But the panel found us in violation of the ELCA constitution and suspended us from membership in the ELCA for five years. By a 6-5 vote, the panel also said that St. Francis will be expelled from the roster of ELCA congregations on December 31, 1995, if we do not withdraw the calls to our lesbian pastors or the ELCA does not change its policies. The ELCA has not changed its policies, nor have St. Francis or First United Lutheran withdrawn our calls to Pastors Frost, Zillhart and Johnson. What has changed at St. Francis Lutheran in the past five years is that we have many more members and our contributions have nearly doubled. Our committees and church life have been energized with an infusion of new people with new ideas. We are as certain of the rightness of our decision today as we were on that fall day in 1989 when with prayer and the movement of the Holy Spirit we called Ruth Frost and Phyllis Zillhart to join our pastoral staff.

 where there is darkness, light;

Ever-present and healing God, we each know the reality of cold, inner darkness. We also know the warmth of your loving, gloriously inviting light that finds us and leads us, if we will open our eyes even just a tiny bit. You have made us in your image, so light is ours to give as well as receive. Sometimes we are a flashlight with a very weak battery; sometimes we are a beacon for all the world to see. But always, let each of us be the light to someone's darkness; let each of us radiate your love as we move daily in the presence of our sisters and brothers. We give you our thanks for life — and light. *~Amen.*

BAKE SALES

In all the business world there is no marketing scheme more perfect, no act of commerce more brilliantly simple than the humble bake sale. It begins with an informal network of mixing bowls, flour-covered hands and trusty rolling pins. The recipes are usually family favorites, perfected over the years to be at their absolute irresistible best.

Part of the appeal is the size of the resulting morsel. Bake sale items are small. They're cute. Each is unique. And they need no label. The irregular shape and wax paper wrapping say it all: homemade and delicious.

Anise Seed Cookies

Extra-Crisp Sugar Cookies

The Clinton Cookie   *California Biscotti*

Trudy's Pecan Cookies   *Butterscotch Brownies*

Pecan Pralines   *Cloud Nine Brownies*

Danish Molasses Cookies   *Lowfat Orange Rum Brownies*

Chocolate Ginger Cookies   *Western Raisin Bars*

Ginger Cookies   *Seven-Layer Bars*

Oatmeal Cherry Cookies   *Carmelitas*

Chocolate-Oatmeal Cookies   *Wayne's Lemon Squares*

                          Dale's Toffee

ANISE SEED COOKIES

Makes 5 dozen

This recipe came from Kirsten Havrehed's aunt who lived in Switzerland. Don't make these cookies on a rainy day as wet weather can influence their texture. Firm cookies are delicious dunked in a glass of sherry or marsala wine.

5 large eggs
2 cups sugar
2½ cups all-purpose flour

3 tablespoons anise seeds
2 teaspoons pure anise
   extract

✤ Preheat oven to 350°. Grease 2 baking sheets.

✤ In large bowl or in the bowl of an electric mixer, beat eggs and sugar together for about 20 minutes, scraping sides and bottom of bowl frequently. Mixture should be light and creamy and sugar completely absorbed. Using a wooden spoon, mix in flour, anise seeds and anise extract. Dough will be quite stiff.

✤ Drop by teaspoonsful onto greased baking sheets. Bake 10-12 minutes. The top crust of cookie will form cracks, which is normal. Store cooled cookies in airtight container.

Per serving: 52.6 calories; 1.12g protein; 10.9g carbohydrates; .521g fat (.137g saturated fat); 17.7mg cholesterol.

EXTRA-CRISP SUGAR COOKIES

Makes 5 dozen

Viola Maatta has been making these simply wonderful cookies for years.

½ cup (1 stick) butter
1 cup sugar plus more
   for rolling
1 egg
½ cup vegetable oil

⅛ teaspoon salt
½ teaspoon vanilla
2½ cups all-purpose flour
1 teaspoon baking soda
1 teaspoon cream of tartar

✤ Preheat oven to 350°. Grease baking sheets.

✤ In a large bowl, cream together butter and 1 cup sugar. Add eggs, oil, salt and vanilla and mix to combine. Add flour, baking soda and cream of tartar and mix until smooth.

✤ Form dough into balls and roll in granulated sugar. Place dough on baking sheet and press down with a fork. Bake until lightly brown, about 10 minutes. Store in airtight container.

Per serving: 63 calories; .658g protein; 7.35g carbohydrates; 3.48g fat (1.16g saturated fat); 7.68mg cholesterol.

THE CLINTON COOKIE   Makes 3½ to 4 dozen

This recipe was developed especially for President Bill Clinton by Tom Roach, owner-baker of Tom's Cookies, located at Macy's in downtown San Francisco. Tom's Cookies were the only specialty food served at all twelve inaugural balls on January 20, 1993. Tom went to Washington, D.C., to bake all 15,000 cookies himself.

1 cup (2 sticks) butter	2½ cups all-purpose flour
1 cup sugar	½ teaspoon salt
1 cup brown sugar (packed)	1 tablespoon baking powder
2 eggs	3 bananas
1 cup chunky peanut butter	

✤ Preheat oven to 350°.

✤ In a large bowl, cream together the butter, sugars and peanut butter until smooth. Add the eggs and mix well. Add the flour, salt, baking powder and beat until well blended.

✤ Using a small ice cream scoop, create golf ball-sized dough balls each weighing about 2 ounces. Place dough balls on a parchment-lined baking sheet. Using the back of a fork handle, make a deep "X" on the top of each dough ball, pushing hard enough to slightly flatten the ball.

✤ Slice the bananas into ¼-inch thick coins and then slice each of these rounds in half to create half-moon wedges. Place four of these banana wedges into the "X"ed depression on the top of each dough ball. Place wedges so that they form an "X" and their flat sides face down so that the wedges will stand upright.

✤ Bake the dough balls with banana wedges until the dough is slightly golden, 16-18 minutes. Remove from the oven and cool.

Per serving: 85.9 calories; 1.43g protein; 8.84g carbohydrates; 5.39g fat (2.39g saturated fat); 15.4mg cholesterol.

TRUDY'S PECAN COOKIES

Makes 3 dozen

Barbara Hack-Wayland, who owns Gwetzli Brownies, recalls her mother's friend, Trudy, serving these cookies at a holiday party a few years ago. She fell in love with them and begged for the recipe. They taste like a praline cookie, almost candy-like. It is tough to eat just one!

1 cup sugar
½ cup butter (1 stick),
   softened

1 egg
1 cup all-purpose flour
2½ cups pecan halves

✤ Preheat oven to 350°. Line baking sheets with aluminum foil.

✤ In a large mixing bowl, cream sugar, butter and egg. Add flour all at once and mix well. Fold in pecans.

✤ Drop by teaspoonsful onto baking sheets about 2 inches apart. Bake until light brown, about 10 minutes. Cool for 5 minutes and lift off with a spatula. Store in an airtight container.

Per serving: 133 calories; 1.36g protein; 13.5g carbohydrates; 8.66g fat (2.83g saturated fat); 19.2mg cholesterol.

PECAN PRALINES

Makes 1 dozen

Clayia Hamilton directs the Senior Center every Wednesday at St. Francis Lutheran. She learned how to make these scrumptious treats in her hometown of New Orleans.

1 cup brown sugar (packed)
1 cup sugar
½ cup light cream
   (half-and-half)

2 tablespoons butter
1 cup pecan halves

✤ In a medium heavy saucepan, over high heat, dissolve sugars in cream and boil to the thread stage (228°F on a candy thermometer), stirring occasionally. Add the butter and pecans and cook until syrup reaches the soft ball stage (236°F on a candy thermometer), or forms a soft ball in water. Let cool about 10 minutes.

✤ Beat mixture with a wooden spoon until it thickens but doesn't lose its gloss. Drop by tablespoonsful onto a greased marble slab or double thickness of waxed paper. The candy will flatten out into large cakes as it cools. Store in an airtight container.

Per serving: 216 calories; .934g protein; 30.3g carbohydrates; 11.1g fat (3.61g saturated fat); 16.2mg cholesterol.

DANISH MOLASSES COOKIES

Makes 4 dozen

Kirsten Havrehed remembers making these delicious molasses cookies during her childhood in Denmark.

½ cup (1 stick)
    butter, softened
¾ cups sugar
½ cup dark molasses
½ teaspoon baking soda
    (dissolved in
    ½ tablespoon warm water)
2 cups all-purpose flour

¼ teaspoon salt
½ teaspoon ground cloves
½ teaspoon ground allspice
½ teaspoon finely grated
    nutmeg
1 teaspoon ground
    cinnamon

✤ Preheat oven to 350°. Grease baking sheets.

✤ In a large bowl, cut butter into small sections. Add sugar, molasses and dissolved baking soda. Mix until well blended.

✤ Sift flour with the salt and spices. Add to first mixture and work it in by hand. When dough is shiny, divide dough into four portions. Form each portion into a roll about 2 inches in diameter. Wrap each roll in aluminum foil and place flat in freezer until frozen, about ½ hour.

✤ Remove each roll separately from freezer as dough softens quickly. With a sharp knife, slice dough into rounds about ¼-inch thick and place 2 inches apart on baking sheets. Bake 8-10 minutes. Store in an airtight container or freeze for longer storage.

Per serving: 55.1 calories; .54g protein; 9.12g carbohydrates; 1.9g fat (1.16g saturated fat); 4.97mg cholesterol.

CHOCOLATE GINGER COOKIES

Makes 3½ to 4 dozen

Micki Fendyan creates and tests recipes for Guittard Chocolate.(What a job!) Chunks of crystallized ginger add spice to these moist, chocolatey cookies, making for a ginger lover's delight. If Guittard products are unavailable, substitute any quality chocolate.

2½ cups unsifted all-purpose flour
1 teaspoon baking powder
½ teaspoon baking soda
1 teaspoon ground ginger
½ teaspoon ground cinnamon
¼ teaspoon ground cloves
⅛ teaspoon salt
2 cups (12 ounces) Guittard semisweet chocolate chips

4 tablespoons (½ stick) butter
2 tablespoons milk
½ cup light molasses
1 large egg
¾ cup coarsely chopped almonds
½ cup chopped crystallized ginger

✤ Preheat oven to 375°. Grease baking sheets.

✤ In a medium bowl, combine flour, baking powder, baking soda, ginger, cinnamon, cloves and salt. Set aside.

✤ Place chocolate chips, butter, milk and molasses in top of double boiler over low heat, stirring until melted and smooth.* Remove from heat and mix in egg. Add dry ingredients and mix to combine. Stir in almonds and crystallized ginger. Cover and let stand at room temperature for 15 minutes.

✤ Roll well rounded teaspoonsful of dough between palms of hands into smooth, shiny balls. Place about 2 inches apart on baking sheet. Flatten slightly with palms. Bake for 7-8 minutes. Let stand 2 minutes before transferring to cooling racks.

✤ Note: *To use a microwave, combine chips, butter, milk and molasses in large micro-proof bowl. Heat at medium power (50% or medium level) for 2 minutes; stir well. Repeat for 30 seconds, stirring until smooth. Proceed as directed above.

Per serving: 89.3 calories; 1.54g protein; 12.4g carbohydrates; 4.32g fat (2g saturated fat); 7.09mg cholesterol.

GINGER COOKIES

Makes 2½ to 3 dozen

Nancy and Paul Barker, former members of St. Francis Lutheran, now make their home in Spokane, Washington. These delicious cookies are perfect for those cold Northwest winters.

1 cup sugar plus more for rolling	1 teaspoon ground ginger
¾ cup (1½ sticks) butter	1 teaspoon ground cinnamon
¼ cup molasses	½ teaspoon baking soda
1 egg	1 teaspoon baking powder
2 cups all-purpose flour	

✤ Preheat oven to 300°. Grease baking sheets.

✤ In a large bowl, cream together sugar and butter. Add molasses and eggs and beat until well blended. Mix together the dry ingredients and add to the butter mixture. Stir well to combine.

✤ Roll a teaspoon of dough into a ball, roll in sugar and place 2 inches apart on a baking sheet. Use a glass dipped in water to press the dough flat. Bake for 15 minutes. Immediately remove from baking sheet and cool on racks.

Per serving: 107 calories; 1.13g protein; 15.1g carbohydrates; 4.86g fat (2.94g saturated fat); 19.5mg cholesterol.

For me, St. Francis Lutheran means being part of a family, in the best sense of that word. It is a place where we are supported for who we are, not for who someone else wants us to be. This may sound presumptuous, but I think St. Francis is a place where the Spirit of God is at work. It is not only a place for worship, but also a place where one is caught up in the work of the Gospel. To have experiences where I have felt God's grace and reconciliation, to see forgiveness happen—that is what it's about.

One of my favorite components of life at St. Francis is my faith group of seven people where we deal with very basic issues of faith and life. For me, my faith is about wholeness, life, completeness. When I look back, I can see that I have always been cared for. When I look forward, I have the faith to move on.

Dale Johnson, 46, grew up in Larimore, North Dakota. He loves music and works as a legal assistant in estate planning. He has been a board member of Lutheran Lesbian and Gay Ministry since its inception.

OATMEAL CHERRY COOKIES   Makes 3 dozen

Since 1899 Deborah Olson's family has grown cherries and apricots on Olson Farms in Sunnyvale, California. A little like raisins, dried cherries can be substituted for raisins in most recipes.

1 cup (2 sticks) butter, softened
1 cup dark brown sugar (packed)
½ cup sugar
2 large eggs
1½ teaspoons vanilla
1½ cups all-purpose flour
½ teaspoon baking powder
½ teaspoon baking soda
1 teaspoon ground cinnamon
Pinch of finely grated nutmeg
2 cups uncooked old-fashioned oats
1 cup dried pitted cherries
½ cup chopped walnuts (optional)

✤ Preheat oven to 350°. Lightly grease baking sheets.

✤ In a large mixing bowl, cream butter and sugars together until well blended. Add eggs and vanilla and beat for several minutes until light and fluffy.

✤ In another smaller bowl, mix together the flour, baking powder, baking soda, cinnamon and nutmeg. Add to butter mixture and beat until well blended. Stir in oatmeal, cherries and walnuts.

✤ Drop batter by tablespoons onto baking sheets. Bake until the edges are just turning brown, about 12 minutes. Let cookies cool on pan for a few minutes, then transfer to racks to cool completely. Store in an airtight container.

Per serving: 152 calories; 2.69g protein; 20.1g carbohydrates; 7.09g fat (3.49g saturated fat); 25.6mg cholesterol.

Homeless people hang out on the steps of our church, panhandling those who walk by. At night, some sleep there. On occasion, they come to church on Sunday, and one man is a regular attendee. Many of these homeless people are addicts who spend their meager income on alcohol and drugs. We've gotten to know them by their street names: Little Bear, Whiner, Jamaica. But when they are sober they tell us their real names and we hear their stories. They are ordinary people who for the most part grew up in ordinary circumstances. Long ago they burned their bridges with their families. We'd like to help, but there is not much we can do except urge them to go to a shelter or to a detoxification center. It is an overwhelming problem.

CHOCOLATE-OATMEAL COOKIES

Makes 6 dozen

Dale Johnson's sister-in-law got this recipe from a friend, who got it from a friend, who got it from a friend—thank you, one and all!

1 cup (2 sticks) butter
1 cup sugar
1 cup brown sugar (packed)
2 eggs
1 teaspoon vanilla
2½ cups oatmeal
2 cups all-purpose flour
½ teaspoon salt
½ teaspoon baking powder
1 teaspoon baking soda
2 cups (12 ounces) chocolate chips
4 ounces milk chocolate, grated
1½ cups chopped nuts

✤ Preheat oven to 375°.

✤ In a large bowl or the bowl of an electric mixer, cream together butter, sugar and brown sugar. Add the eggs and vanilla and beat slowly.

✤ Measure the oatmeal, then grind small amounts in a food processor or blender until it turns to powder. In a second bowl mix the powdered oatmeal, flour, salt, baking powder and baking soda.

✤ Gradually add the oatmeal mixture to the butter mixture and combine. Add the chocolate chips, milk chocolate and nuts and continue beating until all ingredients are thoroughly mixed.

✤ Make golf ball-size cookies by hand or use a small ice cream scoop. Place 2 inches apart on an ungreased baking sheet and bake for 8-10 minutes.

Per serving: 140 calories; 2.21g protein; 17.2g carbohydrates; 7.69g fat (3.53mg saturated fat); 15.8mg cholesterol.

CALIFORNIA BISCOTTI

Makes 4 dozen

Vicki Sebastiani serves these delicious twice-baked cookies at Viansa, the beautiful Sonoma County, California winery she owns and operates with her husband, Sam.

½ cup chopped walnuts
1 cup sugar
½ cup (1 stick) unsalted butter
3 eggs
1½ cups all-purpose flour
1 cup yellow cornmeal

1 teaspoon grated lemon zest
1 teaspoon grated orange zest
½ cup dried currants

✤ Preheat oven to 350°. Toast walnuts in a shallow pan until light brown. Cool and set aside.

✤ In a large bowl, cream together butter and sugar. Add eggs, one at a time. Sift in flour and cornmeal. Add zest, walnuts and currants. Mix just until all ingredients are incorporated.

✤ Roll mixture into several cylinders. Place on parchment-lined sheet pans and bake until light brown, 20-25 minutes. Cool 10-15 minutes.

✤ Reduce oven temperature to 275°. Slice log crosswise into ½-inch cookies. Place cookies on sheet pan and bake 10-15 minutes. Turn cookies over and bake until crisp and light brown, 10-15 minutes. Cool and store in airtight container.

Per serving: 65.8 calories; 1.14g protein; 9.13g carbohydrates; 2.89g fat (1.32g saturated fat); 17.7mg cholesterol.

BUTTERSCOTCH BROWNIES

Makes 16

John Phillip Carroll, author of "California, The Beautiful Cookbook" says that if you want a good butterscotch brownie, this is it. There is no mistaking the flavor, which comes from butterscotch chips and brown sugar. They are moist, chewy-crunchy, and one of the most addictive cookies you will ever make.

4 tablespoons (½ stick)
   butter, softened
⅔ cup all-purpose flour
1 12-ounce package
   (2 cups) butterscotch
   chips
2 eggs

½ cup brown sugar (packed)
1 teaspoon vanilla
1 teaspoon baking powder
¼ teaspoon salt
½ cup shredded coconut
   or chopped walnuts

✤ Preheat oven to 350°. Grease and flour an 8-inch square pan.

✤ In a large heavy saucepan over low heat, combine butter and 1 cup of chips, stirring constantly until about ¾ of the mixture is melted. Remove from heat and whisk vigorously until completely smooth. The mixture should feel faintly warm to your finger. Beat in the eggs and vanilla, then add brown sugar and beat until smooth.

✤ Stir together the flour, baking powder and salt. Add to the first mixture and blend until smooth. Stir in the remaining cup of chips and the coconut or walnuts. Spread evenly in the prepared pan and bake until dry and golden on top, 35-40 minutes. A toothpick inserted in the center should emerge with a few moist crumbs or just a trace of damp batter. (It is better to underbake than overbake these cookies.)

✤ Let cool (cookies may sink a little in the center). Cut in 2-inch squares.

Per serving: 197 calories; 1.9g protein; 24.3g carbohydrates; 10.8g fat (8mg saturated fat); 34.5mg cholesterol.

CLOUD NINE BROWNIES

Makes 16 squares

Micki Fendyan of Guittard Chocolate uses two kinds of chips in this custardy white brownie. Other brands of chocolate may be substituted.

½ cup (1 stick) butter
2 cups Guittard
    Choc-Au-Lait Vanilla
    Milk Chips, divided
2 large eggs
½ cup sugar

¼ teaspoon salt
1 teaspoon vanilla
1 cup all-purpose flour
1 cup Guittard Semi-Sweet
    Chocolate Chips

✤ Preheat oven to 325°. Grease an 8-inch square pan.

✤ Melt butter with ⅔ cup vanilla milk chips in top of double boiler over low heat, stirring constantly until smooth.* Remove from heat; set aside.

✤ In a large bowl or bowl of electric mixer, beat eggs, sugar, and salt at high speed until very pale and thick, about 5 minutes. Blend in melted mixture and vanilla at low speed. Mix in flour just until combined. Stir in remaining vanilla milk chips and semi-sweet chips. Spread in prepared pan. Bake until toothpick inserted in center comes out almost clean, 35-40 minutes. Top will be crusty and browned. (Cover pan with foil if browning too quickly.) Cool before cutting into squares.

✤ Note: *To use a microwave, heat butter and ⅔ cup vanilla milk chips in small micro-proof bowl at medium power (50% or medium level) for 2-3 minutes, stirring well after each minute initially, then at 30 second intervals until smooth. Proceed as directed.

Per serving: 278 calories; 3.39g protein; 32.1g carbohydrates; 16.1g fat (9.44g saturated fat); 46.7mg cholesterol.

Barbara brought me to St. Francis Lutheran after she made just one Sunday visit, and I, too, was hooked. I liked the people instantly, the preaching was good, and there was no pretense or formality about the place.

I cook for the seniors—something I love to do—and inaugurated the now-famous St. Francis Lutheran Thanksgiving Day Dinner with all the trimmings. My, we've fed lots of hungry folks over the years. I wouldn't trade it for anything.

I have been an AIDS caregiver for four years. Ross died in August 1994. I was with him all that time and his life had a profound influence on my own. Caring for him, and for me, was both wonderful and terrible.

I love what St. Francis Lutheran does for our community. I've never had so many good and loyal new friends as I do now.

Jack Kling, 65, is a retired teacher and accomplished artist. A graduate of the California Culinary Academy, he is one of the designated chefs for the St. Francis Lutheran Senior Center.

LOWFAT ORANGE RUM BROWNIES

Makes 12 to 16

Mark Yeager, owner and operator of Mark's Healthy Kitchen, says you won't believe these brownies are lowfat when you taste their deep chocolately flavor and fudgy texture.

½ cup all-purpose flour

¼ cup plus 1 tablespoon cake flour

½ cup Dutch process cocoa plus more for dusting

½ cup ground chocolate

2 whole eggs

1 egg white

1½ cups sugar

5 ounces nonfat ricotta cheese

2 tablespoons unsweetened applesauce

2 tablespoons frozen orange juice concentrate (undiluted)

¼ cup pure maple syrup

2 tablespoons light rum or ½ tablespoon pure vanilla extract

2 tablespoons melted butter

✤ Preheat oven to 350°. Lightly grease 8-inch square baking pan.

✤ In a large mixing bowl, sift flours, cocoa and ground chocolate together.

✤ In another medium bowl, whisk eggs, egg white and sugar until thick and lemon-colored. Whisk in ricotta cheese, apple sauce, orange juice concentrate, maple syrup and rum until smooth.

✤ Add mixture to dry ingredients. Add melted butter and stir with wooden spoon until just incorporated. Transfer batter into prepared cake pan and bake for 25-30 minutes or until top begins to crack and center of pan is firm. Cool in pan on wire rack and loosen sides with knife. When cool, dust top of brownies with additional ground chocolate and cut into squares.

Per serving: 177 calories; 3.33g protein; 31.4g carbohydrates; 4.97g fat (2.74g saturated fat); 33.1mg cholesterol.

WESTERN RAISIN BARS

Makes 3 dozen

Nancy Barker says these are great to make for coffee hour after church.

1 cup raisins	1 teaspoon baking soda
2 cups water	1 teaspoon salt
½ cup solid vegetable shortening	½ teaspoon grated nutmeg
	½ teaspoon ground cloves
1 cup sugar	½ teaspoon ground cinnamon
1 egg	
2½ cups flour	¾ cup chopped walnuts

✤ Preheat oven to 375°. Grease a 10x15-inch jelly roll pan.

✤ In a medium saucepan, combine raisins and water and boil until only about 1 cup of liquid remains. Add shortening, sugar and eggs to the hot raisins and water. Stir quickly until well mixed.

✤ In a medium bowl, mix together flour, soda, salt and spices until well blended. Add to raisin mixture and stir until just mixed. Stir in the chopped nuts.

✤ Spread in prepared pan and bake until toothpick inserted in center comes out clean, about 15 minutes. Frost with powdered sugar frosting, if desired.

Per serving: 99.4 calories; 1.42g protein; 14.7g carbohydrates; 4.19g fat (.836g saturated fat); 5.3mg cholesterol.

SEVEN-LAYER COOKIES

Makes 3 dozen

Dale Johnson's friend, Bonnie Washburn, gave him this incredibly easy bar cookie that is perfect for coffee hour or potluck.

4 tablespoons (1 stick) butter	1 cup chopped walnuts
1 cup graham cracker crumbs	1 cup shredded coconut
1 cup butterscotch chips	1 14-ounce can sweetened condensed milk
1 cup semisweet chocolate chips	

✤ Preheat oven to 350°.

✤ Melt butter and spread evenly in a 9x13-inch baking pan. Sprinkle the graham cracker crumbs over the melted butter.

✤ Make even layers of the butterscotch chips, chocolate chips, walnuts and coconut. Drizzle the condensed milk over top. Bake until barely golden, 20-25 minutes. Cool in the pan on a wire rack. Cut into squares.

✤ Note: These are wonderful plain, but truly heavenly when topped with ice cream, marshmallow cream and hot fudge sauce. You may want to try other toppings as well.

Per serving: 142 calories; 1.97g protein; 16.6g carbohydrates; 8.33g fat (4.45g saturated fat); 7.21mg cholesterol.

CARMELITAS   Makes 16

John Phillip Carroll, cookbook author and baker extra-ordinnaire, likes to serve these chewy, gooey treats in his North Beach home.

¾ cup plus 3 tablespoons all-purpose flour
¾ cup quick-cooking oatmeal
½ cup brown sugar (packed)
½ cup (1 stick) butter, melted
½ teaspoon baking soda
¼ teaspoon salt
½ cup chopped nuts
⅔ cup butterscotch topping

✤ Preheat oven to 350°.

✤ Mix together ¾ cup flour, oatmeal, brown sugar, butter, baking soda and salt. Pat half of this mixture in an 8-inch square pan. Bake for 10 minutes.

✤ Remove from oven and sprinkle with chocolate chips and nuts. Mix butterscotch topping with 3 tablespoons flour (warm topping in microwave or in a saucepan over low heat if it is too stiff) and drizzle over the top. Sprinkle with the remaining oatmeal mixture and return to the oven for 20 minutes. Cut into squares while warm.

Per serving: 209 calories; 2.45g protein; 28.1g carbohydrates; 10.8g fat (5.26mg saturated fat); 15.7mg cholesterol.

WAYNE'S LEMON SQUARES

Makes 2 dozen

Inspired by Stars' pastry chef Emily Luchetti's recipe and adapted with her blessing, these lemon bars are ubiquitous at St. Francis Lutheran. In fact, at the 1994 Congregational Appreciation Banquet, these treats from Wayne Strei were nominated for the "Forbidden Fruit Award" for adding approximately 3,400 pounds to the collective congregation membership. Unfortunately, they didn't win ...

CRUST:

1½ cups all-purpose flour
½ cup powdered sugar

¾ cup (1½ sticks)
    unsalted butter

FILLING:

6 large eggs
2½ cups sugar
1 cup freshly squeezed
    lemon juice

½ cup all-purpose flour
¼ cup powdered sugar

✤ Preheat oven to 325°.

✤ To make the crust, combine the flour and powdered sugar in a medium bowl or the bowl of an electric mixer. Add the butter and mix on low speed or by hand until mixture resembles coarse meal. Press the crust into the bottom of a 9x13-inch pan. Bake the crust until golden brown, 20-25 minutes. Remove from oven.

✤ To make the filling, whisk together the eggs and sugar in a large bowl until smooth. Stir in the lemon juice and then the flour. Pour the lemon filling on top of the crust. Bake until the lemon filling is set, about 30 minutes. Allow to cool for ½ hour, cut into squares and dust with the ¼ cup powdered sugar.

Per serving: 203 calories; 2.74g protein; 32.8g carbohydrates; 7.11g fat (4g saturated fat); 68.5mg cholesterol.

DALE'S TOFFEE

Makes about 1 pound

Dale Leininger makes this very special toffee every year around Christmas and any other time it suits his fancy. It reminds him of his childhood in Indiana.

1½ cups chopped almonds	2 cups (12 ounces)
1 teaspoon salt	semisweet chocolate
¾ cup (1½ sticks) butter	chips
5 tablespoons water	1 cup sugar

✤ Preheat oven to 300°. Toast almonds on a baking sheet for about 10 minutes, being careful not to let them burn.

✤ In a heavy saucepan over medium-high heat, mix together butter, sugar, salt and water and bring to a boil. Boil to hard crack stage (310°F on a candy thermometer). Add toasted almonds and pour onto oiled baking sheet or other large, clean surface. Sprinkle chocolate chips over toffee and spread evenly. Cool. Break into pieces and store in an airtight container.

Per serving: 182 calories; 2.13g protein; 16.7g carbohydrates; 13.2g fat (5.86g saturated fat); 15.5mg cholesterol.

Sometimes I think I stay at St. Francis Lutheran simply because I have been coming here so long—almost 30 years. In 1965 my husband and I emigrated from Holland to the United Sates. We moved into a flat just a few blocks from the church and lived there until 1992. Since the 1960s I've seen the average Sunday attendance grow from about 20 to 100. We've grown similarly in richness and diversity. It seems like a miracle. The friendship among all the different people here, the closeness in Christ, all means a great deal to me.

Erna Dennert, 62, worked at home while she raised her two children—a decision she has never regretted. Since then she has worked as a printer and has finished the culinary program at the City College of San Francisco. She is one of the two designated "congregational chefs" for the senior center and other food events at St. Francis.

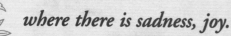 *where there is sadness, joy.*

Father and Mother of us all, thank you for the blessing of balance in life…

the sudden burst of laughter in the midst of tears;

the exquisite feeling of wellness the first day after being sick;

the memories of our grief and sorrow which heighten the joy of today;

our loved ones who, when they were dying, comforted us and reminded us to honor our relationships and to cherish the ordinary;

the countless things you send our way when we are in despair—the love of our families and friends, the unexpected smiles of strangers, rainbows, the little yellow flowers that grow out of the sidewalk.

God of all compassion, teach us to see all the people we walk among as angels who are sent by you to comfort, guide and protect us. Help us to reach out our hands for their healing touch and, in turn, to share that healing touch when someone reaches out to us. *~Amen.*

GIVING THANKS

Thanksgiving is another wonderful seasonal celebration. Though not of religious origin, the day nonetheless has spiritual importance, recognized at St. Francis Lutheran with an annual noon dinner. The church doors are thrown open to the entire community. Neighbors of varied belief and fortune are welcomed with a giant buffet of traditions.

The foods of the season are cooked and presented. Good feelings are passed on, along with the potatoes, and warm wishes are shared. Hopefully, so is that last piece of pumpkin pie.

Curried Pumpkin Soup

Chipotle Chili Pecan-Squash Soup

Honey, Apricot and Cherry Preserves

Mrs. Hildebrand's Red Cabbage with Apple and Bacon

Brussels Sprouts, Apples and Onions Poached in Apple Cider

Brandied Yams

Trio of Roasted Potatoes

Curried Couscous with Toasted Pecans and Cranberries

Squash Apple and Onion Gratin

Chestnut and Wild Mushroom Ragout

Maple-Glazed Chestnuts

Southern Cornbread and Cornbread Stuffing

Pork Roast with Sweet Potatoes and Prunes

Pumpkin Ice Cream Pie

Pumpkin Cheesecake

Cafe's Pecan Pumpkin Pie and Caramel Sauce

Sweet Potato Pie

St. Francis is a very strong part of my identity. I think of it mainly in terms of a community. Some of the most significant moments for me in the church have been when friends have joined, when I can share the things I like about St. Francis.

Lutherans are often apologetic and reluctant to recruit new members, but I think Lutheran doctrine and practice are very rich, powerful things. Once, years ago, I confessed to Pastor DeLange that I had really liked his sermon but couldn't remember anything specific about it. "That's OK," he replied, "the effects of sermons are cumulative." It sounded like a joke, but it's true. Over a long period of time the sermons, the services, and the liturgy have a profound effect. They become intrinsic parts of us.

Tom Tragardh, 48, grew up in Campbell, California, and teaches in the English and English as a Second Language departments at City College of San Francisco. He has been active as a council member and president of the congregation. He and his life partner, David Cortez, have been together for over 26 years.

CURRIED PUMPKIN SOUP

Serves 4

Parker Nolen created this soup in 1989 after experimenting with a basic recipe from "Better Homes and Gardens". Parker's variation is both tasty and extraordinarily hearty. Serve it hot or cold, depending on the season.

4 tablespoons (½ stick) butter
1 cup chopped onion
1-2 garlic cloves, crushed
    through a press
1 tablespoon curry powder
½ teaspoon salt
⅛ teaspoon crushed red
    pepper flakes

3 cups chicken broth
1 16-ounce can pumpkin
1 cup half-and-half
    or milk
Sour cream (optional)
Chives (optional)
Bacon bits (optional)

✤ In a large pot, melt butter over medium heat. Add onion and garlic and cook until soft. Add curry powder, salt and red pepper flakes and stir to combine. Cook about 1 minute, just enough to blend the flavors. Add the chicken broth and bring to a boil. Simmer uncovered, 15-20 minutes.

✤ Carefully stir in the pumpkin and half-and-half or milk and cook 5-7 minutes. Pour mixture into a food processor or blender and puree until creamy. Garnish with a dollop of sour cream, chives or bacon bits if desired.

Per serving: 231 calories; 4.69g protein; 22.5g carbohydrates; 214.5g fat (8.16g saturated fat); 38.1mg cholesterol.

CHIPOTLE CHILE
PECAN-SQUASH SOUP

Serves 8

Although this flavorful soup is a welcome addition to any autumn dinner, Michael Utech especially likes to serve it as a first course on Thanksgiving. Chipotle chiles can pack quite a wallop, but Michael believes they're worth it!

3 tablespoons butter	2 cups shelled pecans plus
1 cup finely diced onion	about 24 whole pecans
2 cloves garlic, crushed	8 cups chicken stock
through a press	1-2 canned chipotle chiles
3 tablespoons tomato paste	Sour cream (optional)
1 small acorn squash	Parsley sprigs (optional)

✤ In a large pot, melt butter over medium-low heat. Add onion and cook until transparent. Add garlic and cook slowly for about 3 minutes to release flavor without browning. Stir in tomato paste, remove from heat and set aside. Cook acorn squash until tender in microwave by cutting in half and covering with plastic wrap (about 5 minutes on high power for a small squash) or bake in a preheated 350° oven for about 30-40 minutes. Remove flesh from squash.

✤ Puree the squash and 2 cups of pecans in food processor or blender Add chicken stock, 1 seeded chipotle chile (2 if you are brave!) and 1 tablespoon of the adobo liquid from the can of chiles and process to combine. Add together pecan mixture with tomato paste, onion and garlic in pot over medium heat and slowly bring to a boil. Cook at least 30 minutes to blend flavors, stirring frequently to avoid burning.

✤ A dollop of sour cream is a nice garnish and compliments the spiciness of the chilies. For an elegant presentation, float three whole pecans in the center of each serving with a small sprig of parsley .

Per serving: 420 calories; 10.9g protein; 25.4g carbohydrates; 32.8g fat (7.32g saturated fat); 37.2mg cholesterol.

HONEY, APRICOT and CHERRY PRESERVES

Makes about 4 cups

Samuel Aller suggests serving this delicious relish with chicken, pork or Thanksgiving turkey. You can make it up to one week in advance—just cover tightly and refrigerate.

1¼ cups apricot nectar
1 cup chopped dried apricots
1 cup (about 4 ounces)
   dried tart cherries
   or cranberries

⅓ cup honey
6 tablespoons sweet white
   wine (such as Reisling)
2 tablespoons sugar

✤ In a heavy saucepan over medium heat, mix together all ingredients and cook, stirring occasionally, until sugar is dissolved and mixture almost comes to a boil. Reduce heat, cover pan and cook about 15 minutes, uncovering to stir frequently. Serve cold or at room temperature.

Per serving: 94.3 calories; .656g protein; 22.6g carbohydrates; .13g fat (.018g saturated fat); 0mg cholesterol.

MRS. HILDEBRAND'S RED CABBAGE with APPLES and BACON

Serves 6

Fran Hildebrand shares her mother's recipe for an excellent Thanksgiving side dish. It's also great with roasted duck, pheasant or pork.

6 whole cloves
6 peppercorns (or 1
   teaspoon ground pepper)
6 slices of bacon, diced
2 cups thinly sliced onion
10 cups coarsely chopped
   red cabbage

4 large tart apples,
   cored, peeled, and
   thinly sliced
½ cup red wine vinegar
1 tablespoon sugar
1 teaspoon salt

✤ Preheat oven to 325°. Combine cloves and peppercorns in a small piece of cheesecloth and tie securely with a piece of kitchen twine.

✤ Cook bacon slowly in a large pot over medium heat until browned, 3-5 minutes. Add the onion and cook, stirring constantly until onions are translucent, about 10 minutes.

✤ Add cabbage, cover and cook over low heat, about 15 minutes.

✤ Gently mix in apple slices, vinegar, cheesecloth-wrapped spices, sugar and salt. Bake covered about 1½ hours. Remove cheesecloth and serve.

Per serving: 152 calories; 1.62g protein; 6.68g carbohydrates; 13.9g fat (1.89g saturated fat); 1.28mg cholesterol.

BRUSSELS SPROUTS, APPLES and ONIONS POACHED in APPLE CIDER

Serves 6

Erna Dennert created this vegetable dish for a family holiday dinner. She says it is especially good with ham or roast pork.

1 pound Brussels sprouts	1½ cups apple cider
2 tablespoons butter	½ teaspoon salt
2 tablespoons olive oil	½ teaspoon ground pepper
1 medium onion, chopped	2 star anise
2 large yellow apples, cored and cut into ½-inch cubes	1/4 cup balsamic vinegar

✤ Trim stems of Brussels sprouts, cutting each one in half lengthwise. In a skillet or heavy saucepan melt butter in olive oil, over medium heat. Add onions and apples and cook for 2-3 minutes. Add Brussels sprouts and cook for 3-4 minutes, stirring gently. Add apple cider, salt, pepper and star anise and stir to combine. Cover, reduce heat to low and simmer 10-15 minutes until Brussels sprouts are tender.

✤ Using a slotted spoon, transfer Brussels sprouts, apples and onions to a serving dish and keep warm. Over high heat, reduce the pan juices by about half. Add balsamic vinegar and cook 2-3 minutes more, scraping bottom of pan while stirring. Discard star anise. Add juices to Brussels sprouts, apples and onions and serve promptly.

Per serving: 148 calories; 1g protein; 18.6g carbohydrates; 8.68g fat (3.06g saturated fat); 10.4mg cholesterol.

BRANDIED YAMS

Serves 10-12

Iris Vaughan makes this extra-special vegetable dish not only at Thanksgiving, but whenever she believes our St. Francis Lutheran pot lucks need some pizazz. You'll love it, too!

8 large Garnet yams*
½ pound (2 sticks) unsalted butter
5 heaping tablespoons dark brown sugar

¼ teaspoon ground cinnamon
Dash of ground cloves
⅓ cup brandy

❖ Preheat oven to 350°. Line oven racks with aluminum foil.

❖ Wash and dry yams and place them on the lined oven racks. Bake about 1 hour or until easily pierced with a fork. (The skins of some of the yams may crack and juice may run down.)

❖ Remove from oven and let cool on wire racks. When cool enough to handle (at least ½ hour), peel and place in a large bowl. Mash, 2-3 at a time, with a fork to remove any lumps.

❖ In a small saucepan, melt the butter over medium heat. Remove from heat and add brown sugar, cinnamon and cloves. Mix together, add brandy and mix again. Pour this mixture into the yams and stir with a wooden spoon until well blended. This dish may be prepared and refrigerated at least one day ahead and simply reheated for about 15 minutes in the oven prior to serving.

❖ Note: *Each yam should be about 1½-2 inches across. Other types of yams can be used, but Garnet yams are the least dry.

Per serving: 233 calories; 1.31g protein; 19.9g carbohydrates; 15.4g fat (9.59g saturated fat); 41.4mg cholesterol.

TRIO OF ROASTED POTATOES

Serves 8

Sweet and Irish potatoes are cooked twice in this recipe from Heidi Cusick, once boiled and once roasted, to make crisp company potatoes to serve with ham, chicken or turkey.

6 medium white potatoes	4 cloves garlic, quartered
2 sweet potatoes	2 tablespoons fresh thyme
2 yams	or rosemary sprigs
½ cup olive oil	Salt and pepper to taste

✤ Preheat oven to 400°. Lightly oil a shallow 9x13-inch baking pan.

✤ Scrub white potatoes, sweet potatoes and yams. In one sauceapn, boil white potatoes in water to cover until just tender. In a separate saucepan, boil sweet potatoes and yams in water to cover until just tender. Cool. Cut the potatoes into wedges and place in oiled baking pan. Drizzle with olive oil. Toss with garlic, herbs, salt and pepper. Bake until crisp and golden, turning occasionally, about 40 minutes.

Per serving: 279 calories; 3g protein; 37.1g carbohydrates; 13.9g fat (1.92g saturated fat); 0mg cholesterol.

In 1993, ten of our members died of AIDS—ten percent of our active members. During the fourteen years we have lived with this epidemic, about 90 people die in San Francisco each month. As Christians, we believe in the Resurrection, so it is not difficult for us to give hope to people who are dying. What is difficult is giving comfort and support to those who are living with AIDS. Several of our members have taken special training at Most Holy Redeemer Roman Catholic Church to become caregivers for people with AIDS. These members, most of whom work full-time, offer emotional support, shop, clean, pick up medications and sometimes bring their clients to church. It's tough to watch people die. But it's tougher still not to offer a cup of water when you've been given the water of life.

CURRIED COUSCOUS with TOASTED PECANS and CRANBERRIES

Serves 5-6

Michael Hiller invented this little dish when Arthur Morris' cousin visited them. They had not seen one another for 10 years and it was a wonderful reunion. For a beautiful presentation, scoop the mixture into brioche or other molds and invert them onto the plates.

1 tablespoon olive oil	Salt and pepper to taste
½ small onion, minced	½ cup chopped pecans, toasted
1 clove garlic, minced	½ cup dried cranberries
1 10-ounce box couscous	
1 tablespoon curry powder	

❖ In a large skillet, heat olive oil over medium heat. Add onion and garlic and cook for 1 minute. Stir in couscous. Season with the curry powder, salt and pepper and stir until all the grains are evenly coated.

❖ Add water as directed on package and bring to a boil. Cover and turn off heat. Let sit for 5 minutes.

❖ Stir in pecans and cranberries. Keep covered until ready to serve.

Per serving: 218 calories; 4.71g protein; 26.2g carbohydrates; 11.1g fat (1.05g saturated fat); 0mg cholesterol.

As a married, heterosexual, white female and life-long Lutheran (and graduate of St. Olaf College), I have been a member of eight different Lutheran congregations. After joining St. Francis in 1987, it was at first sometimes a bit strange being among so many gays and lesbians, yet I always felt welcomed and genuinely cared for. Never before have I been part of a community so diverse, so inclusive, so warm and welcoming.

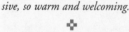

Nancy Barker, 54, worked as a facilities coordinator before retiring with her husband to Spokane, Washington. She was the president of the church council during the controversial ordinations of Ruth, Phyllis and Jeff.

SQUASH, APPLE and ONION GRATIN

Serves 6

This is Marti Lundin's version of a recipe which originally appeared in "Bon Appetit." People who "absolutely don't like squash" have told her they love this dish, making it worth the little bit of extra trouble it takes to put it together.

1 pound butternut squash	¼ cup light brown
¼ cup (½ stick) butter	sugar, divided
2 large onions, thinly sliced	½ cup chicken stock
¾ pound tart green apples,	¾ cup fresh breadcrumbs
peeled, cored and	¾ cup shredded
thinly sliced	Emmenthaler cheese
3 tablespoons flour	6 lean bacon slices, cooked,
½ teaspoon salt	crumbled

✤ Preheat oven to 350°. Heavily butter an oval or 9-inch square baking dish.

✤ Peel squash, cut in half lengthwise and scoop out seeds and stringy parts. Thinly slice squash crosswise.

✤ In a heavy skillet, melt butter and cook onions over medium heat until lightly browned. Set aside. In a large bowl, toss the apples in flour and salt. Arrange half of squash in bottom of baking dish. Top with half of the apple slices. Sprinkle with half of the brown sugar. Top with another layer of squash, then the remaining apples and brown sugar. Cover with onions. Pour stock over all. Bake until squash and apples are tender, about 45 minutes.

✤ Remove from oven. Mix bread crumbs, cheese and bacon. Sprinkle mixture on top and bake another 15-20 minutes, until cheese melts and the crumbs are lightly browned. Serve promptly.

Per serving: 224 calories; 6.81g protein; 23.9g carbohydrates; 12.1g fat (6.75g saturated fat); 31.4mg cholesterol.

CHESTNUT and WILD MUSHROOM RAGOUT

Serves 8-10

A wonderful autumnal dish from the incredible Margaret Fox and her husband Christopher Kump, who run Cafe Beaujolais, the best reason to visit Mendocino, California.

18 pearl onions, peeled
12 baby carrots (greens trimmed to1 inch of carrots), peeled
2½ tablespoons butter, divided
1 to 1½ cups chicken stock
Salt and pepper to taste

1 cup mixed wild mushrooms
Maple-glazed chestnuts (recipe follows)
1 tablespoon minced chives or chopped parsley (garnish)

❖ In a heavy pan that will hold the vegetables snugly in one layer, combine onions, carrots, 1½ tablespoons of butter and stock to just cover the vegetables. Season lightly with salt and pepper and bring to a boil over medium-high heat. Reduce heat, cover and simmer for 5 minutes. Increase heat to medium and cook 2-3 minutes, partially covered. Increase heat to high and cook another 1-2 minutes, uncovered, shaking and swirling the pan until liquid has reduced to syrupy, shiny glaze coating the vegetables. Remove from heat and test carrots and onions (they should be tender but not too soft). If vegetables aren't tender, add 1-2 tablespoons stock, return to heat and cook another 1-2 minutes, or two, partially covered, until tender. Set aside.

❖ If mushrooms are large, cut into bite-sized pieces. In a large skillet or frying pan, melt butter over medium heat. Add the mushrooms and cook quickly over high heat, stirring frequently, about 2 minutes, until mushrooms begin to soften. Season generously with salt and pepper and continue to cook until tender. If there is a lot of liquid, continue to cook to reduce liquid. Add the glazed vegetables and maple-glazed chestnuts to the pan and cook together for 1-2 more minutes to blend flavors. If ragout seems dry, add a little more stock or water. Garnish with minced chives or chopped parsley.

Per serving: 140 calories; 2.89g protein; 20.1g carbohydrates; 5.84g fat (3.01g saturated fat); 12.9mg cholesterol.

MAPLE-GLAZED CHESTNUTS

Serves 8-10

1½ cups (7-8 ounces)
    peeled chestnuts*
1 cup chicken or turkey stock
1½ tablespoons unsalted butter

1 tablespoon maple syrup
Salt and freshly ground
    pepper to taste

✚ Combine all ingredients in the smallest skillet (preferably non-stick) that will allow the chestnuts to sit in one layer. Simmer partially covered for about 15-20 minutes until liquid is syrupy and chestnuts are cooked but not falling apart.

✚ Note: *If starting with unpeeled chestnuts, you will need about 8 ounces. Peel them using a sharp paring knife, cutting a criss-cross through the tough outer shell on the flat side of the chestnuts and scoring the brown outer skin. Heat a couple of cups of either canola oil or water in a small pan. If using oil, heat about 320°F; if water, bring to a boil. With oil, fry the chestnuts in small batches until shells curl away from meat, about 3 minutes. With water, blanch chestnuts in small batches about 1 minute to loosen shells and skin. In both cases, try to work quickly with a paring knife to peel away outer shells and inner skins as soon as they are cool enough to handle as chestnuts become harder to peel as they cool.

Per serving: 69 calories; .887g protein; 11.5g carbohydrates; 2.15g fat (1.17g saturated fat); 4.66mg cholesterol

SOUTHERN CORNBREAD and CORNBREAD STUFFING

Serves 6-8

This authentic Southern dressing comes from Marti Lundin's mother. It keeps well for several days refrigerated, or freezes well for delicious leftovers. Under no circumstances should you use cornbread that has the least bit of sugar, which most ready-made mixes do. This recipe is easily doubled.

CORNBREAD:

1 cup yellow cornmeal	Pinch of salt
½ cup all-purpose flour	½ teaspoon baking soda
1 egg	1 teaspoon baking powder
1 cup buttermilk	

✤ Preheat oven to 400°. Heavily grease a round or 9-inch square baking pan and heat in oven.

✤ Mix together all ingredients and pour into prepared pan. The mix should sizzle as it hits the hot pan. Bake until golden brown, 15-20 minutes.

STUFFING:

1 recipe cornbread (above)	1 tablespoon sage
1 7.5-ounce tube of canned biscuits, baked	1½ celery ribs, chopped
2 tablespoons butter	1½-2 cups chicken broth
1 large onion, chopped	1 teaspoon baking soda
½ tablespoon black pepper	¾ cup buttermilk

✤ Tear cooked cornbread and cooked biscuits into small pieces.

✤ In a heavy pan, melt butter and cook the onion in butter until the onion is translucent. Mix into bread mixture. Add black pepper, sage and celery. Mix in chicken broth so that mixture is very moist. At this point you can refrigerate several hours or overnight. (You may need to add more chicken broth to moisten before proceeding with recipe.)

✤ Preheat oven to 350°.

✜ Just before baking, stir in baking soda and buttermilk until well blended. Use part of the recipe to stuff a turkey and bake the remaining separately in a greased baking pan, or bake the whole recipe in a greased 9x13-inch pan until golden brown, 40-45 minutes.

Per serving: 256 calories; 7.56g protein; 36.9g carbohydrates; 9.18g fat (3.51g saturated fat); 37mg cholesterol.

PORK ROAST with SWEET POTATOES and PRUNES
Serves 6-8

Try this marvelous pork roast from Erna Dennert as an alternative to the traditional turkey on your Thanksgiving table.

6-7 pound pork loin (bone in)	Juice of 2 lemons
4-5 cloves garlic, peeled and quartered lengthwise	Salt and pepper to taste
2 tablespoons dried thyme	2 pounds sweet potatoes, peeled and cut into quarters, parboiled
⅓ cup olive oil	½ pound pitted prunes

✜ Preheat oven to 450°. Grease a large roasting pan.

✜ Scrape pork loin with a knife to remove any large pieces of fat. Stud the meat with garlic pieces.

✜ In a small bowl, mix thyme, olive oil, lemon juice, salt and pepper. Brush generously over the roast. Cook 15 minutes, then reduce heat to 325°. Cook until meat is done but still juicy, 30-35 minutes per pound. Baste the roast regularly with both the drippings and the remaining herb mixture. During the last 30-35 minutes add peeled sweet potatoes and prunes.

Per serving: 935 calories; 105g protein; 48.1g carbohydrates; 34g fat (10.2g saturated fat); 266mg cholesterol.

I tell people, "If you want to find an easy church to join, St. Francis Lutheran is not the one! However, if you want to be part of a combination family/community that shares something very powerful, then you are in the right place." At St. Francis, I am fully accepted. All of me. As a member of that community I have felt myself become stronger and more affirmed in my experience of the love of God. I cannot express the collage of feelings I experienced on my first visit to St. Francis after being away from the church for nearly 20 years. That service started a great change in my life.

God calls us to be servants and gives us faith to go out each day in good courage, not knowing where we will be going. As a congregation, St. Francis is also like that. We can't know the outcome of all that we are doing, but we are faithful in our mission, and we are not afraid. I am confident that in 25 years people will look back and say that we were significant in changing ideas in the church.

Mari Griffiths Irvin, 61, is a professor and administrator at the University of the Pacific in Stockton, California. She grew up in North Dakota, Iowa, and Oregon, and is a St. Olaf College graduate, class of 1955. Mari is currently president of the congregation.

PUMPKIN ICE CREAM PIE

Serves 6-8

This recipe from Leona Lee for an unusual variation on pumpkin pie would be welcome in summer as well as on the Thanksgiving table.

1 quart vanilla ice cream	¼ teaspoon ground nutmeg
1 cup canned pumpkin	¼ teaspoon ground cloves
½ cup brown sugar (packed)	1 8-inch graham cracker
1 teaspoon ground cinnamon	pie crust
¼ teaspoon salt	

✤ In a large bowl, place ice cream to soften.

✤ In another bowl, mix together pumpkin, brown sugar, cinnamon, salt, nutmeg and cloves. Add to ice cream, mix until well blended and pour into prepared pie shell. Freeze until ready to serve.

Per serving: 208 calories; 1.55g protein; 36.2g carbohydrates; 7.01g fat (1.49g saturated fat); .014mg cholesterol.

PUMPKIN CHEESECAKE

Serves 12

Everyone hopes that David Look will bring this cheesecake on Thanksgiving Day. It is a delicious alternative to pumpkin pie.

2 cups graham cracker
   or corn flake crumbs
½ cup (1 stick) butter, melted
¼ cup brown sugar (packed)
2 pounds cream cheese
   at room temperature
1 cup nonfat sour cream
1 cup sugar
7 eggs, lightly beaten
¼ cup all-purpose flour

1 tablespoon ground
   cinnamon
1 teaspoon ground cloves
1 teaspoon ground ginger
1 tablespoon vanilla extract
1 16-ounce can pumpkin
Whipped cream for garnish
½ cup walnut or pecan
   halves (optional)

✤ Preheat oven to 425°.

✤ In a large bowl, combine crumbs, melted butter and brown sugar until well mixed. Press crumbs onto bottom and 2 inches up the side of an 8-inch springform pan. Bake 5 minutes. Let cool.

✤ In another large mixing bowl, mix together cream cheese, sour cream, sugar and eggs. Add flour, cinnamon, cloves, ginger and vanilla, mashed pumpkin and mix until smooth.

✤ Pour pumpkin mixture into prepared crust. Bake 15 minutes. Reduce heat to 275° and bake 1 hour longer. Turn off heat but leave in the oven 3-4 hours until completely cool. Refrigerate until serving. Serve with whipped cream and walnuts or pecans (optional).

Per serving: 570 calories; 12.5g protein; 41.4g carbohydrates; 40.7g fat (22.8g saturated fat); 227mg cholesterol.

CAFE's PECAN PUMPKIN PIE and CARAMEL SAUCE

Makes 2 9-inch pies

Donna Katzl, chef-owner of Cafe For All Seasons, offers this delicious combination pecan and pumpkin pie. The packaged cake mix makes this a very easy recipe.

1 29-ounce can pumpkin
1 5-ounce can evaporated milk
3 eggs, lightly beaten
1 cup sugar
½ teaspoon salt
2 teaspoons ground cinnamon

1 18.25-ounce package yellow cake mix with pudding
1½ cups chopped pecans
½ pound (2 sticks) butter, melted
Whipped cream (garnish)

❖ Preheat oven to 350°. Line the bottom of two 9-inch pie pans with parchment or waxed paper and lightly grease sides.

❖ Mix together the pumpkin, evaporated milk, eggs, sugar, salt and cinnamon. Pour into pans. Sprinkle cake mix over the top. Distribute chopped pecans over cake mix and drizzle melted butter over all. Bake 1 hour. Let cool. Refrigerate.

❖ Invert pies and cut into wedges. Serve topped with a dollop of whipped cream and warm caramel sauce drizzled over the top.

CARAMEL SAUCE:

1 cup (2 sticks) unsalted butter
2 cups light brown sugar (packed)
1 cup heavy (whipping) cream

❖ Cut butter into pieces and melt it in a small heavy pan. Stir in the brown sugar and cream. Cook over very low heat, stirring constantly, until all is melted and blended. Whisking the sauce helps to bring it together. Serve warm. Refrigerate what is not used. Reheat on low heat.

Per serving: 998 calories; 7.83g protein; 97.5g carbohydrates; 67.4g fat (32g saturated fat); 225mg cholesterol.

SWEET POTATO PIE

Serves 6-8

Tom Tragardh has hated pumpkin pies since childhood. This sweet potato pie is very rich, much thicker even before it is cooked than a soupy pumpkin pie. The pie may develop a few cracks as it cooks and cools, but it's a dark, mellow color and still looks good despite any fissures. At St. Francis Lutheran bake sales, Tom always makes several pies and tarts; most are pre-sold. "Am I wrong to go public with the recipe?" he wonders.

Pastry for a 9-inch pie
3 cups mashed cooked yams
¼ teaspoon salt
2 or 3 eggs, well beaten
½-1 teaspoon ground allspice
½ cup sweetened condensed milk or heavy (whipping) cream

½ cup sugar
3 tablespoons light molasses (not blackstrap)
3 tablespoons quality bourbon whiskey or to taste
¼ cup (½ stick) of butter, melted

✤ Preheat the oven to 425°. Line a 9-inch pie plate with pastry.

✤ Steam the yams in their skins until soft. Cool slightly and peel. Mash the yams in a large bowl or the bowl of an electric mixer until completely smooth. Add all other ingredients, mixing thoroughly.

✤ Pour or spoon the mixture into the pastry-lined pie plate. Bake 10 minutes, then reduce the temperature to 300° and bake about 50 minutes. Don't let it burn. Cool on a rack. Refrigerate if not serving immediately.

✤ Notes: *Choose red yams rather than yellow sweet potatoes, disregarding the name of the recipe. "Yam pie" doesn't have the ring of "sweet potato pie." Yams are sweeter, have better texture and require less sugar. To have the most yam flavor in the recipe, reduce the allspice to ½ teaspoon or less. To make it even richer, use three eggs and use heavy cream instead of sweetened condensed milk. The bourbon can be omitted, but why?

Per serving: 406 calories; 5.83g protein; 57.4g carbohydrates; 16.7g fat (7.02g saturated fat); 75mg cholesterol.

O God, we grieve different losses in various ways—

the difficulties of childhood;

the traumas of adolescence;

the misery of lost love;

the disappointments of unfulfilled hopes and dreams;

the loneliness of the forgotten elderly;

the pain of the death of someone we love.

Whether we measure our losses on one hand or in the hundreds, we know that remaining in the pain can sour our lives and limit our usefulness to you. Give us courage to face our fears and walk through our pain that we may be bearers of your love and grace in a world desperate for healing. Loving God, touch us with your comforting hand as we reach out as wounded healers to others. ~Amen.

Grant that we may not so much seek to be consoled as to console;

SUPPER TIME

This is the definitive urban meal. It's got to be quick and simple. No fuss, not after the day you've had. Eight o'clock already? Better make it fast—a quick toss, one-dish specialty.

Of course, it has to be good, too. After all, you could have grabbed something to-go on the way home, so this better be worth the trouble. No problem. Warm a casserole while you're soaking in the tub. Or unwind in the kitchen with a little chopping block therapy. Cooking time is minimal and the clean-up negligible. In between, a relaxing interlude awaits.

Fugi's Special Swiss
Fondue Fromage

Pittsburgh Potatoes

Spaghetti Squash

Epinards a Catalonia

Roasted Red Peppers

Hot Dish Speciale

Sauerkraut and Potato Casserole

Eggplant Casserole

Lamb and Vegetable Orzotto

Spicy Shrimp and Feta Pasta

Spaghetti with Slow-Baked
Tomatoes

Crab Giovanni

Stir-Fry Dungeness Crab

Linguini in Lemon Cream Sauce

Fish in Coconut Sauce

Fish Filets Meuniere with
Vegetable Garnish

Chicken Marsala

Chicken Paprika

Sunday Supper Chicken and Rice

FUGI'S SPECIAL SWISS FONDUE FROMAGE

Serves 4-6

When Jack Lundin was a travel agent based in Paris, he became friends with a flamboyant hotelier by the name of Fugi. This recipe predates the "Americanization" of fondue, especially the prepackaged and typical restaurant variety offered up quickly for appetizers. The Swiss eat this as a main winter dish along with potatoes, salad and, occasionally, sausage. The wine should always be a quality dry white wine, such as sauvignon blanc or chardonnay.

Liquid Sterno or denatured
   alcohol placed under a
   ceramic fondue pot
2½-3 cups dry white wine
1 garlic clove
¾ pound mild Cheddar
   cheese, shredded
¾ pound Emmenthaler or
   Swiss cheese, shredded

½ pound Swiss Gruyere,
   shredded
¼ teaspoon baking soda
½ teaspoon cornstarch
1 ounce quality cognac
   or Kirsch
1 or 2 baguettes or French
   bread, cut into
   bite-size pieces

✤ Light the liquid Sterno to warm the fondue pot. Pour dry white wine into the pot. Peel and crush the garlic clove to allow the garlic juice to seep into the heated wine. Wait until the combination of wine and garlic vapors rise, but are not boiling. Then place the three cheeses into the hot liquid, a handful at a time, continually stirring with a wooden spoon.

✤ Just before the last portions of the three cheeses are put into the pot, take half of the baking soda and half of the cornstarch and sprinkle into the pot, stirring constantly. After all the cheese is in the pot, and just before it melts in the wine, place the rest of the cornstarch and baking soda in the pot. Stir continuously until the mesh of wine and cheese feels easy to stir. Add the Cognac or Kirsch, stir and serve with bread cubes.

✤ Note: You will notice that the top of the pot will have a wine "cover" when you begin serving, but as you dip your bite-size pieces of French bread into the pot the ingredients will gradually begin to emulsify.

Per serving: 961 calories; 43.4g protein; 76.1g carbohydrates; 48.5g fat (28.4g saturated fat); 145mg cholesterol.

PITTSBURGH POTATOES

Serves 6-8

Samuel Aller's mother made this when he was a young boy in Pennsylvania. It was always a special treat for the whole family.

3 medium potatoes,
cubed (about 2 cups)
1 tablespoon chopped onion
1½ tablespoons butter
1½ tablespoons
all-purpose flour
1 cup milk

½ teaspoon salt or to taste
1 teaspoon pepper or to taste
½ cup medium Cheddar
cheese, grated
1 2-ounce jar sliced
pimentos, drained and
chopped

✤ Preheat oven to 350°. Butter a 2-quart deep casserole or baking pan.

✤ In a medium pot over medium heat, cover potatoes with water, bring to a boil and cook 10 minutes. Drain well.

✤ In a heavy saucepan, melt butter over medium-low heat. Mix in flour and cook about 3 minutes. Gradually pour milk into flour mixture, whisking until smooth. Bring to a boil over medium-high heat, whisking constantly. Add salt and pepper. Reduce heat to medium-low and simmer uncovered, stirring often, for 5 minutes. Add the grated cheese and stir into the sauce until melted. Stir in chopped pimentos.

✤ Place the potatoes in the buttered casserole. Pour the cheese sauce over the potatoes and stir gently. Bake until the potatoes are soft, 15-20 minutes. Serve hot.

Per serving: 142 calories; 5.11g protein; 13.8g carbohydrates; 7.66g fat (4.71g saturated fat); 23.2mg cholesterol.

SPAGHETTI SQUASH

Serves 4-6

Greg Jahnke, the Lutheran Brotherhood agent based in San Francisco, offers this vegetarian dish which makes a lovely one-skillet entrée.

¼ cup pine nuts (pignoli)	2 green onions, chopped
1 medium spaghetti squash	(white and green parts)
1 tablespoon olive oil	1 cup grated Parmesan
4 garlic cloves, minced	cheese

✤ Preheat oven to 350°. Roast pine nuts in baking pan until lightly browned, about 10 minutes. Set aside.

✤ Halve and seed spaghetti squash. In a covered saucepan large enough to hold squash, bring about ½ inch of water to a simmer. Add squash and steam until "meat" becomes stringy but remains firm when separated with a fork, 15-20 minutes. Do not let squash become mushy. Cool squash and remove meat with fork. Set aside.

✤ In a large skillet, heat olive oil over medium-low heat. Add garlic and cook until soft. Add onions and squash, stirring just to combine. Do not overmix. When squash is heated through, remove from heat and sprinkle with pine nuts and Parmesan cheese. Serve promptly.

Per serving: 222 calories; 9.65g protein; 8.57g carbohydrates; 18.9g fat (5.28g saturated fat); 13.1mg cholesterol.

EPINARDS a CATALONIA

Serves 4-6

In 1987 Arthur Morris visited his friend Dan in Barcelona, Spain, where he was often served this spinach dish. Arthur and Dan tried many variations before deciding on these proportions.

1 medium onion	2-3 tablespoons olive oil
¼ cup pine nuts (pignoli)	3 slices of thick bacon,
1 pound (2-3 bunches)	cooked and chopped
spinach	

✤ Slice the onion very thinly, separate into rings and set aside. Toast the pine nuts in a cast-iron skillet on the stove or in the oven until medium brown, using no oil. Put in a small bowl and set aside.

✤ Wash the spinach and discard tough stems. Chop the spinach and set aside in a large bowl.

✤ In a large skillet or frying pan, heat the oil over medium-high heat. When hot, cook the onion until translucent. Add bacon and immediately add as much spinach as you can and still be able to stir. Stir the spinach until you coat the leaves. Cover and lower the heat. After 2 minutes add more spinach, stir to mix and cover. Continue until all of the spinach is wilted. Quickly stir in the pine nuts and serve promptly.

Per serving: 303 calories; 12g protein; 11.5g carbohydrates; 27.3g fat (4.48g saturated fat); 4.05mg cholesterol.

ROASTED RED PEPPERS   Serves 6-8

Michael Utech says these peppers are great served alone or as an addition to pastas or salads. Use in sandwiches or serve on slices of toasted French bread as an appetizer.

4 large red bell peppers	1 teaspoon sugar
2 tablespoons olive oil	1 teaspoon salt
½ tablespoon balsamic	
vinegar	

✤ Preheat broiler to high.

✤ Cut peppers in half lengthwise. Remove seeds and core. Flatten with the palm of your hand and place on a baking sheet, skin side up. Roast peppers under the broiler until skins are charred black. Remove from broiler and place in plastic bag, tie bag shut and let peppers sweat for 15-20 minutes. Remove peppers from bag and scrape off charred skin. Cut roasted peppers in 1-inch strips.

✤ In a large skillet, heat olive oil and peppers. Add remaining ingredients. Cook about 5 minutes over medium heat until sugar dissolves. Serve hot or refrigerate for later use.

Per serving: 42 calories; .33g protein; 2.95g carbohydrates; 3.45g fat (.467g saturated fat); 0mg cholesterol

One of the exciting things about St. Francis Lutheran is that we try to embody Christ's love and compassion not only for lesbians, gays, and bisexuals but also for seniors, children, the neighborhood, and the homeless. The senior program exemplifies how St. Francis helps people in simple but important ways. One active participant is Grace, a survivor of the 1906 earthquake. When I pick her up to come to the Wednesday program at St. Francis, she always exclaims, "Oh, today is the day of days!" With limitations of hearing, sight, and mobility, Grace loves the meaningful contact with other people that the senior program makes possible.

I also love the monthly birthday events that Faye Robinson has invented for the whole congregation's Sunday coffee hour. She makes sure there is a cake for the occasion, and leads the birthday song with genuine gusto and pleasure.

Phyllis Zillhart, 37, and her partner Ruth Frost served as pastors with Lutheran Lesbian and Gay Ministry, and are now associate pastors at St. Francis. Phyllis is also pastor for the congregation's ministry with the elderly. She and Ruth Frost are the mothers of Joy Noelle Hart, born October 3, 1993.

HOT DISH SPECIALE

Serves 6-8

St. Francis Lutheran Church member Parker Nolen, presently studying in Montreal, tells us this dish is guaranteed to get you a date if you're single!?

1 8-ounce jar artichoke hearts, drained	1 cup sour cream
2 10-ounce packages frozen creamed spinach	1 cup mayonnaise
	¼ cup lemon juice
	½ pound mushrooms, sliced

❖ Preheat oven to 350°. Lightly grease a 9x13-inch baking dish.

❖ Lay the artichokes in the bottom of the prepared dish. Cook the spinach according to package directions. Pour the spinach over the artichoke layer.

❖ In a small bowl, combine sour cream, mayonnaise, lemon juice and mushrooms. Pour over spinach layer. Bake until bubbly and hot, about 20 minutes.

Per serving: 391 calories; 5.81g protein; 11.7g carbohydrates; 37.8g fat (9.4g saturated fat); 38.6mg cholesterol.

SAUERKRAUT and POTATO CASSEROLE

Serves 6

Dale Leininger, raised a Missouri Synod Lutheran in Tipton, Indiana, makes this German dish when he wants to remember the comfort foods of his youth.

1   pound potatoes, sliced
1   large yellow onion, diced
½   pound cooked summer sausage, sliced
½   pound ham, cut into ½-inch pieces
1   pound white sauerkraut, rinsed and drained

½   cup beer or dry white wine
1   cup sour cream or plain yogurt
½   pound Emmenthaler or Swiss cheese, shredded

✤   Preheat oven to 425°.

✤   In a large baking dish, layer potatoes, onion, sausage and ham. Cover with the sauerkraut. Pour the beer or white wine over entire mixture. Cover and bake until potatoes are softened, about 1 hour.

✤   Top with sour cream and cheese. Bake uncovered until cheese is melted and beginning to brown, 15-20 minutes. Serve promptly.

✤   Note: For a more authentic version, substitute ¼ pound of shredded Gruyere for ¼ pound of the Emmenthaler or Swiss cheese (not for the faint of heart!).

Per serving: 529 calories; 30.3g protein; 23.3g carbohydrates; 34.7g fat (17.4g saturated fat); 105mg cholesterol.

EGGPLANT CASSEROLE

Serves 6

Kirsten Havrehed's eggplant casserole has graced the table at St. Francis Lutheran at numerous potlucks and church dinners where it's always a hit. When purchasing eggplant look for a firm, smooth, glossy purple fruit. Avoid those that are large and rough or spongy surface with brown marks—they are overripe and contain lots of mature brown seeds.

2 medium eggplants
⅓ cup half-and-half
1 10¾-ounce can cream of mushroom soup
2 eggs, lightly beaten

½ cup finely chopped onion
1 cup crushed packaged herb-seasoned stuffing mix
½ cup grated Parmesan cheese

✤ Preheat oven to 350°. Butter or grease a 2-quart casserole or baking dish.

✤ Peel and cube the eggplant and place cubes in a medium bowl. In a separate small saucepan, boil enough water to cover eggplant. Add eggplant cubes, cover and continue to boil for 5 minutes. Drain well.

✤ In a large bowl, mix half-and-half with cream of mushroom soup. Add eggs to soup mixture and combine. Add eggplant, chopped onion and the stuffing mix and stir to blend. Pour into prepared pan sprinkle with the Parmesan cheese. Bake 30-40 minutes.

✤ Note: This dish can be frozen. It is also excellent with chicken or turkey as a substitute for dressing.

Per serving: 196 calories; 9.39g protein; 18.5g carbohydrates; 9.96g fat (4.07g saturated fat); 97.7mg cholesterol.

LAMB AND VEGETABLE ORZOTTO   Serves 6

Donna Katzl is chef-owner of Cafe For All Seasons, two American restaurants in San Francisco and San Mateo that serve only fresh dishes like this easy risotto.

2 tablespoons olive oil
12 ounces lamb steak, chopped coarsely
4-5 tablespoons butter
½ cup minced yellow onion
1 tablespoon minced garlic
1 cup white wine
2 cups orzo (rice-shaped pasta)

6-8 cups hot chicken stock
1 large red bell pepper, roasted, peeled and finely chopped
⅓ cup chopped parsley, divided
Salt to taste
½ cup grated Asiago cheese

✤ In a medium frying pan, heat olive oil. Add lamb and cook until lightly golden. With a slotted spoon, remove lamb and drain.

✤ In a separate heavy pot, melt 2 tablespoons butter over medium-low heat. Add onions and garlic and cook 2-3 minutes or until soft. Add lamb and white wine. Cook until reduced by half, 3-4 minutes.

✤ Stir in orzo and coat evenly. Add 2 cups of chicken stock and cook, stirring until absorbed, 5-6 minutes. Continue to add as much stock as needed, 1 cup at a time, until orzo is creamy and tender but still firm in center.

✤ Remove from heat and stir in remaining butter, chopped roasted red pepper, ¼ cup parsley and salt to taste, if needed. Sprinkle with grated Asiago cheese and remaining chopped parsley.

Per serving: 540 calories; 25g protein; 29.2g carbohydrates; 33.3g fat (14.1g saturated fat); 90.9mg cholesterol.

In the mid-1980s Pastor DeLange preached a sermon about Central America—a situation that was sounding too much like the beginnings of Viet Nam. At the same time, the sermon sparked my interest in the sanctuary movement as one way to work for peaceful change. I soon found myself heavily involved in St. Francis Lutheran's many committees, including the Social Justice Committee. A highlight for me came in 1989 when I was one of 13 people of faith in a sister-parish delegation to El Salvador. I visited Resurrection Lutheran, our congregation's sister church in the city of San Salvador. There, in spite of the military presence and economic poverty of the country, I saw the power of the church as a place of hope.

Peter Quam, 52, is a graduate of Pacific Lutheran University. He started working in the insurance industry after a five-year stint (including a year in Viet Nam) as a helicopter pilot and flight instructor in the U. S. Marine Corps. Peter's 15-year-old daughter, Alexandra, helps to keep him young.

SPICY SHRIMP and FETA PASTA   Serves 4-6

Valerie Wagner and John Crimaldi live in San Francisco where Valerie is an attorney and John is finishing his doctorate in engineering at Stanford University. When they find time to cook it's often a pasta dish like this one. The crushed red pepper makes a fairly spicy dish, so be careful!

1 pound linguini	6-8 oil-packed sun-dried
2 tablespoons olive oil	tomatoes, finely
4 tablespoons (½ stick) butter	chopped
⅔-1 pound medium shrimp,	½-1 teaspoon crushed red
peeled and deveined	pepper flakes
1 clove garlic, crushed	¼ cup dry sherry
through a press	½ pound feta cheese,
6 green onions,	crumbled
finely chopped	

✤ In a large pot of salted water, cook pasta until tender.

✤ In a medium saucepan, melt butter in olive oil over medium heat. Add shrimp, garlic, onions, sun-dried tomatoes, red pepper flakes and sherry and cook, stirring occasionally, until shrimp are just pink, 5-7 minutes.

✤ Drain pasta and return to pot. Pour shrimp mixture over pasta. Add feta cheese and toss. Serve promptly.

Per serving: 412 calories; 25.1g protein; 26.5g carbohydrates; 22.1g fat (11.4g saturated fat); 169mg cholesterol.

SPAGHETTI with
SLOW-BAKED TOMATOES

Serves 4

Janet Fletcher is a San Francisco Bay Area food writer and restaurant critic who has written a number of cookbooks, including "More Vegetables, Please." This vegetarian pasta dish is one of her favorites.

1½ pounds large vine-ripe tomatoes
Salt and pepper to taste
2 large cloves garlic, minced
¼ cup extra virgin olive oil plus a little for oiling the baking dish

4 quarts salted water
1 pound spaghetti
½ cup chopped fresh basil leaves
¾ cup freshly grated Parmesan or Pecorino Romano cheese

✤ Preheat oven to 300°. Lightly oil a 9x13-inch baking dish.

✤ Core tomatoes and cut them in half horizontally. Trim the bottoms if necessary to make the halves sit up straight. Place halves in baking dish. Season with salt and pepper. Sprinkle surfaces with garlic, then drizzle with olive oil. Bake uncovered for 2 hours, basting the tomatoes with their rendered juices occasionally.

✤ Transfer tomatoes to a chopping board and chop coarsely. Put the chopped tomatoes and their juice, and any juice from the baking dish, into a large bowl and place in a low oven to keep warm while you cook the pasta.

✤ Bring a large pot of salted water to a boil. Add pasta and cook until tender. Drain and transfer to bowl with tomatoes. Toss. Add basil and cheese and toss again. Serve on warm plates.

Per serving: 567 calories; 24.6g protein; 94.3g carbohydrates; 21.5g fat (5.73g saturated fat); 14.8mg cholesterol.

CRAB GIOVANNI

Serves 8-10

Erna Dennert has lived in the Netherlands, Curacao and now in San Francisco. This hearty crab dish is easy to make and great for company. You can make it or two days ahead and refrigerate until ready to bake.

2 cups chopped onions
½ pound fresh mushrooms, sliced
2 cloves garlic, minced
½ cup butter, melted
12 ounces spaghetti, cooked
2-3 cups crab meat
½ cup stuffed green olives, sliced
1 pound shredded sharp Cheddar cheese

½ cup sour cream
1 28-ounce can tomatoes, drained and coarsely chopped
1½ teaspoon salt or to taste
1 teaspoon white pepper
½ teaspoon dried basil

✤ Preheat oven to 375°. Grease a 3-quart casserole or baking dish.

✤ In a large frying pan, melt butter over medium heat. Cook onions, mushrooms and garlic tender, 5-10 minutes.

✤ In a pot of salted boiling water, cook the spaghetti until tender. Combine with the onion mixture. Add crab meat, green olives, Cheddar cheese, sour cream, tomatoes, salt, pepper and basil and mix well, careful not to break the crab into too small pieces. Pour into prepared baking dish and bake uncovered until hot and bubbly, 35-40 minutes. (If dish has been refrigerated, allow about 1 hour for baking.) Serve hot.

Per serving: 513 calories; 28.6g protein; 23.4g carbohydrates; 34.6g fat (21.2g saturated fat); 131mg cholesterol.

STIR-FRY DUNGENESS CRAB

Serves 2-4

Well-known in San Francisco and across the country for her Chinese stir-fry sauces, Maggie Gin gave us this recipe which has become a staple in her family.

1 large live dungeness crab (about 2 pounds)	1 tablespoon oyster sauce
2 tablespoons peanut oil	1 tablespoon light soy sauce
2 green onions, cut in 2-inch lengths	1 tablespoon rice wine or dry sherry
2 garlic cloves, bruised	1 teaspoon Asian sesame oil
3 slices ginger root	½ cup crab butter or water
	Coriander sprigs (garnish)

✤ Drop live crab into a large pot of boiling water and cook for 5 minutes. Remove immediately and plunge into cold water. Drain and separate body and claws from hard shell. Discard any soft spongy parts of crab. Reserve the smooth yellow crab butter inside crab shell. Split body section in half or quarters and crack claws.

✤ Heat peanut oil in a wok or large skillet over high heat and stir-fry onion, garlic and ginger for 30 seconds. Add crab pieces and stir-fry for 30 seconds.

✤ In a small bowl, combine oyster sauce, soy sauce, wine, sesame oil and crab butter. Add to wok and stir until well blended. Cover, letting steam rise to surface and cook about 5-7 minutes. Garnish with coriander.

Per serving: 337 calories; 51.2g protein; 4.53g carbohydrates; 11.1g fat (1.79g saturated fat); 174mg cholesterol.

Not everything is serious at St. Francis Lutheran. We take what we do seriously, but try not to take ourselves too seriously. The annual congregation banquet features the "Franny Awards," with nominees for "The Forbidden Fruit Award," the "Burned at the Steak Award" and the "Pillar of Salt Award," among others. There are formal presenters and fanfares and we really camp it up. We've learned a lot from watching the Oscars. We invited them to come and watch us, but so far we've had no takers. They would love the food because we use some of the recipes in this book.

Gay and lesbian Lutherans are the Church's prodigal children, and for many years I was one of them. I was raised in a devout Norwegian Lutheran household in Iowa, and attended a Lutheran parochial school. Yet, for 15 years as an adult, I never found a place or a people where I could share my spiritual journey. As a lesbian, the church seemed to be an enemy camp, not a place of sanctuary and redemption. Yet I could not renounce my Lutheranism so I became a Lutheran-in-exile.

I joined St. Francis Lutheran after reading the newspaper story about the church's decision to call a lesbian minister. The first Sunday I worshipped at St. Francis was a profoundly moving experience. I felt as though I had come home. The diverse composition of the congregation, the traditional liturgy, the eloquent sermon, the references to Scandinavian heritage, the call to social justice—this unusual collage was wonderfully surprising. I would hope for everyone the kind of experience that St. Francis has made possible for me.

Bev Ovrebo, 42, is a Professor and Acting Chair of the Health Education Department at San Francisco State University. She studied at the University of California, Berkeley, and was a Peace Corps volunteer in Togo and Ecuador.

LINGUINE with CRAB in LEMON CREAM SAUCE

Serves 4

This delightful dish is from Grissini Trattoria & Wine Bar, an Italian restaurant in the Hilton Hotel in Concord, California.

4 tablespoons (½ stick) unsalted butter	Grated zest of 2 lemons
1 fresh leek, thinly sliced	Salt and pepper to taste
½ pound fresh Dungeness crab meat	¾ pound lemon-flavored linguine or other pasta
½ cup dry white wine	2 tablespoons chopped parsley
¾ cup heavy (whipping) cream	

✥ In a large skillet, heat butter over medium heat. Add leeks and cook for 1 minute. Add crab meat and cook 1 minute. Add white wine and cook until reduced by half. Add cream and cook 1 minute. Mix in lemon zest and salt and pepper to taste.

✥ Bring a large pot of boiling salted water to a boil. Add pasta and cook until tender. Drain and toss with sauce and fresh parsley. Serve promptly.

Per serving: 477 calories; 18.3g protein; 30.6g carbohydrates; 29.4g fat (17.6g saturated fat); 135mg cholesterol.

FISH in COCONUT SAUCE

Serves 6

Heidi Cusick learned to make this from Dona Conceicao, who owns a restaurant, Casa da Gamboa, in Bahia, Brazil, when Heidi was traveling researching African influences on cooking in the New World. This is a great opportunity to sample coconut milk, which is available in Asian markets or the imported food section of many supermarkets.

4 firm white fish fillets, about 5 ounces each
Salt and pepper to taste
2 tablespoons olive oil
1 yellow onion, cut lengthwise into narrow strips
1 green bell pepper, seeded and cut lengthwise into narrow strips
4 tomatoes, cut into wedges

½ cup coconut milk, fresh or canned
½-1 cup water, depending on thickness of coconut milk
2 tablespoons tomato sauce or paste
2 white potatoes, boiled until tender, peeled and cut into 1-inch pieces
1 lime, cut in half or in wedges

✤ Season the fish with salt and pepper. In a skillet or frying pan, heat the oil until almost smoking. Add the fish and sear to brown on both sides. Transfer to a platter.

✤ In the same pan, add the onions and peppers and cook over medium heat until wilted, about 5 minutes. Add the tomatoes, coconut milk and water. Cook until the sauce thickens and the vegetables are tender, about 5 minutes. Stir in the tomato paste.

✤ Return the fish fillets to the pan and add the potatoes. Cook until heated through, about 5 minutes longer. Pour sauce over fish. Squeeze lime juice over all or serve wedges with each plate.

Per serving: 227 calories; 19.4g protein; 15.6g carbohydrates; 10.4g fat (4.97g saturated fat); 43.5mg cholesterol.

FISH FILETS MEUNIERE with VEGETABLE GARNISH

Serves 4

In this attractive presentation Jay Harlow, who writes a seafood column for the San Francisco Chronicle, surrounds golden-brown filets with a mixture of finely shredded leeks, carrots and zucchini. To keep calories down, the vegetables are "cooked" in stock, with just a bit of oil added for flavor.

¼ cup all-purpose flour
½ teaspoon salt
Pinch black or cayenne
   pepper to taste
2 tablespoons olive oil
8 small fish filets
   (tilapia, sole, flounder),
   about 1¼ pounds in all
1½ ounces dry white wine

4 tablespoons (½ stick)
   butter
2 tablespoons chopped
   fresh mild herbs (chervil,
   parsley, tarragon
   or chives)
Lemon juice
Salt and pepper to taste

✤ In a shallow dish, combine the flour, salt and pepper. Dredge the filets in the seasoned flour and shake off the excess. Heat the oil in a skillet over medium-high heat. Add the fish and cook until lightly browned, about 3 minutes. Turn and cook or until a skewer easily enters the thickest part, 2-3 minutes.

✤ When the filets are done, transfer them to warm individual plates or a serving platter. Deglaze the pan with wine and reduce by half. Remove the pan from the heat and swirl in the butter and herbs. Taste the sauce for seasoning and adjust if necessary with lemon juice, salt or pepper. Spoon the sauce over the fish and arrange the vegetables around the outside.

VEGETABLE GARNISH:

1 large or 2 small leeks
¼ cup chicken or
   vegetable stock
1 teaspoon olive oil

1 medium carrot, cut into
   fine strips
1 medium zucchini, cut into
   fine strips
Salt and pepper to taste

✤ Wash and trim the leeks Cut the white and pale green parts into 2-inch lengths. Split the sections lengthwise and cut into thin ribbons. Soak in a bowl of cold water, separating all the pieces and swirling to wash away any dirt. Lift out and drain. Heat the stock and oil in a small skillet, add the vegetables and cook until the vegetables are just tender and the liquid is nearly gone. Season to taste and serve.

Per serving: 436 calories; 35.1g protein; 22g carbohydrates; 22g fat (8.85g saturated fat); 113mg cholesterol.

CHICKEN MARSALA   Serves 4

When Susie Cohen's mother went to Italy in 1969, she "discovered food" and started cooking this dish. Susie admits it's still really good.

4 chicken breast halves, pounded	¼ cup or more dry Marsala wine
¼ cup all-purpose flour	¼ cup grated Parmesan cheese
2 tablespoons butter	¼ cup lemon juice
2 tablespoons olive oil	¼ cup chicken stock

✤ Coat chicken lightly with flour. In a large skillet, melt butter in olive oil over medium heat. Add chicken and cook until golden brown. Pour marsala over chicken and let bubble for 2 minutes. Cover each half breast with grated cheese, moisten with lemon juice and chicken stock. Cover pan and cook over medium heat for 5 minutes. Serve promptly.

Per serving: 317 calories; 19g protein; 8.18g carbohydrates; 21.3g fat (7.67g saturated fat); 66.9mg cholesterol.

CHICKEN PAPRIKA

Serves 4

Diane Nelson DeLange married Pastor James DeLange in the newly refurbished sanctuary of St. Francis Lutheran Church in May of 1992. This is one of her favorite quick and easy recipes.

2 large onions, chopped	2 tablespoons all-purpose
¼ cup plus 1 tablespoon	flour
butter, divided	1 tablespoon tomato paste
3-4 pounds chicken, cut into	2 teaspoons paprika
serving pieces	½ teaspoon curry powder
Salt and pepper to taste	1 cup sour cream
2 cups vegetable stock, divided	

✤ In a large frying pan or skillet, melt ¼ cup butter. Add onions and cook without browning. Add chicken, salt, pepper and 1 cup stock. Cover and cook 30 minutes.

✤ In a small bowl, make a paste of 1 tablespoon butter, flour and remaining vegetable stock. Add tomato paste, paprika and curry powder. Stir carefully into chicken mixture. Cook 15 minutes over medium-low heat. Add sour cream and cook slowly 5 minutes. Do not let boil. Serve promptly.

Per serving: 1288 calories; 90g protein; 16.6g carbohydrates; 94.4g fat (34.7g saturated fat); 399mg cholesterol.

This may sound odd at first, but one of the things I find most remarkable about St. Francis Lutheran is that it is so ordinary—it is not outrageous, as some people expect. The congregation is extraordinary in that the people usually work so well together.

A moment that epitomizes St. Francis for me occurred in my Bible class in 1983, when I was not yet out to the congregation. The class only wanted to talk about the sermon Pastor DeLange had just preached on homosexuality. At one point, Erna Dennert turned to me and simply said, "Michael, tell us what it's like." That open-minded question, coming from a straight person raised in the conservative Dutch Reformed tradition, gave me permission to be out at St. Francis and in my ministry.

Michael Hiller, 49, is one of the associate pastors at St. Francis and vice president of human resource development at Stanford Federal Credit Union. He and his partner, Arthur Morris, celebrated their holy union in August 1994.

SUNDAY SUPPER
CHICKEN AND RICE

Serves 4-6

When Paul Groth invites people over for dinner they are likely to say, "Oh, sure. I just love your chicken and rice dish." The moral here is not to overuse your favorite recipes!

¼ pound bacon	4 large carrots, halved
4 pounds frying chicken, cut into serving pieces	2 medium onions, sliced
Juice of 1 lemon	1 large clove garlic, chopped
½ to 1 cup all-purpose flour	1 teaspoon fresh chopped tarragon or ½ teaspoon dried
½ teaspoon salt or to taste	
1 teaspoon pepper or to taste	½ cup chopped parsley
1½ cups rice	1-2 cans chicken broth
2-4 tablespoons butter (optional)	

✤ Grease a large covered casserole dish.

✤ In a heavy skillet or frying pan, cook bacon until crisp. Drain bacon, chop finely and place bacon in the bottom of the casserole dish. Rub the chicken pieces with lemon juice, then shake or dredge in flour mixed with salt and pepper. In the same frying pan, cook chicken in the bacon fat, a few pieces at a time, browning all sides.

✤ Brown the rice in the same pan, adding butter if necessary. Add the rice in an even layer over the bacon pieces. Layer chicken, halved carrots, onions, garlic and tarragon and top with parsley. Cover and refrigerate until cooking time (overnight is fine).

✤ Preheat oven to 375°.

✤ Pour in enough chicken broth (at least one can) to cover the rice in the bottom of the dish. Cover and bake for about 1 hour or until the rice is done and the liquid entirely cooked away. If liquid cooks away before rice is soft, add a little more broth. Serve promptly.

Per serving: 1256 calories; 105g protein; 76.9g carbohydrates; 85.5g fat (25.6g saturated fat); 367mg cholesterol.

There's an air of enthusiasm at St. Francis Lutheran. We have various groups to meet different needs in our community. We all thrive on habits, but we can grow stale—the church needs to move forward. If we become static, we become dead.

I personally hope that St. Francis can serve as a beacon to the rest of America. We are a community that values difference, tradition and service to others.

St. Francis is a church sustained by prayer. We have shared many strains over the past years. The 1989 earthquake left our building with severe damage that we have repaired. But we know that a building is not God's church, the people who worship in the building are the church. In that respect our church has endured a blow far greater than any earthquake could ever accomplish—the death of many of our young people from AIDS. We sustain one another during theses difficult times by offering a small kindness, by sharing an encouraging word, and by uniting in prayer to the God of love and hope.

Kirsten Ilavrehed has been a member of St. Francis Lutheran for over 40 years. Since her retirement she has been a dedicated and faithful volunteer offering small kindness to countless people through hospice programs and other San Francisco community organizations.

 to be understood as to understand;

There is so much in this world, O God, that challenges our understanding:

How can there be homelessness and selective medical care in the midst of affluence that has never before been seen in our human history?

Who will speak up for the rights of those who cannot speak for themselves?

When will our peace heroes receive the same accolades as our war heroes?

What price must we pay to find the means of conquering cancer, AIDS, and other life-threatening diseases?

O All-Knowing One, give us but a portion of your omniscience that we might resolve these and other such questions for the betterment of all humankind. Equip us to be your agents of love, compassion and healing. Give us the wisdom and understanding of Jesus: our brother, our friend, and our God. *Amen.*

PARTY FLAVORS

To the chef, appetizers — those marvelous little nibbles set seductively about the room—are a paradox. The goal is to make arty, beckoning creations that are always within fingers' reach of being consumed by a crowd that arrives hungry. Keep things moving with an ingenious array of hors d'oeuvres. Invent a stand-up culinary act big on variety.

The dilemma is that the guests will be unable to stop eating the delightful little bundles and become too stuffed to enjoy dinner. The answer, of course, is to forego the sit-down altogether. An amusing evening of tidbits, nibbles, conversation and entertainments.

Celebration Frost

Slush

St. Louis Pickles

Mushroom Almond Pate

Eileen's Tortilla Rolls

Sweet and Salted Almonds

Palo Alto Pear Spread

Crostini di Fagioli

Hummus

Cheesy Fudge

Brie with Pesto

Pesto a la Genovese

Hot Artichoke Dip

Caviar Pie Romanoff

Layered Crab Dip

Garlic Mushrooms

Coconut Fried Shrimp

Quajado de Spinaca

Tinga

Sesame Beef Strips

Fresh Fruit Salsa

Fennel and Vodka Cured Salmon

CELEBRATION FROST

Serves about 25-30

Jack Kling makes this for many of our St. Francis Lutheran events, and we're glad he does! It isn't too sweet and it doesn't taste like punch—two thumbs up!

1 6-ounce can frozen
  lemonade concentrate
1 6-ounce can frozen
  orange juice concentrate
1 6-ounce can frozen
  pineapple juice
  concentrate

2 quarts water
1½ cups apricot nectar
½ cup freshly squeezed
  lemon juice
1 quart lemon sherbet
1 28-ounce bottle
  ginger ale

✤ Combine concentrates with water, apricot, nectar and lemon juice. Mix together until smooth.

✤ Just before serving, add sherbet and ginger ale and mix together gently. Serve promptly.

Per serving: 80 calories; .537g protein; 19.6g carbohydrates; .377g fat (.192g saturated fat); .8mg cholesterol.

SLUSH

Makes about 1 quart

Lois Reinke usually has this staple in her freezer in Cecil, Wisconsin.

9 cups water, divided
4 bags green tea
2 cups sugar
1 12-ounce can frozen
  orange juice

1 12-ounce can frozen
  lemonade
2 cups brandy or vodka*
Sparking soda

✤ In a small saucepan, bring 2 cups of water to a boil. Add 4 green tea bags, remove from heat and cool. In a larger saucepan, combine sugar and the remaining 7 cups of water. Bring to a boil and cook until dissolved. Let cool. Add tea to sugar water and mix to combine. Add cans of frozen orange juice and lemonade, brandy or vodka. Mix well and place in freezer. Mixture will not freeze but remain "slushy."

✤ To serve, place scoops of slush in a glass and fill with sparkling soda.

✤ Note: *At Christmas, use sloe gin instead of brandy or vodka for a pretty red color.

Per serving: 188 calories; .458g protein; 34.6g carbohydrates; .078g fat (.011g saturated fat); 0mg cholesterol.

ST. LOUIS PICKLES   Serves 10-12

Somehow these come from St. Louis, Missouri. Arthur Morris' Irish mother has made them as long as he can remember. There is not much in Irish history to indicate wide-spread acceptance of pastrami, pickles or even cream cheese, so he thinks his mother either made this up or stole it from a neighbor. When his parents came to San Francisco for a visit, Arthur and his partner, Michael Hiller, hosted a party for them. Arthur asked his mom to make these pickles— they were the most popular thing at the party and disappeared very quickly.

8 ounces cream cheese	¼ to ½ pound thinly
6 whole dill pickles	sliced pastrami

✤ Place the cream cheese in a food processor or blender and puree for 2 minutes. Completely cover pickle with cream cheese. (Don't even try using kitchen tools; fingers work better than any of them.) Wrap the cream cheese-covered pickle with pastrami. Wrap in foil or plastic wrap and refrigerate at least 1 hour.

✤ Cut the wrapped pickle into ¼-inch thick slices and serve.

Per serving: 98.5 calories; 5.11g protein; 2.16g carbohydrates; 7.83g fat (4.51g saturated fat); 31mg cholesterol.

MUSHROOM ALMOND PATÉ   Makes 1½ cups

Barbara Hack Wayland admits she's a great one for stealing recipes and this is one she took from her friend Shirley. Barbara asked her for the recipe and has made this simple, tasty appetizer many times since. It's delicious!

1 cup slivered almonds	¾ teaspoon salt
4 tablespoons (½ stick) butter	¼ teaspoon ground thyme
¾ pound mushrooms, sliced	⅛ teaspoon white pepper
1 small onion, chopped	2 tablespoons vegetable oil
1 clove garlic, minced	
or pressed	

✤ In a wide, heavy frying pan, toast slivered almonds over medium-low heat, stirring frequently, until light browned, about 10 minutes. Turn out of pan and cool.

✤ In the same frying pan, melt butter over medium-high heat. Add mushrooms, onion, garlic, salt, thyme and white pepper. Cook, stirring occasionally, until most of the liquid is absorbed, about 10 minutes.

✤ Chop 2 tablespoons of the toasted almonds and reserve. Chop remaining nuts in a food processor or blender until finely ground. With machine running, gradually add vegetable oil until mixture is creamy and smooth. Add mushroom mixture and blend until smooth.

✤ Stir in reserved chopped almonds. Press mixture into serving dish, garnish with slivered almonds, if desired, and refrigerate until needed. Serve at room temperature with crackers or raw vegetables.

Per serving: 130 calories; 2.98g protein; 4.31g carbohydrates; 12.1g fat (3.18g saturated fat); 10.4mg cholesterol.

EILEEN'S TORTILLA ROLLS

Makes 36 pieces

Jim Sherman's friend, Eileen (who else?), first made these rolls as an appetizer. Now it seems they're everywhere, even in "Those People At That Church."

1 pound ham, diced
18 ounces cream cheese
1 7-ounce can diced
   green chilies

1 8-ounce can chopped
   black olives
About 6-7 whole wheat
   tortillas

✤ In a large bowl, mix together ham, cream cheese, green chilies, and black olives.

✤ Spread mixture sparingly on a tortilla and roll into a long roll. Trim ends. Repeat process with remaining mixture. Place rolls in a casserole and cover with a damp towel. Refrigerator several hours or overnight.

✤ Cut each roll into 1-inch slices and serve. Serve with salsa for dipping.

Per serving: 97.4 calories; 3.8g protein; 4.34g carbohydrates; 7.72g fat (3.92g saturated fat); 22mg cholesterol.

SWEET and SALTED ALMONDS

Makes 1½ cups

Food stylist and cookbook author Peggy Fallon offers this tantalizing tidbit to munch at your next party.

½ pound whole blanched
   almonds (about 1½ cups)
2 teaspoons extra virgin olive oil

1 teaspoon sugar
½ teaspoon salt

✤ Preheat oven to 350°. In a large baking pan, combine almonds and oil, tossing to coat. Roast for 10-15 minutes, tossing occasionally, until light golden brown.

✤ Remove from oven and immediately add sugar and salt, tossing to coat. Let cool. Drain almonds on paper towels to remove excess oil.

✤ If made in advance, store airtight up to 2 weeks.

Per serving: 143 calories; 4.63g protein; 4.64g carbohydrates; 12.8g fat (1.25g saturated fat); 0mg cholesterol.

PALO ALTO PEAR SPREAD

Serves 8-12

Another of Arthur Morris' inspired creations, this was first served in Palo Alto, California. The pear preserves and curry are an interesting taste combination.

8 ounces cream cheese	1 teaspoon curry powder
½ cup pear preserves	Whole wheat crackers

✤ Combine cream cheese, pear preserves and curry powder in a food processor or blender. Puree about 2 minutes. Refrigerate at least 1 hour to allow flavors to blend.

✤ Serve at room temperature in a bowl surrounded by whole wheat crackers.

Per serving: 85.9 calories; 1.47g protein; 5.58g carbohydrates; 6.64g fat (4.16g saturated fat); 20.8mg cholesterol.

CROSTINI di FAGIOLI

Makes about 2 cups

John B. Shulman has worn many hats in his life. Right now he is a respected and admired food professional. This Italian appetizer is easy, healthy and good—what else could you ask for, bella? It is also wonderful served on pasta.

1 15½-ounce can garbanzo beans, drained	Salt to taste
5 garlic cloves, coarsely chopped	1 tablespoon lemon juice
1 tablespoon freshly ground black pepper	½ teaspoon hot pepper powder (of choice)
½ cup coarsely chopped parsley	Baguette or dense Italian bread, sliced, brushed
½ cup extra virgin olive oil	with olive oil and toasted (crostini)

✤ Place garbanzo beans, garlic, black pepper, parsley, olive oil, salt, lemon juice, and hot pepper in a food processor or blender and puree.

✤ Spread a tablespoon of the bean paste on the crostini and garnish with chopped parsley. Arrange on a platter to serve.

Per serving: 170 calories; 3.86g protein; 20.6g carbohydrates; 8.09g fat (1.2g saturated fat); 0mg cholesterol.

HUMMUS

Makes 1½ to 2 quarts

Tom Rice and Karl Breitzman, vegetarians who live in Berkeley, enjoy Middle-Eastern foods. Add more oil if you choose; more of anything else may suit you as well. Hummus is pretty addictive, especially with pita bread or fresh sourdough. Tahini is available in Middle-Eastern Markets or the imported food section of many supermarkets.

2 cups dry garbanzo beans
   (about 5 cups cooked)
4 medium to large garlic
   cloves, minced
½ cup tahini
1 heaping tablespoon
   ground cumin

2 heaping teaspoons salt
⅔-¾ cup fresh
   lime juice (juice of
   5-7 limes)
1⅓ cups olive oil

✤ Soak dry beans overnight. Drain. In a large pot, cover beans with water and bring to a boil over medium heat. Lower heat and simmer until tender, about 1½ hours. Drain.

✤ Mix together beans and garlic in a food processor or blender and puree until well ground, about 1 minute. Add the tahini, cumin and salt and process to combine.

✤ While the machine is running, add the lime juice. Add the olive oil in a slow, steady stream, scraping down the bowl as necessary. Continue processing until the mixture is smooth. Serve promptly or refrigerate.

Per serving: 134 calories; 2.82g protein; 7.97g carbohydrates; 10.6g fat (1.42g saturated fat); 0mg cholesterol.

CHEESY FUDGE

Serves 12-15

This hors d'oeuvre from Doug Varner is extremely simple and especially good.

1 pound mozzarella cheese,
  shredded
1 pound Cheddar cheese,
  shredded

4 eggs, lightly beaten
1 8-ounce jar picante sauce

❖ Preheat oven to 350°. Lightly grease a 9x13-inch pan.

❖ Mix together cheeses in prepared baking pan. Pour eggs over cheese mixture. Drizzle picante sauce over top. Bake until lightly browned, about 30 minutes. Let cool. Cut into squares and serve.

Per serving: 138 calories; 10.4g protein; 1.25g carbohydrates; 10.1g fat (6.16g saturated fat); 66.1mg cholesterol.

BRIE with PESTO

Serves 24-30

Everyone seems to love Brie, but cookbook author Peggy Fallon thinks that sometimes it's fun to dress it up for a party. This same technique can be used on a wedge of cheese for a smaller group.

1 8½-inch wheel of Brie
  cheese (about 2 pounds)
½ cup Pesto a la
  Genovese, purchased
  or homemade
  (recipe follows)

2 tablespoons pine nuts
  (pignoli)
Crackers or baguette slices
Fresh basil sprigs
  (garnish)

❖ To facilitate slicing, freeze Brie until just firm but not frozen, about 1 hour.

❖ Preheat oven to 325°. With a long sharp knife, split Brie horizontally in half. Spread pesto in an even layer over cut side of bottom half to about ¼-inch from edge. Set top of Brie in place and press gently to sandwich layers.

✤ Spread pine nuts in a shallow pan and bake, shaking pan once or twice, until lightly browned, 7-10 minutes. Scatter toasted pine nuts over top of Brie, pressing them in gently. Let cheese return to room temperature. Serve with crackers or baguette slices and garnish with fresh basil.

Per serving: 156 calories; 7.72g protein; .803g carbohydrates; 13.9g fat (6.3g saturated fat); 31.6mg cholesterol.

PESTO a la GENOVESE   Makes about 1½ cups

Not only is this great with Brie, but try it on hot pasta or toasted bread with tomatoes and melted mozzarella cheese.

2 cups (packed) fresh basil leaves	2 garlic cloves, coarsely chopped
½ cup freshly grated Parmesan cheese	1¼ teaspoons salt
1 tablespoon pine nuts (pignoli)	¼ teaspoon freshly ground pepper
	½ cup extra virgin olive oil

✤ In a food processor or blender, combine basil, Parmesan cheese, pine nuts, garlic, salt and pepper. Puree until a coarse paste forms. With machine on, slowly add oil. Use pesto immediately, or store in an airtight container in refrigerator up to 4 days, or freeze.

Per serving: 227 calories; 5.02g protein; 1.99g carbohydrates; 23g fat (4.39g saturated fat); 6.56mg cholesterol.

A lot of people leave the church as adolescents, but almost everyone does if they discover they are gay or lesbian. When people check out St. Francis Lutheran, they usually slip in the back and listen to see if we are who we say we are. We try to be; we're not sure we always succeed. If people come back, they are invited to attend an information class—twenty hours of intensive group discussions and lectures stretched over two weekends. They are most surprised by the gospel of grace. Somehow in this era of feeling good, a lot of people feel really bad. We believe Christ came to change that.

HOT ARTICHOKE DIP

Serves 10-15

Michael Utech loves this simple dip—everyone swears there's crab in it!

2 14-ounce jars artichoke
   hearts, drained, and
   finely chopped
2 cups mayonnaise
1 0.7-ounce package
   dry Italian dressing mix

1 tablespoon fresh
   lemon juice
½ cup grated Parmesan
   cheese
Melba toast rounds

✤ Preheat oven to 350°. Lightly grease a shallow casserole or 9-inch baking pan.

✤ In a large bowl, mix together artichoke hearts, mayonnaise, Italian dressing mix, lemon juice and Parmesan cheese until well blended. Spread mixture in prepared baking pan and bake until the top begins to brown slightly, about 20 minutes. Serve hot surrounded by Melba toast rounds.

Per serving: 299 calories; 3.47g protein; 8.25g carbohydrates; 29.3g fat (4.83g saturated fat); 20mg cholesterol.

CAVIAR PIE ROMANOFF

Serves 10-12

Jack and Marti Lundin have always loved to entertain, especially now that they have retired to the beautiful wine country of Sonoma County, California after Jack's 35-year career as a Lutheran pastor. This is one of their most special hors d'oeuvres.

6 hard boiled eggs, shelled
3 tablespoons mayonnaise
1½ cups minced sweet onion,
    white or yellow*
8 ounces cream cheese,
   softened

⅔ cup sour cream
3½-4 ounces Romanoff
    Lumpfish Fish Caviar
Party rye slices for serving

✤ Finely chop eggs and mix with mayonnaise. Spread the mixture evenly in a well greased 8-inch springform pan or tart pan with removable bottom. Sprinkle onions over egg mixture.

✤ In a blender or food processor, blend cream cheese and sour cream until smooth. Spread over onions using wet spatula. Cover and chill 3 hours or overnight.

✤ Before serving, spread caviar over the entire surface. Remove bottom from pan. Cut into 10-12 wedges to serve. Party rye makes a perfect accompaniment.

✤ Notes: *Use onions that are very sweet, like Texas, Maui or Vidalia, if available. If you wish to make this without the caviar, use chopped well drained ripe olives as the top layer. The flavor is very good, but of course the dish is not as elegant without caviar.

Per serving: 192 calories; 7.62g protein; 3.59g carbohydrates; 16.7g fat (7.64g saturated fat); 191mg cholesterol.

LAYERED CRAB DIP
Serves 8-10

German Lutherans have a rich history of potluck dinners for special occasions such as anniversaries and birthdays, as well as post-funeral gatherings. Andrew Olson, chef at Now We're Cooking, San Francisco caterers, says this recipe is one his grandmother makes for fancier events and it is always a crowd-pleaser.

12 ounces cream cheese
2 tablespoons mayonnaise
1 tablespoon fresh
   lemon juice
1 tablespoon Worcestershire
   sauce
1 tablespoon minced green
   onion (white and
   green parts)

6 ounces (½ bottle)
   chili sauce
½ pound cooked crab meat
   (picked through for
   shell fragments)
3 tablespoons finely
   chopped parsley
Crackers for serving

✤ In a medium bowl or the bowl of an electric mixer, cream together the cream cheese, mayonnaise, lemon juice, Worcestershire sauce and green onions. Spread cream cheese mixture evenly into the bottom of a 9x9-inch glass serving dish. Pour chili sauce over cream cheese mixture and spread evenly into a thin layer. Evenly distribute the crab over the chili sauce. Sprinkle the chopped parsley evenly over the crab. Refrigerate until ready to serve. Serve with crackers.

Per serving: 167 calories; 7.45g protein; 2.18g carbohydrates; 14.5g fat (7.88g saturated fat); 59.2mg cholesterol.

GARLIC MUSHROOMS

Alejandro Cejudo is from Mexico City and loves hot and spicy food. These mushrooms are already hot, but feel free to add more chilies for extra zest, if you dare.

2 pounds fresh large
   mushrooms, cleaned
3 tablespoons butter, divided
10 fresh garlic cloves, chopped
2 Serrano chiles, chopped

1 Roma tomato, chopped
Salt to taste
Juice from ½ lemon
Fresh parsley sprigs (garnish)
Lemon slices (garnish)

✤ Cut off bottom ¼-inch of mushroom stems and slice lengthwise into ¼-inch slices.

✤ In a large frying pan or skillet, melt 1 tablespoon butter over medium heat. Add sliced mushrooms and cook until all moisture is released and evaporated, 20-30 minutes. The mushrooms should be fairly dry. Remove mushrooms from pan and set aside.

✤ In the same pan, melt remaining 2 tablespoons of butter. Add chopped garlic and Serrano chiles and cook over medium-low heat until tender, about 5 minutes. Return mushrooms to pan and cook for about 5 minutes. Be very careful not to burn garlic.

✤ Add chopped Roma tomato and salt to taste and cook until tomato is soft, 2-3 minutes.

✤ Drizzle with fresh lemon juice to accent flavor. Thin slices of lemon and a few sprigs of parsley make a nice garnish. Serve warm or at room temperature.

Per serving: 70.8 calories; 2.27g protein; 5.9g carbohydrates; 5.02g fat (2.93g saturated fat); 12.4mg cholesterol.

COCONUT-FRIED SHRIMP

Makes 24-30 pieces

Jill Brennan teaches cooking classes and creates her own exquisite recipes at Jill's Kitchen in Danville, California. Try this simple hors d'oeuvre at your next gathering.

DIPPING SAUCE:

½ cup honey

3 tablespoons prepared
  horseradish

BATTER:

½ cup all-purpose flour
¼ cup cornstarch
½ teaspoon salt
½ cup water
1 egg white

1 pound large shrimp,
  shelled and deveined
  (tails left on)
2 cups shredded coconut
2 cups oil for deep frying

✤ In a small bowl, mix together honey and horseradish until well blended. Set aside.

✤ In another larger bowl, mix together flour, cornstarch, salt, water and egg white until blended (a few lumps are okay). Dip shrimp in batter and then in coconut. Place on wax paper. Heat oil in a 10-inch skillet or wok. Add battered shrimp in small batches and cook until golden brown. Remove and drain on paper towels. Serve promptly with dipping sauce.

Per serving: 385 calories; 18.1g protein; 52.3g carbohydrates; 12.4g fat (10g saturated fat); 115mg cholesterol.

Other than brief soirées into playing jazz and a few years taking tours to Europe, ministry has been my life. Now that I've completed a good number of very happy and wonderful years in the parish, I find that "pew-sitting" has a new kind of appeal I never expected. But it's easy to like such things at St. Francis Lutheran. The liturgy is precise, flowing and inviting. The homilies are timely and well-grounded, and the whole experience is deeply Christian and warmly human.

I must also say that I think very highly of those times and occasions when people honestly struggle with their faith. St. Francis is a setting which honors and appreciates those who keep on "wrestling with the angel." It is also a church where you don't get talked down to. One can be "saved" only so many Sundays in a row before wondering who's going to help get the car of salvation running in the very real traffic of the day. Fear not. We're in the midst of the traffic of life here at St. Francis.

Jack Lundin is a "retired" Lutheran pastor who directs the Center for Imagination, Interchange and Incredulity, dealing with clergy health and healing. He and his wife, Marti, have been married for 35 years, and he is an accomplished jazz pianist and drummer.

QUAJADO de SPINACA
(Spinach Pie)

Serves 16-20

Laurence Whiting, owner of San Francisco catering company "Now We're Cooking," tells us this recipe has been handed down through his family on his mother's side, who were Sephardic (Mediterranean) Jews from Greece and Turkey. It is an easy hors d'oeuvre that is guaranteed to please and a great contribution to any party.

3 10-ounce boxes frozen spinach, fully thawed (do not use fresh)

8 eggs, beaten

4 ounces Bleu cheese,* crumbled

4 ounces Romano cheese,* grated

✤ Preheat oven to 350°.

✤ Mix all ingredients together in a 9x13-inch baking dish and heat in oven until top starts to brown and center feels fairly solid when a knife is inserted in the center, about 45 minutes. Pie should be the consistency of quiche. Cool before cutting into small squares or diamonds.

✤ Note: *Use cheese quantities to taste, but equal amounts of Bleu and Romano work best.

Per serving: 279 calories; 21.7g protein; 5.5g carbohydrates; 19.4g fat (11.2g saturated fat); 192mg cholesterol.

TINGA (Mexican meat dip)

Serves 10-15

Michael Utech says this Mexican dip is definitely worth the extra effort.

½ cup raisins

6 medium tomatoes

4 cups chicken broth

2 garlic cloves

1 canned chipotle chile, seeded, not drained

1 teaspoon salt

1-2 tablespoon sugar

1½ pounds ground beef

1½ pounds ground pork

3 small onions, thinly sliced and chopped

✤ In a small saucepan, boil raisins in water (about 5 minutes) to soften. Set aside. In another saucepan, bring about 2 quarts of water to a boil. Drop whole tomatoes in boiling water and cook until skin begins to break. Immediately remove tomatoes from boiling water and place in cool water. Skin can now be easily removed from tomatoes.

✤ Combine tomatoes and raisins with chicken broth, garlic, chipotle chile and 1 tablespoon of juice from the canned chiles, salt and tomatoes in food processor or blender. Puree and balance hot/sweet taste to your preference by adding sugar as needed.

✤ Remove mixture from food processor or blender and place in large saucepan or stock pot. Bring mixture to a boil over medium-heat. Add meat and onions and bring to a boil again. Cook 10-15 minutes until most of the liquid has been absorbed. Pour into serving dish. Serve warm with tortilla chips.

Per serving: 198 calories; 16.7g protein; 7.41g carbohydrates; 11.2g fat (4.12g saturated fat); 55.6mg cholesterol.

SESAME BEEF STRIPS   Serves 6-8

These "kabobs" from cooking teacher Jill Brennan will spice up any party!

Bamboo skewers
2 tablespoons Asian sesame oil
¼ cup soy sauce
2 cloves garlic, minced
½ tablespoon rice wine
   vinegar
1 teaspoon grated ginger root
¼ teaspoon cayenne
¼ cup sherry
2 tablespoons brown sugar
1 green onion, thinly sliced
2 tablespoons sesame seeds,
   toasted finely chopped
1 pound flank or
   top round steak, cut
   about 1½-inches thick

✤ Soak bamboo skewers in water to prevent burning.

✤ In a large bowl, food processor or blender, mix together sesame oil, soy sauce, garlic, rice wine vinegar, ginger, cayenne, sherry, brown sugar and green onion until well blended. Add 1 tablespoon sesame seeds and stir to combine.

✤ Slice steak across grain into thin slices. Cover with sauce and marinate in a plastic bag at least 4 hours or overnight in the refrigerator.

✤ Thread on bamboo skewers and barbecue or broil. Sprinkle with remaining sesame seeds and serve hot.

Per serving: 241 calories; 22.1g protein; 4.96g carbohydrates; 13.9g fat (4.19g saturated fat); 50.9mg cholesterol.

FRESH FRUIT SALSA

Makes 2½ cups

This is a variation of a recipe which appeared in a book Peggy Fallon co-authored with Lonnie Gandara, "365 Snacks, Hors d'oeuvres and Appetizers." Serving this salsa with blue corn tortilla chips makes an attractive presentation, but it is equally good with grilled fish or chicken.

2 Fuji apples, Bosc pears
   or Asian pears
   (about 1 pound total)
4 dried apple slices or
   2 dried pear halves,
   finely chopped
½ cup chopped red onion
¼ cup chopped fresh mint
   or cilantro
Juice and grated zest of 1 lime

1 tablespoon minced
   fresh ginger
1 jalapeno or serrano
   pepper, seeded and
   minced
1 garlic clove, crushed
   through a press
¾ teaspoon salt
¼ teaspoon crushed hot
   red pepper flakes

✛ Core apples or pears and cut into a ½-inch dice. In a medium bowl, gently toss cubed fruit with dried fruit, onion, mint, lime juice and zest, ginger, jalapeno, garlic, salt and pepper flakes until well mixed. Cover and refrigerate at least 30 minutes or as long as 4 hours to blend flavors.

✛ Note: This salsa is best served the same day it is made.

Per serving: 413 calories; 3.19g protein; 106g carbohydrates; 2.4g fat (.278g saturated fat); 0mg cholesterol.

I'm still a Presbyterian at heart but I love St. Francis, not because it's a Lutheran Church but because of the people here. When I walked in for the first time I didn't know anyone except Wayne Strei, but I sensed the love and the caring immediately. I had a feeling that it was a special place, a special group of people. Communion on a weekly basis helps me focus as I become centered and at peace. I can come in with the world on my shoulders, but as soon as we break bread together I have a sense of the bigger picture. Suddenly I don't have to mess with the little details of life. That's really helpful to me.

Pam Blair describes herself as "a woman of faith."

FENNEL and
VODKA-CURED SALMON

Serves 24-30

Benjamin Davis, chef at Cypress Club in downtown San Francisco, says this is the only way to serve gravlax. Try it and see for yourself!

1 side salmon (4-6 pounds) pin boned, skin on	1 tablespoon fennel frond, chopped
½ cup coarse (kosher) salt	1 bulb fennel, thinly sliced
½ cup dark brown sugar (packed)	2 ounces lemon vodka
1 tablespoon fennel seed, toasted and ground	Cheesecloth
	Kitchen twine

✤ In a stainless steel bowl, mix together salt, sugar, fennel seed and frond. Rub this mixture on both sides of the salmon so that the fish is well coated with the curing mixture. Spread the fennel bulb on the flesh side of the fish and pour the vodka over the length of the fish.

✤ Rinse the cheesecloth under cold running water and spread on a table. Place the salmon on the cloth and wrap as tightly as possible. Tie with the twine so that the cloth is secure but the fish is not scarred. Place in a stainless steel pan, preferably one with holes to allow for moisture to drip through. Weight with something heavy enough to compress the fish. Place in refrigerator and chill 24 hours.

✤ Drain off the moisture and turn over the fish. Reweigh and chill, weighted, for another 24-36 hours. The fish is "done" when it is firm to the touch and has a shiny appearance on the surface.

✤ Rinse under cold running water. Pat dry with a paper towel and store wrapped in plastic wrap until ready to serve.

Per serving: 395 calories; 45.6g protein; 14.2g carbohydrates; 14.9g fat (2.24g saturated fat); 125mg cholesterol.

to be loved as to love.

O Blessed Christ-Child, who, held in a Mother's arms and adored by shepherds, knew a world's love, grant that we may soon know the grace to love as we have been loved. In this holy season remind us of those who have mirrored your love in their giving and joy, and grant us the gift to return love for love, for you are love. *~Amen.*

MERRY CHRISTMAS

At which time the foods of holidays past and present converge. Old traditions are observed, new bonds celebrated. Like joyous get-togethers of yesteryear, Christmas brings the community of St. Francis Lutheran together. A diverse clan, linked by kindred spirits and beliefs, this is a family of choice rather than blood.

We are a modern alliance, our urban family. Yet the ties are strong, a precious link celebrated and indulged at table. The food is hearty and, much like the revelers themselves, speaks of both the old and new.

Glögg

Wassail

Tom and Jerry Mix

Swedish Meatballs

Potato Lefse

Timballo

Terry's Party Pork Roast

Faerie Food

Popcorn Balls

Seafoam Candy

Berlinerkranswer

Bella's Holiday Spritz

Danish Rice Pudding

The Best Ever Bread and Butter Pudding

Alda Johnson's White Dessert

Arni's Cheesecake

Venetarta

Linzer Torte

GLÖGG

One of Tom Tragardh's first memories of Christmas was the sting of alcohol vapors in his eyes while drinking a tiny cup of very hot glögg at his grand-mother's home. In Sweden, glögg is a warming, welcoming winter and Christmas drink. Adding honey was suggested to Tom years ago by an old Swede named Axel Olsson, who found it gave the glögg more body. After a demitasse or two of glögg with dessert or cookies, people glow.

4 cups of premium red wine
1 cup raisins, rinsed and dried
1 cup currants, rinsed and dried
1 cup (or less) of whiskey or brandy (this ingredient could be reduced a great deal, if necessary)
2 cups sugar or more, to taste
½ cup honey
1 tablespoon orange marmalade or a piece of fresh or candied orange peel
⅛ teaspoon (or less) of ground cardamom
10 whole cloves
10 whole allspice
1 stick cinnamon
½ teaspoon almond extract

✤ Place all the ingredients in a large stainless steel, glass or enamel pot over medium-low heat (do not use an iron or aluminum pan). Stirring often, heat mixture to the boiling point. Cover the pan if you wish to prevent the evaporation of the alcohol. Refrigerate the glögg overnight or longer to allow flavors to blend. Serve it very, very hot, preferably in demitasse cups.

✤ Note: Sweetness is truly a matter of taste, but with glögg the sweeter the better. More raisins, more currants, and more sugar will not harm the glögg!

Per serving: 358 calories; 1.23g protein; 68.6g carbohydrates; .268g fat (.065g saturated fat); 0mg cholesterol.

WASSAIL

This is a traditional Christmas holiday drink that Michael Utech says tastes great on a cold night next to the fireplace.

2 quarts apple juice
   or cider
1 pint cranberry juice
¾ cup sugar
1 teaspoon aromatic bitters

2 cinnamon sticks
1 teaspoon whole allspice
1 small orange studded
   with whole cloves

✤ Combine all ingredients in a crock pot or stock pot. Cover and cook over high heat for 1 hour. Reduce heat to low and simmer for 4-8 hours. Serve warm.

Per serving: 101 calories; .081g protein; 25.6g carbohydrates; .17g fat (.036g saturated fat); 0mg cholesterol.

TOM and JERRY MIX

Makes 2 quarts

This really warms up Wisconsin winters where Wanda and Noel Nienstedt live with their daughter, Lindsey.

1 pound (4 sticks) butter
1 pound brown sugar
1 pound powdered sugar
2 tablespoons vanilla

2 quarts vanilla ice cream
1 ounce rum
1 ounce brandy
Ground nutmeg (optional)

✤ Melt butter in a heavy saucepan over medium-high heat. Add brown sugar and bring to a boil, stirring constantly. Remove from heat. Add powdered sugar and vanilla and mix to combine. Add ice cream and beat until well blended. Store in freezer until ready to use.

✤ To serve, scoop 2 tablespoons of mixture into a large mug. Add rum and brandy and fill mug to the top with boiling water. Shake a dash of ground nutmeg on top, if desired.

Per serving: 333 calories; .931g protein; 42.8g carbohydrates; 17.8g fat (11.1g saturated fat); 51mg cholesterol.

SWEDISH MEATBALLS
(Kottbullar)

Makes about 48

No two Swedes make meatballs the same way, but Tom Tragardh believes the meatballs nonetheless taste remarkably similar. If you have time, refrigerate the mixture overnight for the flavors to mellow and the meatballs will hold their shape better if the mixture is cold. Besides, it's all too much work to do in one day!

2 pounds lean ground beef
½ pound ground pork
⅔ cup breadcrumbs soaked
   in water to make a
   very thick paste
2 eggs, lightly beaten
1 teaspoon brown sugar
1 tablespoon
   Worcestershire sauce
¾ teaspoon salt or to taste
½ teaspoon dry mustard

½ teaspoon ground
   black pepper
½ teaspoon ground
   allspice
2-4 tablespoons butter,
   divided
½ cup finely chopped
   onions
¼ cup finely chopped celery
2 tablespoons chopped
   parsley

✤ In a large bowl, mix together meat, breadcrumbs, eggs, brown sugar, Worcestershire sauce, salt, dry mustard, pepper and allspice thoroughly with your hands, keeping your fingers wet with water to prevent the mixture from sticking.

✤ In a medium frying pan melt 2 tablespoons butter. Cook the onions, celery and parsley until the onions are translucent. Add to the meat mixture, mixing thoroughly. Refrigerate overnight if possible.

✤ Keeping your hands wet with water, shape the mixture into balls the size of small walnuts. Swedish meatballs are not large—just bite-size. Roll each of the meatballs thoroughly in the palms of your hands so they are firm. Refrigerate until ready to cook.

✤ Preheat oven to 375°.

✤ In a large, heavy skillet or frying pan, melt remaining 1-2 tablespoons butter. The pan should be fairly hot, almost smoking. Quickly but gently place several meatballs in the skillet so they fill up about half the surface of the pan. Immediately start shaking and rolling the meatballs in the pan to brown their entire surface working fast to move the meatballs around constantly. If the meatballs are sticking, gently push them with a spoon. Place the browned meatballs in a casserole or baking dish. Bake for 30 minutes.

✤ Serve with gravy, if desired, or with sour cream and dill on the side.

Per serving: 458 calories; 42.9g protein; 4.2g carbohydrates; 28.7g fat (11.1g saturated fat); 194mg cholesterol.

POTATO LEFSE   Serves 8

Lefse is a Scandinavian bread that is served at Thanksgiving and Christmas festivities. Here is a traditional recipe from Johanna Berg.

8 cups mashed potatoes	4 cups all-purpose flour
½ cup (1 stick) butter	Vegetable oil
½ cup heavy (whipping) cream	Ground cinnamon
1 tablespoon salt	Sugar

✤ In a large bowl, combine warm mashed potatoes, butter, whipping cream and salt. Cool mixture to room temperature. Mix in flour.

✤ Lightly flour a pastry board or flat clean surface. Take a big handful of dough and roll out with a rolling pin into paper-thin rounds.

✤ Lightly grease a griddle or electric frying pan. One at a time, cook round on greased griddle or frying pan turning to lightly brown both sides. Cool on clean dish towels. Keep lefse separated by stacking one on top of another. Grease griddle or frying pan as needed until all dough has been used.

✤ To serve, spread with butter, sprinkle with cinnamon and sugar and fold in half or quarters.

Per serving: 543 calories; 10.9g protein; 85.1g carbohydrates; 18.9g fat (11.4g saturated fat); 55.6mg cholesterol.

TIMBALLO (Spaghettini)

Serves 8-10

Weezie Mott developed this recipe at home in Alameda, California, after a friend served Weezie and Howard this dish in his home in Italy.

¼ ounce imported dried Italian mushrooms	8-10 ounces spaghettini
12-15 slices prosciutto, thinly sliced	4 tablespoons butter
1 10-ounce package tiny frozen peas	1½ cups heavy (whipping) cream, divided
½ cup water	1 cup freshly grated Parmesan cheese
	Salt and pepper to taste

✤ In a small bowl, soak dried mushrooms in water to cover for 30 minutes. Drain and coarsely chop. Set aside.

✤ Line the buttered baking dish by overlapping thin slices of prosciutto, allowing the prosciutto to hang over the dish. About 9-10 slices will do for this. Coarsely chop 2-3 slices of prosciutto and set aside.

✤ In a heavy saucepan, over medium heat, place the peas, water, drained and chopped mushrooms and chopped prosciutto. Cook together until peas are barely tender, about 5 minutes. Remove from heat and drain.

✤ Preheat oven to 375°. Generously butter a 1-quart souffle or baking dish.

✤ Cook the spaghettini in 5 quarts of boiling salted water until tender. Drain. In the same pot in which the pasta was cooked over medium heat, mix together the butter and 1 cup cream until almost boiling. Add the peas, prosciutto and mushrooms and mix well. Add Parmesan cheese and remaining ½ cup of heavy cream. Stir in the cooked and drained spaghettini. Season to taste with salt and pepper. Mix well. Turn entire mixture into the prosciutto-lined dish. Cover top with the overlapping prosciutto slices. Cover with 1 or 2 more slices of prosciutto, if necessary, to enclose completely. Bake in oven for 10 minutes. Turn oven off, open oven door, and allow dish to stand for 5 minutes. Unmold on a heated platter. Slice into individual wedges and serve.

Per serving: 1132 calories; 14.8g protein; 17.8g carbohydrates; 114g fat (70.5g saturated fat); 329mg cholesterol.

TERRY'S PARTY PORK ROAST

Serves 10-12

Our friend, Terry Frye, lives in Washington, D.C. He suggests this as a perfect entrée for Christmas dinner.

5 pound boneless pork loin roast, slit and tied	1 tablespoon chopped garlic
12 prunes	½ teaspoon ground black pepper
12 dried apricots	½ teaspoon ground thyme
1 cup Dijon mustard	1 teaspoon ground sage
½ cup honey	

✚ Preheat oven to 450°.

✚ Wash pork roast and place in large rectangular glass baking pan. Stuff the prunes and apricots into the sides of the roast.

✚ In a small bowl, mix together the mustard, honey, garlic, pepper, thyme and sage. Brush mixture over roast.

✚ Insert meat thermometer into center of roast. Cover with aluminum foil. Place roast in oven and immediately reduce heat to 350°. Bake about 25-35 minutes per pound.

Per serving: 537 calories; 55.4g protein; 17.1g carbohydrates; 25.7g fat (8.55g saturated fat); 172mg cholesterol.

I was raised Roman Catholic—baptized at Our Lady of Lourdes in St. Louis, Missouri and confirmed at St. Monica's in Creve Coeur. I struggled with that church and my adult spiritual needs for nearly 15 years; the last time was just prior to the baptism of my nephew and godson, Andy. I find St. Francis Lutheran to be spiritually meaningful. My intense involvement at St. Francis is contemporaneous with my personal life with Pastor Hiller—but not only because of him, although it is enhanced by having a theologian around the house. I'm involved because of the ministry of St. Francis Lutheran to the very young and the very old, to lesbians and gay men, its high standards of worship and music and for its support for the ELCA's larger mission in El Salvador.

Arthur Morris, 39, is a manager in local government who describes himself as "an out-of-the-ordinary pastor's wife."

FAERIE FOOD

Makes about 4 dozen

This is Wayne Strei's favorite memory from childhood Christmases at Christ Lutheran Church in Hintz, Wisconsin. Be sure to use a large pot to make this candy because the mixture really puffs up when you add the baking soda.

2 cups sugar	1 heaping teaspoon baking soda
1 cup light syrup	
2 tablespoons vegetable oil	1 pound dipping chocolate, melted
1 teaspoon vanilla	

✤ Grease 2 large shallow baking pans. Set aside.

✤ In a large pot over high heat, mix together sugar and light syrup until dissolved. Boil until mixture reaches the thread stage (255°F on a candy thermometer). Add vegetable oil and boil 2 minutes more, stirring constantly so mixture doesn't burn. Remove from heat.

✤ Stir in vanilla. Add baking soda and quickly stir to combine. Mixture will immediately puff up. While still foaming, pour mixture into prepared pans. Cool.

✤ Break into pieces. Dip into melted chocolate to coat and place on waxed paper to set chocolate. Store in an airtight container.

Per serving: 123 calories; .127g protein; 28.2g carbohydrates; 1.7g fat (.441g saturated fat); .403mg cholesterol.

POPCORN BALLS

Makes 1 dozen or more

Fran Johnson of Shawano, Wisconsin gave us the recipe for these addictive temptations that are welcome at Christmas, Halloween—well, just about anytime!

¾ cup unpopped yellow popcorn	½ cup butter
	1 cup brown sugar
¼ cup vegetable oil (optional for popping)	15 whole marshmallows

✤ Pop popcorn in a hot-air popper or in a pot with hot vegetable oil and place in a large bowl.

✤ In a heavy saucepan mix together butter, brown sugar and marshmallows. Heat until marshmallows are melted. Pour over popcorn. Using your freshly washed hands, form into balls. Wrap in plastic wrap and store in an airtight container or freeze.

Per serving: 215 calories; .45g protein; 29g carbohydrates; 11.6g fat (7.19g saturated fat); 31.1mg cholesterol.

SEAFOAM CANDY

Makes 2-3 dozen

It always meant Christmas was really close whenever Clarice Strei made this candy years ago on the family farm.

3 cups sugar	¼ teaspoon salt
1 cup dark syrup	1 cup walnuts,
⅔ cup water	finely chopped
2 egg whites	1 teaspoon vanilla

✤ In a medium saucepan over high heat, boil sugar, syrup and water until it starts to thread (255°F on a candy thermometer). Lower heat and continue to boil slowly.

✤ In a separate bowl, beat egg whites until soft peaks begin to form. Add about ½ of the syrup mixture, leaving the remaining syrup to boil slowly until it forms a hard ball and cracks in cold water or reaches hard crack stage (310°F on a candy thermometer). Add hot syrup to the egg whites and stir constantly until mixture stands in peaks. Add nuts and vanilla and mix to combine. Drop by teaspoonsful on waxed paper. Cool. Store in an airtight container.

Per serving: 254 calories; 1.51g protein; 54.5g carbohydrates; 4.64g fat (.419g saturated fat); 0mg cholesterol.

BERLINERKRANSWER
(Norwegian Christmas Wreath Cookies)

Makes 36 cookies

Doug Varner gave us this treasured family heirloom. Although it takes a little extra effort to make these delicacies, watch them disappear in no time!

½ cup sugar plus more
  for decorating
2¼ cups all-purpose flour
1 cup (2 sticks) butter,
  softened
2 egg yolks
2 teaspoons grated orange peel

¼ teaspoon salt
1 egg white, lightly beaten
Maraschino cherries
  (halved) for
  decorating
1-2 drops green food
  coloring

✤ Preheat oven to 400°.

✤ In a large bowl, combine ½ cup sugar, flour, butter, egg yolks, orange peel and salt. Mix together and beat for about 4 minutes, scraping side of bowl often. Mixture will be dry.

✤ Roll a heaping teaspoon of dough at a time into a 6-inch rope. Put on baking sheet in the shape of a wreath with the ends overlapping at the bottom. Brush cookies with egg white and sprinkle with sugar. Bake until light golden brown, 10-12 minutes. Mix together 1 tablespoon sugar and 1 or 2 drops of green food coloring and sprinkle on baked cookies. Decorate with Maraschino cherry halves.

Per serving: 88.2 calories; 1.11g protein; 8.78g carbohydrates; 5.47g fat (3.29g saturated fat); 25.6mg cholesterol.

Without the clergy and congregation of St. Francis Lutheran, I could not carry on my own life with dignity, let alone make sense of the suffering I confront in the lives of my clients, friends, and others in the human community.

I have the HIV virus, and that makes me keenly aware that I "walk through the valley of the shadow of death." Yet the gifts from a faith, still fledgling, that has been nourished and strengthened at St. Francis Lutheran have helped me able to "fear no evil" and to look forward to a bountiful future, on this planet and beyond.

David Neely, from a 1990 statement. With a degree from Yale Law School, David did community law for the desperately poor people of East Palo Alto. He also served as a member and president of the commission which directs the budget and policies of the San Francisco Department of Social Services. David died of AIDS at age 37 in 1991.

BELLA'S HOLIDAY SPRITZ   Makes 48-60 cookies

This is the "most special" Christmas cookie Mari Irvin's mother (Bella) ever made. A Norwegian delicacy, the recipe was passed on orally from one generation and family to another. After much prodding from Mari when she was a young woman, Bella finally wrote it down. Although Mari seldom bakes, according to her family and her sister's family she is the best Spritz-maker of her generation, an honor of which she is extremely proud. You will need a cookie press to make these treats.

2 cups (4 sticks) butter
1½ cups white sugar
2 egg yolks
¼ teaspoon salt

1-2 teaspoons almond
     flavoring or to taste
3½-4 cups all-purpose flour

✤ Preheat oven to 325°.

✤ In a large bowl, cream together butter and sugar until well blended.

✤ In a separate bowl, lightly beat egg yolks. Add salt and almond flavoring to beaten yolks and stir to combine. Add egg yolks to creamed mixture a little at a time, beating constantly. You cannot overbeat! Add the flour gradually, mixing thoroughly with each addition.

✤ Before putting dough in cookie press, dust the palms of your hands with flour and knead the dough well. (Slightly chilled, not cold, dough is easier to handle.) Fill cookie press with dough, place press over ungreased baking sheets and turn handle to squeeze out dough. Experiment with the press until you get the size of cookies you want and the design remains intact. Tip press away from baking sheet to release dough. Cookies are usually made in the shape of wreaths, candy canes or other holiday shapes. Test bake 1-2 cookies until baked cookie holds its shape and is lightly browned, 8-10 minutes. Add flour, if needed, and bake remaining dough.

Per serving: 128 calories; 1.14g protein; 13.2g carbohydrates; 7.97g fat (4.87g saturated fat); 29.5mg cholesterol.

DANISH RICE PUDDING with
RED FRUIT SAUCE

Serves 8

This is a traditional Christmas Eve dessert that Kirsten Havrehed says involves a little game. Danes place one whole almond in the pudding. The person who gets that almond wins a decorated marzipan pig or some other special candy treat. Of course, you may have to eat all of the pudding to reveal the winner!

4 cups milk	½ cup sugar
1 tablespoon vegetable oil	2 tablespoons pure
½ cup white rice, uncooked	almond extract
1 cup almonds,	4 cups heavy (whipping)
toasted and ground	cream, whipped
2 envelopes unflavored	1 single whole almond
gelatin, dissolved in	(optional)
¼ cup water	

❖ In a heavy 2-quart saucepan over medium-high heat, combine milk and oil and bring to a boil. Add rice. Lower heat, cover and cook until rice is cooked, about 30 minutes. Uncover and stir occasionally to avoid sticking. Remove from heat.

❖ Add ground almonds, dissolved gelatin, sugar and almond extract. Cool. Gently fold in the whipped cream. Pour into a large serving bowl. Serve cool with red fruit sauce.

RED FRUIT SAUCE:

1 quart pure juice (cherry	3 tablespoons cornstarch
is the Danish favorite)	½ cup cold water

❖ In a medium saucepan over medium heat, bring juice to a boil. Mix together cornstarch and cold water and add to the juice. Bring to a boil, stirring constantly, and cook until thickened. Cool and spread over rice pudding.

Per serving: 785 calories; 11.7g protein; 59.8g carbohydrates; 56.8g fat (30.7g saturated fat); 180mg cholesterol.

THE BEST EVER BREAD and BUTTER PUDDING

Serves 8-10

Ralph Burgin, chef of the incredible Carnelian Room on the 52nd floor atop the Bank of America World Headquarters, tells us this is the most popular dessert on their menu. It tastes great with stewed fruit or rum sauce.

1 cup milk
1 cup heavy (whipping) cream
1 teaspoon pure
   vanilla extract
3 large eggs
¾ cup sugar
10-12 slices French bread,
   sliced ½-inch thick

3 tablespoons butter,
   softened
¼ cup raisins, soaked in
   water or port wine
2 tablespoons warmed
   apricot jam
Powdered sugar for dusting

✤ Preheat oven to 375°. Butter an 8x8-inch baking dish.

✤ In a small saucepan over medium heat, bring milk, cream and vanilla extract to a boil. Meanwhile, mix eggs and sugar. In a large bowl strain simmering cream egg mixture, stirring thoroughly. Butter the french bread. Drain the raisins and sprinkle over the bottom of the prepared baking dish. Arrange the bread slices to cover the bottom of the dish. Pour the cream and egg mixture over the bread slices.

✤ Place the baking dish in a larger pan filled with about 1 inch hot water. Bake until pudding is set and a knife inserted in center comes out clean, about 45 minutes. Remove from oven. Spread with warmed apricot jam and dust with powdered sugar. Serve warm.

Per serving: 456 calories; 6.88g protein; 52.9g carbohydrates; 15.4g fat (8.58g saturated fat);107mg Cholesterol.

If you come to our church for worship on Sunday morning, you will see that everything is programmed and there is not much opportunity for spontaneity. Lutherans like things organized. Still, we needed to have a time and place where we could talk freely about issues of faith and life and learn from each other as well as our pastors. Groups of eight to ten meet informally in homes twice a month where we just talk and pray for each other. Life can be hard and sometimes it is confusing. We find it helpful to have a support group right in our church community.

ALDA JOHNSON'S
WHITE DESSERT

Serves 4-6

Paul Groth got this recipe from Alda Johnson, well-known entertainer and Red Owl Grocery manager in his home town of Mayville, North Dakota. Alda served this dessert as a salad at the Luther League Christmas Banquet in 1971 and the dish became an immediate hit with Paul's family because it contains four of the Midwestern food groups—cream, sugar, coconut and raspberries.

1 tablespoon unflavored gelatin
2¼ cups milk, divided
¼ cup sugar
½ teaspoon salt
1 teaspoon vanilla
1 cup flaked coconut

2 cups heavy (whipping) cream, whipped
1 10-ounce package frozen raspberries, thawed
1½ teaspoons cornstarch
½ cup currant jelly

✤ In a heavy saucepan over medium heat, mix together the gelatin and 1¼ cup of the milk until dissolved and cook about 5 minutes. Add sugar and salt to the gelatin mixture and stir until the sugar is dissolved. Do not boil. Remove from heat and chill in refrigerator or in a bowl filled with ice. While chilling, stir occasionally to prevent a film from forming.

✤ After the mixture has thickened, add the vanilla and coconut and stir to blend. Fold in the whipped cream and pour into a 1½ quart bowl or mold. Cover and chill in refrigerator for 2-3 hours.

✤ To make the topping, crush the thawed raspberries. In a heavy saucepan over medium-low heat, place about one cup of the raspberries. Add cornstarch and stir to combine. Add remaining berries and mix together thoroughly. Add jelly and bring to a boil over medium heat. When mixture has thickened slightly, remove from heat and strain to remove raspberry seeds.

✤ To serve, divide the cream and coconut base among 4-6 individual glass dishes. Pour raspberry topping over each serving, or bring serving bowl to table and divide among guests. Leftover topping is great on ice cream.

Per serving: 437 calories; 8.74g protein; 51.2g carbohydrates; 23.3g fat (15.9g saturated fat); 66.8mg cholesterol.

ARNI'S CHEESECAKE

Serves 8-10

St. Francis Lutheran Church secretary, Arni Lovitt, former assistant pastry chef at the Stanford Court Hotel in San Francisco, believes cheesecake tastes best when made a day in advance and finishing it off the day it is served.

CRUST:

1½ cups Arrowroot
     cookie crumbs

⅓ cup melted butter

FILLING:

1½ pounds cream cheese
     at room temperature
1 cup sugar

1 tablespoon vanilla
4 extra large eggs
     at room temperature

TOPPING:

1 cup sour cream

2 teaspoons sugar

✤ Preheat oven to 350°.

✤ Mix cookie crumbs with butter and press evenly in the bottom of a 9-inch springform pan. Bake 15 minutes. Let cool. Lower oven temperature to 300°.

✤ In a medium bowl, mix cream cheese and sugar together until well blended. Stir in vanilla. Beat in eggs one at a time, scraping bowl well after each addition. Pour mixture over cooled crust and place springform pan in a larger pan filled with 1 inch of hot water. Bake until top is puffed and lightly brown, about 1½ hours. Remove baking pan from oven and springform pan from larger pan; place springform pan on a rack to cool. Cover with plastic wrap and refrigerate overnight, if possible.

✤ To make the topping, mix sour cream and sugar together until smooth. Pour over top of cheesecake and bake at 350° about 12 minutes.

Per serving: 466 calories; 8.54 g protein; 26 g carbohydrates; 37.1 g fat (22.5 g saturated fat); 188 mg cholesterol.

VENETARTA
(Traditional Icelandic torte)

Serves 12-14

Proud of her heritage, Diane DeLange offers us this traditional Christmas dessert from Iceland.

1 cup (2 sticks) butter	1 teaspoon almond extract
1½ cups sugar	4 cups all-purpose flour
2 eggs	1 teaspoon ground
2 tablespoons heavy	cardamom
(whipping) cream	1 teaspoon baking soda

✤ Preheat oven to 375°. Line seven 8-inch cake pans with wax paper.

✤ In a large bowl cream together butter and sugar. Add eggs, cream, almond extract and beat until well blended. Add flour, cardamom and baking soda and mix to combine.

✤ Divide batter into 7 parts. Pat into lined cake pans. Bake until light golden, 7-8 minutes. Remove and cool on racks.

FILLING:

1 pound prunes	1 teaspoon vanilla
½ cup water	1 teaspoon cinnamon
1 cup sugar	

✤ In a small bowl, cover prunes with water and let soak at least four hours or overnight.

✤ Transfer to a medium saucepan and stir in sugar, vanilla and cinnamon. Cook over medium heat until thickened (mixture should be the consistency of jam).

✤ Beginning with a cake layer spread filing to edges of cake. Cover with another cake layer and repeat until all seven cake layers are used. Do not spread filling on top layer. Frost with butter cream frosting, if desired. Cover and store at room temperature for several days to allow flavors to blend.

Per serving: 241 calories; 2.81g protein; 41.9g carbohydrates; 7.59g fat (4.5g saturated fat); 34.3mg cholesterol.

LINZER TORTE

This is yet another of our Arni Lovitt's incredible pastries. Be careful to keep the dough chilled until the last minute or it will fall apart when you try to roll it out!

¾ cup (1½ sticks) butter
1 cup all-purpose flour
1½ cups almonds
   (with skins), grated fine
½ cup sugar
⅛ teaspoon ground cloves
⅛ teaspoon ground cinnamon

2 egg yolks
1 egg white, lightly beaten
⅓ cup seedless raspberry
   jam (or with seeds
   if you prefer)

✜ In a large bowl, mix butter into flour until mixture resembles coarse meal. Add grated almonds and mix lightly.

✜ In another medium bowl, mix together sugar, cloves, cinnamon and egg yolks. Add to almond mixture and mix until well blended. There should be no visible butter in dough. Press one-half of dough into the bottom of 9-inch springform pan. Place springform pan and remaining dough in refrigerator to chill for at least 1 hour.

✜ Preheat oven to 325°.

✜ Remove springform pan and remaining dough from refrigerator. Roll out remaining dough to ¼-inch thick. Cut into ½-inch strips and make a border around the outside edge of springform pan. Fill center with raspberry jam and spread jam until smooth and it touches border. Cut more ½-inch strips and make lattice over top of raspberry jam. Brush lattice with egg white.

✜ Bake until the top is light to moderately brown, about 1 hour and 15 minutes. To brown evenly, rotate in oven every 20-30 minutes. Cool before serving.

Per serving: 451 calories; 7.9g protein; 38.1g carbohydrates; 31.4g fat (12.4g saturated fat); 99.6mg cholesterol.

God of goodness and delight,

We thank you for all things that sweeten the tongue and warm the heart:

For puff pastries and kept promises;

For fresh fruit and close friends;

For aromatic coffee and quiet conversation.

Bless this dessert and the moments we share, O God, that we might savor the sweetness of your grace and delight in the warmth of your love.

~Amen.

For it is in giving that we receive;

SWEET INSPIRATIONS

Most cooks are drawn immediately here, to the cake plate and the pie tin. Perhaps it is because sweets elicit the highest praise for cooks. Maybe the process of kneading, rolling and shaping fulfills some sort of artistic and creative urge. Most likely it is as simple as that delightful smell coming from the oven.

There's an extra incentive for the cook to deliver a winning dessert since it leaves the meal's final impression. The question is, once they've had a slice, will the guests ever leave at all?

Hun's Apple Pie

Coconut Pie

Custard Pie

Deborah's Classic Cherry Pie

Macadamia Nut Pie

Fresh Apricot Pie

*Old-Fashioned Southern
Apple Rhubarb Pie form Connecticut
(or Somewhere)*

Unnie's Lemon Meringue Pie

Butterscotch Pie

Apple-Banana Cake

Grandma's Applesauce Chocolate Cake

Persimmon Cake

Pear Cake

Plum or Apricot Cordial

David's Cordial Cake

Rich Hot Fudge Sauce

Chocolate to Die For

Lowfat Chocolate Mousse

HUN'S APPLE PIE

Makes one 9-inch pie

Jim Sherman's mother showed him the basics on pie making and he has been improvising ever since. This recipe is submitted in memory of Nick Teramani, who was a big fan of this particular dessert and jokingly gave the pie its name.

½ cup lemon juice	1 tablespoon all-purpose flour
6-8 Granny Smith or Pippin apples, peeled	¼ teaspoon ground nutmeg
1½ cups sugar	Pastry for a 2-crust, 9-inch pie
¾ teaspoon cinnamon	

✤ Preheat oven to 425°.

✤ Pour lemon juice into a large pan or sink of cold water. Peel the apples and leave in the water while preparing the other ingredients.

✤ In a small bowl, mix sugar, cinnamon, flour and nutmeg together.

✤ Core apples and slice into ½-inch slices. Line a 9-inch, deep pie dish with half of pastry and cover with the apples. Sprinkle the sugar mix on the slices as you layer the apples. When you have used all the apples, making a mound well above the rim, pour the remainder of the sugar mixture on top. Cover with the top pie crust and sprinkle sparingly with cinnamon.

✤ Bake for 15 minutes. Reduce heat to 350° and bake until the pie is brown and bubbling, about 45 minutes.

Per serving: 384 calories; 2.79g protein; 63.7g carbohydrates; 14g fat (3.5g saturated fat); 0mg cholesterol.

I've never been part of a church where so many people do so much more than just go to church on Sunday. I'm proud to be a member of St. Francis Lutheran because of the breadth of the congregation's commitments—not just to gays and lesbians, but also activities like the childcare center and senior center.

Alejandro and I literally found St. Francis by accident. We had planned to visit another church and couldn't find it. The doors of St. Francis were open, so we walked in. And here we stayed.

Michael Utech, 36, works for a surety bonding company. He grew up in Topeka, Kansas, lived in Dallas and New York, and moved to San Francisco in 1988. Michael chairs the annual fundraising dinner for the childcare center, and is a member of the center's board, along with his partner, Alejandro Cejudo.

COCONUT PIE

Makes one 9-inch pie

Joanne Karns likes to make this pie in the middle of winter. It seems to bring a hint of the tropics to her Cedar Rapids, Iowa home.

1¼ cups sugar
½ cup (1 stick) butter
1 tablespoon all-purpose flour
3 eggs
1 teaspoon vanilla

¼ cup buttermilk
1 6-ounce package
 frozen fresh coconut
1 9-inch pie crust, unbaked

✤ Preheat oven to 325°.

✤ In a large bowl, mix together sugar, butter, flour, eggs, vanilla and buttermilk until creamy. Add coconut and combine. Pour into 9-inch pie crust. Bake until golden brown, 45-50 minutes.

Per serving: 334 calories; 3.53g protein; 35.9g carbohydrates; 20.6g fat (14.1g saturated fat); 111mg cholesterol.

CUSTARD PIE

Makes one 9-inch pie

Another of Wisconsin cook Evelyn Frank's best recipes, this can be made without the crust for the ultimate comfort food.

6 eggs, slightly beaten
1 cup sugar
½ teaspoon salt
½ teaspoon grated nutmeg

½ tablespoon vanilla
4 cups scalding hot milk
1 9-inch pie crust
 (optional)

✤ Preheat oven to 375°. Grease a 9-inch square baking pan if you don't wish to use a baked pie crust.

✤ In a large bowl, beat eggs until well mixed.

✤ In another bowl, beat together sugar, salt, nutmeg, vanilla and hot milk. Add to egg mixture and combine.

✤ Pour into prepared baking pan or unbaked 9-inch pie crust and bake until set, about 45 minutes.

Per serving: 461 calories; 17.4g protein; 62.7g carbohydrates; 15.7g fat (7.46g saturated fat); 351mg cholesterol.

DEBORAH'S CLASSIC CHERRY PIE

Makes one 9-inch pie

Every June, Deborah Olson finds time to bake a cherry pie for her dad for Father's Day (together they own and operate Olson's Farms in Sunnyvale, California). It's a two-day process, pitting the cherries one day and baking the next, but it's really worth the extra work.

PASTRY:
2 cups all-purpose flour
1 teaspoon salt
⅓ cup plus 1 tablespoon

⅓ cup plus 1 tablespoon shortening
4-5 tablespoons cold water
butter

FILLING:
¾ to 1¼ cups sugar, depending on sweetness of cherries
⅓ cup all-purpose flour
2 tablespoons butter

8 cups pitted Bing, Royal Ann or Tartarian cherries (about 3½ pounds)
¼ teaspoon almond extract

✤ Preheat oven to 350°.

✤ Place flour and salt into a medium mixing bowl or into a food processor. Cut in shortening and butter and work with a fork or pastry cutter until mixture is like coarse corn meal. Sprinkle in cold water 1 tablespoon at a time, mixing until all flour is moistened and forms a ball. Refrigerate until needed. (Be sure not to overwork the dough.)

✤ In a large mixing bowl, stir together sugar and flour. Mix well with cherries. Roll pastry out on a lightly floured board. Place bottom crust in 9-inch pie plate. Add cherry mixture. Sprinkle with almond extract and dot with butter. Cover pie with top crust, crimping edges, and make slits in top crust to allow for steam to escape. Cut a piece of aluminum foil about 3 inches wide and cover the edge of the pie to prevent excess browning. Bake until crust is brown and juices are bubbly, 35-45 minutes. (Remove foil during last 15 minutes of baking.)

✤ Freeze pie unwrapped; when frozen wrap carefully and return to freezer. Pie will keep 4-6 months.

Per serving: 713 calories; 8.18g protein; 95.9g carbohydrates; 34.7g fat (12.6g saturated fat); 28.5mg cholesterol.

MACADAMIA NUT CREAM PIE

Makes one 9-inch pie

Barbara Kling and her husband, Jack, love to travel to Hawaii where they especially enjoy feasting on macadamia nuts. This brings a bit of Hawaii to their San Francisco home.

⅔ cup sugar
¼ cup cornstarch
½ teaspoon salt
3 cups heavy (whipping) cream or half-and-half
¾ cup chopped, macadamia nuts, divided

3 egg yolks, slightly beaten
1 tablespoon butter
1 teaspoon vanilla
1 9-inch pie crust, baked

✤ In a heavy saucepan, mix together sugar, cornstarch and salt. Gradually stir in the cream or half-and-half. Add ½ cup of the macadamia nuts. Cook over low to medium heat, stirring constantly (wooden spoon to start—then switch to wire whisk) until mixture thickens and boils. Boil 1 minute, being careful not to scorch.

✤ Remove from heat. In a medium bowl, lightly beat egg yolks. Stir the milk mixture into the egg yolks one spoonful at a time until at least half of the hot milk mixture has been added. Blend the egg mixture back into the remainder of the hot milk mixture. Using a whisk, stir constantly until mixture comes back to a boil. Stir and boil for 1 minute. Again, being careful not to let mixture burn.

✤ Remove from heat. Blend in butter and vanilla. Immediately pour into baked pie crust. Sprinkle remaining finely chopped nuts over top of pie. Let cool at room temperature and serve or refrigerate for later use. If refrigerating, cover top with plastic wrap, tapping the wrap down lightly onto the surface of the pie to prevent drying.

Per serving: 607 calories; 6.33g protein; 35g carbohydrates; 50.3g fat (24.8g saturated fat); 206mg cholesterol.

When I first visited St. Francis Lutheran in 1988, the church had not yet taken its courageous stand in relation to the ordination of gays and lesbians. Instead, I stayed and joined because at St. Francis there were no stepchildren in the family of God. Later, the ordinations of Jeff, Ruth and Phyllis were the high point of my life in the church. It was a coming-out as gay to the Christian world and as a Christian to the gay world.

Edward Grey is a graduate student in theology at Emory University in Atlanta.

FRESH APRICOT PIE

Makes one 10-inch pie

At food writer and cookbook author Elaine Corn's house in Sacramento, California, no summer begins without this pie. Because apricot season is short, the small window of opportunity makes this pie a very special treat. All you do is halve the 'cots—they moosh down by themselves during baking.

CRUST:

2 cups all-purpose flour
⅜ teaspoon salt
¼ teaspoon sugar

1 tablespoon butter
3 tablespoons shortening
3-3½ tablespoons ice water

APRICOTS:

8 cups halved fresh
   apricots
¼ cup brown sugar
¼ cup white sugar
3 tablespoons all-purpose
   flour or cornstarch
1 egg, separated (white
   for brushing bottom
   crust, yolk for
   brushing top crust)

¼ cup clarified butter
1-2 tablespoons Calvados
   (or cider or orange juice)
White sugar (for
   sprinkling)
1 tablespoon milk,
   (for egg yolk-milk wash)

❖ Preheat oven to 400° and place rack in center of oven.

❖ To make the crust, mix flour, salt, sugar, butter and shortening with hands until crumbly. Stir in ice water and mix dough until it forms a ball. Form into 2 disks, wrap in plastic and put in freezer while you prepare the apricot filling.

❖ Mix apricots with sugars and flour. Set aside at room temperature while you prepare the remaining ingredients, mixing now and then.

❖ To build the pie, have ready the separated egg, butter, liqueur and white sugar. Roll out the bottom crust. Place in a deep 10-inch pie plate. Brush with egg white. Fill with apricots. Dribble butter and Calvados over apricots. Sprinkle with sugar.

❖ Roll out top crust and place over filling. Cut an even overhang with scissors, then fold overhang under itself and crimp to look like a rope.

Beat yolk and tablespoon milk lightly. Brush yolk-milk wash over top crust. If making decorations with extra dough, do so now. Brush decorations with yolk-milk wash. Cut four 1-inch slits in the middle of the pie to act as steam vents. Set pie on a cookie sheet, and place in preheated oven.

✦ Bake for 20 minutes. Reduce heat to 375° and continue baking until pie is golden brown and bubbly, about 30 minutes. Cool on a wire rack. Cut when cool.

Per serving: 324 calories; 4.51g protein; 36.4g carbohydrates; 18.7g fat (10g saturated fat); 56.7mg cholesterol; 222mg sodium.

OLD-FASHIONED SOUTHERN APPLE RHUBARB PIE from CONNECTICUT (or SOMEWHERE)

Makes one 9-inch pie

This was inspired by a visit to a cafe in North Carolina where food writer Jeanette Ferrary became enamored with all the typically Southern food and the typically Southern proprietors—who turned out to be from Connecticut.

Pastry for a 2-crust 9-inch pie	1 cup brown sugar (packed)
2 cups sliced rhubarb	2 tablespoons grated orange zest
3 tart apples, cored, peeled and diced	¼ cup raisins
	2 tablespoons all-purpose flour

✦ Preheat oven to 350°.

✦ Roll out bottom crust and fit into pan.

✦ In a large bowl, combine rhubarb, apples, brown sugar, orange zest, raisins and flour. Fill pie shell and cover with top crust. Make slits in crust to vent. Bake until golden brown, 45-50 minutes.

Per serving: 316 calories; 3.29g protein; 45.6g carbohydrates; 14.1g fat (3.48g saturated fat); 0mg cholesterol.

UNNIE'S LEMON MERINGUE PIE

Makes one 9 or 10-inch pie

Kerry Kelly remembers her grandmother serving this pie when Kerry was growing up in Fresno, California. She is happy to report it tastes just as wonderful today as she remembers.

4 egg whites at room temperature	4-5 tablespoons lemon juice
¼ teaspoon cream of tartar	Grated zest of 2 lemons
1½ cups sugar, divided	½ pint heavy (whipping) cream
4 egg yolks	

✤ Preheat oven to 250°.

✤ In a large bowl, beat egg whites until soft peaks form. Add cream of tartar and sugar and beat until whites are shiny. Place mixture in ungreased 9 or 10-inch pie pan and bake 20 minutes. Increase oven temperature to 300° and bake another 40 minutes. Cool.

✤ In another bowl, beat egg yolks well. Add sugar, lemon juice and lemon rind. Cook in double boiler over hot water until mixture thickens, stirring constantly until the mixture is the consistency of thick pudding. Let cool.

✤ In a large bowl, whip cream. Spread ½ of the whipped cream over the cooked meringue. Cover with all the lemon mixture and then spread with the remaining whipped cream.

✤ Refrigerate at least overnight or up to 24 hours before serving.

Per serving: 212 calories; 3.37g protein; 39.2g carbohydrates; 5.33g fat (2.51g saturated fat); 116mg cholesterol.

I first visited St. Francis Lutheran in 1987 as the pall-bearer for my friend, John Hanson. Pastors DeLange and Lokken had helped my dying friend find peace with God; a gay man had found acceptance with a mainstream church. Back then I was't ready to join a church, but eventually my lover Michael Jordan and I came to a service at St. Francis. We were amazed when the topic of AIDS was woven into the sermon, we were genuinely welcomed, and the congregation was getting ready to ordain Ruth, Phyllis, and Jeff. Finally, here was a church I could accept after 25 years of rejection.

Thomas Heck, 42, has worked in advertising for the *Milwaaukee Journal*, and after his move to San Francisco in 1978 for the *Santa Rosa Press Democrat*. He is an avid opera fan.

BUTTERSCOTCH PIE

Makes two 9-inch pies

Wayne Strei's neighbors Evelyn and Clifford Frank lived about a mile away on another dairy farm in northeastern Wisconsin. Evelyn passed away in 1991, but to Wayne she was always the best cook in the neighborhood (sorry, Mom!). This butterscotch pie was one of her family's favorites.

2 cups brown sugar (packed)
2 cups water
3 tablespoons butter
⅓ cup cornstarch (dissolved in 2 tablespoons water)
4 egg yolks, lightly beaten
1 teaspoons vanilla

1 9-inch pie shells, baked
4 egg whites at room temperature
⅓ cup sugar
¼ teaspoon salt
½ teaspoon vanilla

✤ In a large saucepan, bring brown sugar and water to rolling boil.

✤ Remove from heat and add butter and cornstarch mixture. Add egg yolks slowly, stirring constantly. Add 1 teaspoon vanilla and stir to combine. Divide into baked pie shells.

✤ Preheat broiler.

✤ To make meringue, place the egg whites and sugar in a large bowl. Place this bowl into a larger bowl filled with about 2 inches of hot water. Stir constantly until mixture is warm. Add salt and ½ teaspoon vanilla and stir to combine. Remove the smaller bowl from the hot water and beat egg white mixture with an electric mixer until stiff and shiny. Spread meringue over filled pie shells to the inner edge of the crust. Place pie under broiler until meringue peaks brown, only 1-2 minutes.

Per serving: 267 calories; 1.98g protein; 43.6g carbohydrates; 9.73g fat (3.91g saturated fat); 102mg cholesterol.

APPLE-BANANA CAKE

Serves 12-16

This recipe comes from Parker Nolen's grandmother's kitchen. When he was a child, every Thanksgiving and Christmas the smell of baking apples and bananas permeated the house. Even now when Parker visits her in Dallas, there is a fresh, hot apple-banana cake on the table. Serve this cake with or without icing.

2 cups all-purpose flour	2 red apples, unpeeled and
1 teaspoon baking soda	diced
½ teaspoon salt	2 large bananas, mashed
1 cup vegetable oil	1 teaspoon vanilla
2 cups sugar	1 cup walnuts, chopped
2 eggs	(optional)

✤ Preheat oven to 300°. Grease and flour a 9x13-inch baking pan.

✤ In a small bowl, sift together flour, soda and salt, set aside.

✤ In a large mixing bowl, combine the oil, sugar and eggs and beat until smooth. Add the flour mixture and stir to combine. Add apples, bananas, vanilla and walnuts and mix well.

✤ Pour into prepared pan. Bake 30 minutes. Reduce temperature to 275° and continue to bake until top springs back when lightly touched, about 45 minutes more.

Per serving: 532 calories; 5.61g protein; 85g carbohydrates; 21.3g fat (3.76g saturated fat); 26.3mg cholesterol.

In the 1980s, thousands of people from El Salvador came to San Francisco to escape the civil war. In 1985, St. Francis Lutheran voted to become a Sanctuary Church. Since then our Social Justice Committee has raised money for local needs and we have sent about $12,000 to El Salvador. The Lutheran Bishop of El Salvador, Medardo Gomez, visited St. Francis in 1988. He told us he used our gifts to purchase land for people who had been forced off their own land by the Salvadoran army.

GRANDMA'S APPLESAUCE
CHOCOLATE CAKE

Serves 8

This recipe was passed down to Brian Knittel from his great-grandmother, who emigrated from Italy to Ukiah, California in the 1880s. For Italians, food is the embodiment of love and this cake has been a special token of affection in Brian's family for as long as he can remember. It is offered here as a grateful acknowledgment of the love and support he has always had from his family.

2 cups all-purpose flour
1 cup sugar
3 tablespoon cocoa powder
1 tablespoon cornstarch
½ teaspoon ground cloves
½ teaspoon ground nutmeg
1 teaspoon ground cinnamon

2 teaspoons baking soda
1 cup walnuts, chopped
1 cup raisins
½ cup vegetable oil
1½ cup applesauce
Powdered sugar for dusting

✤ Preheat oven to 350°. Lightly grease and flour 8x8-inch baking pan or a 12-inch cast-iron skillet.

✤ In a large bowl, mix together flour, sugar, cocoa powder, cornstarch, clover, nutmeg, cinamon and baking soda. Add walnuts and raisins, oil and applesauce and stir only until just combined. Pour batter into prepared pan. Bake for 40-50 minutes, until toothpick inserted in center comes out clean. (Be careful not to overbake if using skillet.) When cool, lightly dust with powdered sugar.

✤ Note: You might want to use half dark and half golden raisins, or omit the nuts and/or raisins altogether.

Per serving: 519 calories; 6.54g protein; 75.3g carbohydrates; 23.7g fat (2.37g saturated fat); 0mg cholesterol.

PERSIMMON CAKE

Makes 2 loaves

Bill Shoaf brought this cake to St. Francis Lutheran one Sunday morning and lots of people asked for the recipe. His friend, Kay Miyoko, was glad to oblige. If you have never tried persimmons, well, here's your chance!

Juice and zest of 1 lemon
½ cup raisins
1 cup sugar
¼ cup butter
1 egg
2 teaspoons baking soda
1 cup ripe persimmon pulp

1½ cups all-purpose flour
1 teaspoon ground cinnamon
½ teaspoon cloves
½ teaspoon allspice
½ cup chopped walnuts

✤ Preheat oven to 300°. Grease and flour two 5x9-inch loaf pans.

✤ Pour lemon juice over raisins and let stand a few minutes.

✤ In a large mixing bowl, cream together sugar, butter and egg.

✤ In a separate small bowl, mix together baking soda and persimmon pulp and add to egg mixture, stirring to combine. Sift flour, cinnamon, cloves and allspice together. Add to persimmon mixture and mix well. Add nuts, raisins and lemon zest and stir just to combine. Pour into prepared pans. Bake until toothpick inserted in the center comes out clean, about 1 hour and 10 minutes. This loaf will keep as well as a fruitcake.

Per serving: 266 calories; 3.82g protein; 44.3g carbohydrates; 9.1g fat (3.42g saturated fat); 33.6mg cholesterol.

PEAR CAKE

Serves 10-12

Faye Robinson is St. Francis Lutheran's "Birthday Lady." On the last Sunday of every month she bakes a cake for everyone who is celebrating a birthday during the month and leads us all in a rousing chorus of "Happy Birthday." This is one of her favorites—and ours as well.

1½ cups vegetable oil
2 cups sugar
3 eggs
3 cups all-purpose flour
1 teaspoon salt
1 teaspoon baking soda
1 teaspoon ground cinnamon

1 teaspoon vanilla
2 cups cored and unpeeled chopped pears
1 cup chopped walnuts or pecans
Powdered sugar (optional)

✤ Preheat oven to 325°. Grease and lightly flour a 9 or 10-inch tube pan with a removable bottom or a 10-inch Bundt pan.

✤ In a large bowl, cream together vegetable oil, sugar and eggs.

✤ Sift flour, salt, baking soda and cinnamon together. Add to creamed mixture. Stir in vanilla. Fold in pears and nuts until just combined. Pour into prepared pan. Bake until a toothpick inserted in the center comes out clean, about 1 hour and 20 minutes. Remove from oven. Cool 20 minutes and invert cake onto serving platter. Top with powdered sugar, if desired.

Per serving: 701 calories; 7.6g protein; 76.1g carbohydrates; 42.1g fat (4.17g saturated fat); 63.6mg cholesterol.

PLUM or APRICOT CORDIAL   Makes 1 quart

Longtime St. Francis Lutheran member David Look makes this marvelous cordial at different times during the year, taking advantage of seasonal fruits. He made it in an impromptu cooking class one evening and now lots of eager students have cordial sitting in their closets waiting for the holidays. It makes a very nice housewarming or Christmas gift.

5-6 pounds small black   1.5 liters vodka
     plums or apricots*
1 cup sugar

✤ Wash fruit. Prick fruit many times with fork and place in large glass jar. Add sugar. Cover with vodka until all fruit is covered. Screw lid on tightly and place jar in a dark cupboard or closet for 3-6 months. (Sugar and alcohol will interact reducing the alcohol content.)

✤ After 3-6 months, remove jar from darkness. Line a colander with cheesecloth. Set colander in a large bowl or pan. Drain liquid from fruit. Pit fruit and put into a sterile glass jar or bottle and keep in refrigerator until ready to serve. Serve cordial in small glasses after dinner, over ice cream or make David's Cordial Cake (recipe follows). Drink within one to two months. Light in refrigerator will degrade the color but not the quality of the cordial.

✤ *Notes: After all sugar has disappeared, taste for sweetness. If cordial tastes too strong, add a little more sugar. If too sweet, use less sugar next time. The smaller the fruit, the more surface area in contact with the vodka; the more surface area, the better the color.

Per serving: 277 calories; 1.07g protein; 27.7g carbohydrates; .841g fat (.068g saturated fat); 0mg cholesterol.

DAVID'S CORDIAL CAKE

Serves 16-24

First make the cordial, then you can bake this incredible cake.

¾ cup vegetable oil
4 eggs
1 cup sugar
2½ cups pitted plum or
   pitted apricot meat
   from making cordial*
   (recipe above)
2 cups all-purpose flour
2 teaspoons baking soda

½ teaspoon salt
3 teaspoons cinnamon (only
   1 teaspoon for apricots)
1 teaspoon grated nutmeg
   (none for apricots)
1 cup raisins (use white
   raisins with apricots)
2 cups chopped walnuts
   or pecans

✤ Preheat oven to 350°. Grease and flour a 10-inch Bundt pan.

✤ Pour vegetable oil into food processor or blender. Add eggs and sugar. Mix together. Add meat of cordial fruit a little at a time and process until smooth with no lumps.

✤ In a large bowl, mix together flour, baking soda, salt, cinnamon and nutmeg. Add cordial mixture and mix together. Remove stems from raisins, if any, and fold raisins and nuts into batter.

✤ Pour into prepared pan. Bake until toothpick comes out clean, about 1 hour. Remove cake from oven and set on rack to cool for about 15 minutes. Invert to remove cake from pan.

✤ Note: *Fresh fruit can be substituted for cordial mixture.

Per serving: 348 calories; 5.75g protein; 36.9g carbohydrates; 21.1g fat (2.24g saturated fat); 53mg cholesterol.

RICH HOT FUDGE SAUCE

Serves 4-6

Barbara Holzrichter owns Grand Finale, California's smallest licensed candy factory. The recipe's simple name says it all.

¼ cup cocoa
½ cup Karo syrup
2 cups half-and-half
   (light) cream

¼ pound bittersweet
   chocolate
3 tablespoons butter
1 teaspoon vanilla

✤ In a heavy saucepan, make a paste of the cocoa and karo syrup. Cook over low heat, slowly adding the half-and-half, chocolate and butter. Continue cooking over medium heat, stirring constantly, for 15 minutes. Remove from heat and add the vanilla. Serve over vanilla ice cream (if you dare!).

✤ The longer the sauce simmers, the harder it will firm over ice cream.

Per serving: 333 calories; 4.59g protein; 35.5g carbohydrates; 23g fat (13.8g saturated fat); 45.3mg cholesterol.

CHOCOLATE TO DIE FOR

Serves 10-12

Jill Brennan teaches very popular cooking classes in Jill's Kitchen, her school in Danville, California. This dessert is appropriately named!

1 cup (2 sticks) unsalted butter
   at room temperature
1 cup sugar
½ pound semisweet
   chocolate, melted

1 teaspoon instant coffee
   granules dissolved in
1 tablespoon hot water*
8 eggs, separated

✤ Preheat oven to 325°. Grease the bottom only of a 9-inch spring-form pan.

✤ In a medium bowl, beat butter and sugar together. Add melted chocolate and dissolved coffee granules and stir to combine. Add egg yolks one at a time, beating well after each addition. Beat well for about 15 minutes.

✤ In another bowl, beat egg whites until stiff peaks form. Fold gently into chocolate batter. Pour ¾ of the batter into the prepared pan and bake for 50 minutes. Remove from oven and cool. Spread remaining batter on top. Chill well and serve with whipped cream.

✜ Note: *One tablespoon of any liqueur can be substituted for coffee and water.

Per serving: 340 calories; 5.13g protein; 29g carbohydrates; 24.3g fat (13.9g saturated fat); 183mg cholesterol.

LOWFAT CHOCOLATE MOUSSE   Serves 6-8

Mark Scott Johnson has been associated with Lutherans Concerned since its inception twenty years ago. Tofu helps to give this delicious dessert its lowfat label.

8-10 ounces soft tofu
¾ cup plus 1 tablespoon sugar
¼ cup Grand Marnier
      or other orange liqueur
6 ounces semisweet
      chocolate

¼ cup strong coffee
4 egg whites
Pinch cream of tartar
      (optional)

✜ In a food processor or blender, puree the tofu until completely smooth. Add ¾ cup sugar and Grand Marnier with the machine running.

✜ In a double-boiler, melt the chocolate and coffee together over boiling water, stirring constantly.* With food processor or blender running, add the chocolate mix to the tofu base.

✜ Place egg whites in a bowl and let them warm to room temperature. Begin beating slowly. If the bowl isn't unclad copper, add a pinch of cream of tartar. Beat on high speed until whites form soft peaks. Add the remaining tablespoon of sugar and beat to stiff shining peaks.

✜ Stir about a quarter of the egg whites into the mousse base to loosen it. Gently fold the mousse base into the whites. Pour into a mold or molds and chill until set, at least 4 hours. It can also be frozen.

✜ Note: To melt the chocolate in a microwave, break the chocolate into bits and place in a microwave-proof bowl. Add the coffee and cover. Microwave on medium-low setting for 1 minute, then stir. Repeat until the chocolate is smooth. Be careful not to burn.

Per serving: 62.9 calories; 2.99g protein; 5.73g carbohydrates; 3.06g fat (.929g saturated fat); 9.18mg cholesterol.

O
God, our help in ages past, our hope for years to come:
Thank you for not not discarding people when we grow old or pass from the favor of the moment. Rather, you unpack layers of memory and meaning hidden deep in the flesh, now grown fuller and richer through the rising and falling of the years. Stirred by a fragrance or flavor from times and places long ago, you retrieve the buried treasure of memory, of cherished connections and once-forgotten faces and touches. Their loving power lives again in the pleasure of this moment, twice-blest by the gifts of experience and reminiscence.

Spirit of Never-Failing Love, when we feel old and useless, remind us of the increased value of heirlooms, whose beauty is appreciated by the eye and the heart. Help us to prize people, not only reclaimed objects, as they age. Teach us the wisdom of love-laden tradition and time-invested care for daily we impart the values and memories the next generation must discover and treasure. *–Amen.*

it is in pardoning that we are pardoned;

EDIBLE HEIRLOOMS

If tradition was a tangible thing it might very well be meatloaf. Or paella. It could be a soup or stew, or take form in a more personal (and secret) seasoning of a baked chicken. From the homeland or the old hometown, favorite recipes are handed down through the years to constitute an intimate family chronicle. An oral history in more ways than one.

Inevitably, some upstart will throw an innovative twist into the mix. Grandma swears by her gravy; Mom, polite but firm, claims her version is better. The hungry third generation, learning something of diplomacy, if not cooking, offers a non-committal shrug. After all, it's impolite to talk with your mouth full.

Egg Custard

Dolmas

Kaali Laatikko

Jansson's Temptation

Grandma's Paella

*Carribbean Red Snapper
with Funchi*

Prawn Tandoori

Beef Rouladen in Brown Sauce

Same-Day Sauerbraten

*Celestial Clouds Captured
on Earth Lake*

Singapore Noodles

Dragon Noodles

Dutch Crepes and Crêpe Cake

Danish Apple Cake

Jericalla

*Almost Better than
Ostakaka Bread Pudding*

Ostakaka

EGG CUSTARD

Serves 4

Although she's been making this custard for over 20 years, Norman Chan just asked his mother for this recipe. He says it is easy to make, especially for someone who doesn't feel he is much of a cook, such as Norman himself.

4 eggs
4 teaspoons sugar (depends on how sweet you want it)
2 bowls of milk or coconut milk (bowl is size of a rice bowl)

✤ In a large mixing bowl, beat eggs about 1 minute. Add sugar and beat again until fluffy, about 10 minutes. Add milk and beat until well blended. Pour mixture into four individual bowls. Take out the bubbles as much as you can by using a chopstick or spoon.

✤ Fill steamer with water. Place bowls in the steamer and steam over medium heat for 5 minutes or until custard sticks to an inserted chopstick or spoon handle. Remove from heat and let cool about 5 minutes.

Per serving: 165 calories; 10.3g protein; 10.5g carbohydrates; 9.08g fat (4.09g saturated fat); 229mg cholesterol..

DOLMAS

Makes 4 dozen

Fran Hildebrand was baptized at Angsar Lutheran Church, now St. Francis Lutheran, in 1954. She first discovered dolmas on a trip to London in the 1960s. Unable to find a recipe when she returned to San Francisco, she created her own.

4 cups cooked rice
¼ cup olive oil
2 medium onions, chopped
1 pound ground lamb

Juice of 1 lemon
Salt and pepper to taste
1 8-ounce jar grape leaves
2 cups water

✤ In a large skillet or frying pan, heat olive oil over medium heat. Add and cook until onions are limp and golden. Add ground lamb to onions and cook until browned. Add lemon juice, salt and pepper to taste. Remove from heat and combine with cooked rice.

❖ Remove stems from grape leaves. Place about a tablespoon of lamb mixture on a grape leaf and roll up. Place filled leaves seam side down in a 9x13-inch baking pan. Repeat until all of the lamb mixture is used. Pour water over leaves and cover baking pan with aluminum foil.

❖ Preheat oven to 250°. Bake until leaves are dark green, checking occasionally to make sure leaves stay moist, about 2 hours. Add a little olive oil if leaves are dry. Refrigerate. Serve at room temperature.

Per serving: 62.9 calories; 2.99g protein; 5.73g carbohydrates; 3.06g fat (.929g saturated fat); 9.18mg cholesterol..

KAALI LAATIKKO (Cabbage Dish)   Serves 8

When Leona Lee and her mother visited Finland, their hostess served this at the evening meal with boiled potatoes and described it as a "Finnish peasant main dish." At one of our church suppers, we discovered that adding a pinch of nutmeg to the mixture really wakes up the flavor.

1 medium head cabbage, chopped	Salt and pepper to taste
¼ cup water	2 eggs
2 tablespoons butter	1½ cups whole milk
1 pound ground beef	Pinch of grated nutmeg (optional)

❖ Preheat oven to 350°. Lightly grease a 7x11-inch or 8-inch square baking dish.

❖ Cook chopped cabbage in water and butter until cabbage is soft, 8-10 minutes. Drain in colander.

❖ In a heavy skillet or frying pan over medium heat, brown beef. Season with salt and pepper. Remove grease. Add cabbage to beef and stir to combine. Place mixture in baking dish.

❖ In a small bowl, mix eggs, milk and nutmeg (optional) and pour over cabbage. Bake uncovered until hot and bubbly, about 30 minutes.

Per serving: 242 calories; 20.1g protein; 3.27g carbohydrates; 16.1g fat (7.23g saturated fat); 123mg cholesterol.

JANSSON'S TEMPTATION

Serves 6-8

Respected San Francisco food professional Ann Segerstrom tells us that Jansson's Temptation is found on every Swedish smorgasbord. Her grandfather immigrated from Sweden to the United States at the turn of the century and to her knowledge this wonderful potato dish was never served at his California table. Ann's introduction to this memorable experience came much later at a Swedish friend's gracious and laden table. To American palates the recipe will sound exotic and strange, but don't be fooled—it tastes great. Swedish "anchovies" are actually Baltic herring, but if you can't find them use regular anchovies. The dish will still taste wonderful, if not totally authentic.

6 medium Russet potatoes, sliced into matchstick thin strips
3 medium yellow onions thinly sliced
3 tablespoons butter

15 Swedish anchovy fillets
1½ cup half-and-half or milk
Salt and pepper to taste
Finely chopped fresh dill

✤ Preheat oven to 350°. Grease or butter an oven proof casserole.

✤ In a small skillet or frying pan, melt butter over medium heat. Add onions and cook until limp and golden.

✤ In the baking dish, alternately layer the potatoes, onions and anchovy fillets, ending with a layer of potatoes.

✤ In a small bowl, season the cream with salt and pepper. Stir in chopped dill and pour liquid over the potatoes and onions to cover. Bake until potatoes are soft, about 50 minutes. Serve warm.

Per serving: 342 calories; 5.77g protein; 28.3g carbohydrates; 23.6g fat (14.3g saturated fat); 86mg cholesterol.

Before joining St. Francis Lutheran I attended virtually every other Lutheran church in San Francisco. More than any other church, St. Francis reaches out to its surrounding community and connects to key issues facing our society. Of our regular activities, the sacraments and preaching are important, but most of all I enjoy Pastor Hiller's Bible study class. Learning and intellectual stimulation are central concerns for me, and Michael artfully ties our meandering class comments with his own impressive knowledge of Judaism and early Christianity.

Werner Bachmann, 58, is a retired foreign language and English teacher. He began teaching in the San Francisco public schools in 1965 and loves to travel, which he often does with friends from St. Francis.

GRANDMA'S PAELLA

Serves 8-10

Jeannette Ferrary, who writes for "The New York Times" and "The San Francisco Chronicle," offers her Gibraltarian grandmother DeeTee's recipe for paella, although DeeTee never called it anything so fancy as that. In fact, she never used anything so fancy as a recipe, but Jeannette's food memory lingers and is reproduced, at least in spirit, by her granddaughter's earnest attempt.

1 pound spicy sausage
3-6 tablespoons olive oil
3 whole boneless chicken
    breasts, cut into
    2-inch pieces
1 onion, chopped
4 garlic cloves, minced
½ teaspoon saffron
    (not optional)
½ teaspoon ground
    coriander
1 teaspoon thyme
2 tablespoons chopped
    parsley
2 cups long grain rice,
    uncooked

3 cups chicken broth,
    homemade or canned
½ cup white wine
1 cup chopped tomatoes,
    fresh or canned,
1 red pepper,
    seeded and chopped
1 package frozen
    artichoke hearts
1 cup peas, fresh or frozen
1 pound shrimp, shelled
    and deveined
2 dozen mussels or
    clams

✤ In large frying pan or paella pan over medium-high heat, brown sausages in olive oil, about 15 minutes. Add chicken and cook for 5 minutes, stirring occasionally. Remove chicken and reserve. Cut sausage into 1-inch lengths and return to pan, adding more oil if necessary.

✤ Add onion and garlic and continue to cook, stirring until onion is softened, about 5 minutes. Stir in herbs, spices and rice. When rice is coated, add broth, wine, tomatoes, peppers, artichokes and peas. Bring to a boil and simmer, stirring occasionally, until rice is cooked, 20-30 minutes.

✤ Add shrimp and clams. Cook until shrimp turns pink and clams open, about 5 minutes. Serve promptly.

Per serving: 456 calories; 36.8g protein; 39.8g carbohydrates; 14.7g fat (3.61g saturated fat); 149mg cholesterol.

CARIBBEAN RED SNAPPER
with FUNCHI

Serves 4

Erna Dennert, who spent much of her youth in Curacao, tells us that funchi, a distant cousin of polenta, is served with most meals in the islands. Leftovers may be reheated and topped with sliced aged cheese such as Gouda.

8 thin small red snapper fillets
4 teaspoons Cajun blackened fish seasoning
3 tablepoons all-purpose flour
1-3 tablespoon butter
1 tablespoon olive oil
1 medium onion, chopped

3 medium tomatoes, chopped with juice
2 tablespoons chopped parsley
2 tablespoons white wine vinegar
1-2 dashes Tabasco sauce

✤ Rinse and dry fish fillets. Sprinkle with blackened fish seasoning and flour.

✤ In a large heavy skillet, melt 1-2 tablespoons butter in olive oil over medium heat. Cook the fillets until cooked through and crisp on the outside. Place on paper towels to drain.

✤ In the same skillet over medium heat, cook onions, about 5 minutes, adding more butter if necessary. Add tomatoes and mash with a fork. Add parsley, white wine vinegar and Tabasco sauce and simmer about 10 minutes, stirring once or twice. Sauce should be thick.

✤ Add fish to sauce and reheat over low heat.

FUNCHI:

2 cups water
1 teaspoon salt

1 cup cornmeal

✤ In a small saucepan over low heat, bring water and salt to a boil. Lower heat and add cornmeal all at once, stirring vigorously and pressing lumps against the sides of the pot until smooth. This process is called "haleren" in the local language of the islands (Aruba, Bonaire and Curacao). Cook about 5 minutes.

✣ Lightly moisten 2 plates with water. Scoop funchi onto one of them and cover with the other plate to form a flat cake. Before cutting into pie-shaped pieces, bless the funchi by making a cross with a knife on the top.

Per serving: 649 calories; 93.3g protein; 33.2g carbohydrates; 14g fat (2.37g saturated fat); 161mg cholesterol.

PRAWN TANDOORI   Serves 4

Inspired by the ancient cuisine of Indian kings and queens, this dish from Appam Restaurant's owner-chef Irene Trias bursts with exotic flavors, yet it is light, refreshing and very kind to the heart.

1½ pounds fresh prawns, rinsed, peeled and deveined	2 tablespoons fresh minced ginger
1 cup plain lowfat yogurt	1 tablespoon olive oil (optional)
¼ cup fresh lemon juice	1 tablespoon turmeric
6 whole green cardamom, crushed	2 teaspoons paprika
2 tablespoons freshly minced garlic	¼ teaspoon crushed red pepper flakes (optional)
	Salt to taste

✣ Place prawns in a shallow baking dish.

✣ In a large bowl, mix remaining ingredients together. Pour half the sauce mixture over the prawns, completely coating them. Marinate in refrigerator at least one hour.

✣ Grill prawns over hot coals or on a wire rack in a baking pan in preheated 350° oven until they turn pink, about 5 minutes on each side. Brush the remaining sauce mixture onto the prawns as they cook. Serve promptly.

Per serving: 250 calories; 39.1g protein; 7.56g carbohydrates; 6.39g fat (1.6g saturated fat); 335mg cholesterol.

BEEF ROULADEN in BROWN SAUCE

Serves 10

This hearty German favorite comes to us from Buddy Murphy of Virginia Beach, Virginia.

2½ pounds bottom or
   top round steak
½ pound bacon, chopped
¼ pound smoked ham,
   chopped
¼ pound ground beef
1 small onion, chopped
2 eggs, lightly beaten

1 cup bread crumbs
1 tablespoon chopped
   parsley
Thin pickle strips
¾ cup all-purpose flour
Salt and pepper to taste
1 cup vegetable oil, divided
2 8-ounce cans beef broth

✤ Preheat oven to 350°. Slice beef into ¼-inch thick pieces and flatten with a meat mallet.

✤ In a small bowl, combine bacon, ham, ground beef, onions, eggs, bread crumbs and parsley. Mix well.

✤ Put 1 tablespoon filling and 1 pickle strip on each piece of meat. Roll up the meat and secure with toothpicks. Dredge rolls in ¼ cup flour seasoned with salt and pepper.

✤ In a large skillet or frying pan, heat ½ cup vegetable oil over medium-high heat. Brown on all sides in hot oil and place in 9x13-inch baking dish.

✤ In a large saucepan, mix together beef broth, ½ cup flour and ½ cup oil and bring to a boil over medium heat. Pour over beef rolls. Cover tightly and cook until tender, about 1½ hours, turning rolls over once. Strain sauce and serve over rouladen.

✤ Note: Sauce may also be flavored with dry red wine and garlic.

Per serving: 501 calories; 48.7g protein; 11.2g carbohydrates; 27.8g fat (6.87g saturated fat); 166mg cholesterol.

SAME-DAY SAUERBRATEN

Serves 8

This recipe was given to Joyce Soules by her mother Elda Schueller, who lives in Ohio.

4-5 pound pot roast
1¾ cup water, divided
¾ cup malt vinegar
2 teaspoons salt
3 tablespoons brown sugar
⅛ teaspoon cloves

⅛ teaspoon ground allspice
1 teaspoon ground ginger
1 bay leaf
½ teaspoon pepper
¾ cup chopped onion

✤ In a heavy skillet or frying pan, brown meat. Remove meat from skillet and place meat on a rack in a large roasting pan. Add ¾ cup water, cover and simmer over low heat for 1 hour. Remove meat from liquid and cut into thin slices. Return to skillet.

✤ In a small saucepan, place 1 cup water, malt vinagar, salt, brown sugar, cloves, allspice, ginger, bayleaf and pepper and bring to a boil over medium-high heat. Pour over meat. Cover and simmer until meat is tender, about 1½ hours, adding more water if necessary. Serve with potato pancakes and gravy.

Per serving: 642 calories; 65.6g protein; 5.62g carbohydrates; 38.4g fat (14.5g saturated fat); 218mg cholesterol.

CELESTIAL CLOUDS
CAPTURED on EARTH LAKE

Serves 4-6

Wai-Ching Lee, born and raised in Singapore, serves this beautiful dish by spooning a little sauce on individual dishes (Earth Lake) and arranging a filled mushroom cap (Celestial Clouds) on the thin lake of sauce. Garnish with your choice of chives, onions, garlic, finely shredded green onions, sprigs of herbs, any edible unsprayed flowers, or deep-fried golden ginger shreds.

FILLING:

3 fresh or dried Shiitake
  mushrooms per person
3 ounces soft bean curd
  (tofu)
¼ teaspoon dark toasted
  sesame oil, preferably
  Japanese

1 teaspoon finely sliced
  green onions, chives or
  any other herb for
  East-West flavor
Pinch of sea salt or
  herb salt

SAUCE:

¼ cup water
4 slices tender ginger,
  thinly sliced and
  shredded
¼ teaspoon soy sauce

¼ teaspoon honey
¼ teaspoon sherry
  or dry white wine
¼ teaspoon corn flour

❖ Clean fresh shiitake caps and remove stalks. If using dried shiitake, soak in hot water for 10 minutes. Squeeze dry gently and cut off stalks.

❖ In a small bowl, mash tofu. Add sesame oil, green onions, chives or other herbs and salt. Adjust flavor to personal taste.

❖ Prepare steamer. Bring water to a boil. Add mushrooms and steam until tender. Gloss over mushroom caps with a touch of sesame oil. Dust the insides with corn-flour. Fill caps with tofu filling, making sure some mushroom shows through. Steam for 5 minutes on a plate.

❖ To make sauce, bring water to a boil in a small saucepan over medium-high heat. Reduce heat, add ginger slices, soy sauce, honey and sherry or wine and simmer until ready to serve.

✤ In a small bowl, mix corn flour and a little water or broth together. Add to sauce, stirring until translucent and thickened. Spoon a little sauce on individual plates and arrange a filled mushroom cap on top. Serve promptly.

Per serving: 55.4 calories; 2.86g protein; 9.63g carbohydrates; 1.43g fat (.219g saturated fat); 0mg cholesterol.

SINGAPORE NOODLES

Serves 5-6

"This is one of the most popular items on our menu," says Michelle Sampson, executive chef of Silks Restaurant in the beautiful Mandarin Oriental Hotel in San Francisco.

12 ounces udon or rice noodles	½ cup yellow bell pepper chopped
1-2 tablespoons sesame oil	¼ cup soy sauce
1 tablespoon minced garlic	½ cup chicken stock
1 tablespoon minced ginger	½ cup green onions, chopped
1 jalapeno, minced	2 ounces Chinese sausage, diced into ¼-inch pieces
1 tablespoon curry powder	Salt and pepper to taste
½ cup red bell pepper chopped	

✤ In a large pot of unsalted boiling water, cook noodles until tender, about 3 minutes. Drain.

✤ In a large skillet or frying pan, heat sesame oil over medium heat. Add garlic, ginger, jalapeno, curry powder and bell peppers and cook for 2-3 minutes. Add noodles and toss to combine. Add soy sauce, chicken stock, green onions and Chinese sausage and toss to combine. Add salt and pepper to taste. Serve promptly.

Per serving: 217 calories; 3.26g protein; 14.8g carbohydrates; 16.6g fat (3g saturated fat); 7.18mg cholesterol.

We chose to join St. Francis Lutheran in order be in a church where we can actually work on social issues rather than argue with people over whether we can even deal with the issues—much less work on them—for the sake of bringing about justice. Specific concerns like the gay/lesbian question are far from my Texas Methodist roots, and I suppose my ancestors might turn over in their graves over them. At the same time, my motivation toward dealing with such issues is very close to those same Texas Methodist roots.

I am also here to say that after over thirty-five years as a pastor's spouse, I like having a "non-husband" pastor.

Marti Lundin is a retired educator, devoted grandmother and extraordinary cook. She and her husband, Jack, live in Sonoma, California.

DRAGON NOODLES

Serves 3-4

Barbara Tropp, owner-chef of China Moon in San Francisco and cookbook author, dedicates this recipe to her dear friend Jean Ives Le Ferre who was the "talented dragon" that gave us our China Moon. A great spicy cold noodle dish, served on its own or alongside fish, poultry or grilled steak, this recipe first appeared in "The China Moon Cookbook," published by Workman in 1992.

1 pound very thin Chinese or Italian egg noodles
¼ cup black soy sauce
¼ cup unseasoned Japanese rice vinegar
2½ tablespoons fresh lemon juice
¼ cup hot chili oil or China Moon chili-lemon oil
¼ cup plus 1 tablespoon sugar
1 teaspoon kosher salt
Grated peel of 1 lemon
½ cup thinly sliced green and white onion rings, divided
2 tablespoons toasted black sesame seeds (optional)

✤ Fluff the noodles to separate the strands. Cook in a large pot of unsalted boiling water until tender, about 3 minutes. Drain and immediately plunge into ice water to chill. Drain again. Spread the noodles in a large shallow bowl.

✤ In a small bowl, combine soy sauce, rice vinegar, lemon juice, hot chili oil, sugar and salt, whisking to blend. Add to noodles. Grate the lemon evenly on top and toss to mix. Let the noodles stand for 10 minutes, then toss again. Sprinkle in most of the scallion rings and sesame seeds and toss again. Serve on plates of contrasting color, garnished with the remaining green onion and sesame seeds (optional).

Per serving: 338 calories; 6.6g protein; 45g carbohydrates; 15.3g fat (2.3g saturated fat); 37.4mg cholesterol.

DUTCH CRÉPES and
DUTCH CRÉPE CAKE

Serves 14-16

Erna Dennert enjoys making these delicious crépes. Ask her nicely and she might make the Dutch Crépe Cake for special occasions.

½ cup plus 2 tablespoons all-purpose flour	2 cups milk

½ teaspoon salt	4 tablespoons (½ stick)
	    butter or more
	    as needed

2-3 eggs, slightly beaten	

✤ In a medium bowl, mix flour and salt together. Add eggs and mix to blend. Add the milk a little at a time, stirring constantly to combine until batter is smooth.

✤ In a small crépe pan or small frying pan, melt 1 tablespoon of butter over medium heat. Add a thin layer of batter, swirling pan to cover bottom. Immediately lower heat. When top of crépe is dry, turn it over and lightly brown other side. Crépes cook very fast. Remove crépes to a heated plate and repeat with remaining batter. To serve, sprinkle liberally with sugar, roll up and serve.

✤ To make a Dutch Crépe Cake, place a crépe on a heated plate larger than the crépes. Spread liberally with your choice of preserves, syrup, custard, chocolate custard, fruit compote or brown sugar. Top with another crépe and spread with same filling. Repeat until all crépes are used. Sprinkle powdered sugar on top. Serve in wedges at room temperature or cold.

Per serving: 67.6 calories; 2.22g protein; 4.48g carbohydrates; 4.56g fat (2.63g saturated fat); 38.4mg cholesterol.

establishment readily admits it has nothing to offer and won't have for several years, that hope becomes very elusive.

So, where do I find this hope? I find some hope from my community of friends, especially here at St. Francis Lutheran, where I draw a lot of strength and support. I also find some hope from my family, especially the adoring love of my niece and my nephews. I find a great deal of hope from my lover, Bob. The love he has for me can always strengthen my hope. But my greatest source of hope is my religious faith. The beautiful images that many of the stories bring to mind are often a source of both strength and hope. Like Harvey Milk said, "Even hope that can be hard to find is not just an important thing, it's everything."

Michael Johnson, from a faith talk given in front of the St. Francis Lutheran congregation on October 10, 1993, about four months before he died of AIDS at age 31.

DANISH APPLE CAKE

Serves 8-10

This refreshing dessert from Kirsten Havrehed was a big hit at one of our St. Francis Lutheran recipe-testing potlucks. This is a traditional Danish Christmas Eve dessert, but the Danes eat it anytime—so will you!

10-12 medium apples, peeled, cored and diced into ¼-inch pieces	2 cups crushed zwieback or graham cracker crumbs
½ cup water	1 teaspoon ground cinnamon
1½ cups sugar, divided	1 pint heavy (whipping) cream, whipped (garnish)
2 teaspoons vanilla	
½ cup (1 stick) butter	

✤ In a heavy saucepan, cover apples with water. Stir in ½ cup sugar and vanilla. Cover and simmer until apples are translucent. Apples should remain chunky so it is best not to stir. With lid held tightly, shake saucepan occasionally to keep apples from sticking.

✤ In a heavy skillet or frying pan, place 1 cup sugar, crumbs and cinnamon. Stir with wooden spoon to keep from burning. When crumbs are lightly browned, remove from heat using a slotted spoon for apples, layer crumbs and apples alternately in a large glass bowl so that the layers will be visible when served. Finish with a layer of crumbs.

✤ Refrigerate. Serve cold with whipped cream.

Per serving: 470 calories; 2.69g protein; 85g carbohydrates; 14.8g fat (7.85g saturated fat); 35.9mg cholesterol.

JERICALLA (pronounced hair-e-hy-ya)   Serves 8

Alejandro Cejudo tells us this version of the traditional Mexican dessert flan originated in the Mexican state of Jalisco. It is generally lighter and creamier than flan and has a very refined taste with just a hint of cinnamon and vanilla.

4 cups whole milk
1 14-ounce can sweetened
    condensed milk
1 12-ounce can
    evaporated milk
1 teaspoon vanilla

1 cinnamon stick
6 egg yolks, beaten
Fresh fruit (garnish)
Splash of brandy
    (optional)

✤ Preheat oven to 350°.

✤ In a large saucepan or stock pot, combine all three milks, vanilla and cinnamon stick. Slowly bring to a boil over medium heat, being careful not to burn. Gently boil for 30 minutes, stirring constantly. Remove from heat and cool.

✤ Once mixture has cooled, whisk in beaten egg yolks. Divide among 8 heat-resistant dessert dishes or ramekins. Place dessert dishes or ramekins in one or two pans filled about 1 inch of hot water. Bake until a toothpick inserted in center comes out clean and tops are lightly browned, about 45 minutes.

✤ Refrigerate for 2 hours. Unmold on small plates and serve with seasonal fruit garnish, such as strawberries or blueberries, or make a fruit sauce in a food processor or blender by pureeing fresh fruit with a splash of brandy.

Per serving: 218 calories; 9.24g protein; 20g carbohydrates; 11.4g fat (5.88g saturated fat); 189mg cholesterol.

ALMOST BETTER than OSTAKAKA BREAD PUDDING

Serves 6-8

Max Kirkeberg's mother got this recipe from her sister-in-law, Mindy, who was living in Boston at the time. Max guesses that makes this a New England bread pudding. Unlike ostakaka, this is super easy to make, or so Max is told. (Check out Michael Utech's recipe for ostakaka on the next page and decide for yourself!)

4 cups milk (not lowfat)	½ cup sugar
2 cups white bread, torn into 2-inch squares (crusts on or removed)	½ teaspoon salt
	½ teaspoon vanilla
	1 tablespoon butter, melted
2 eggs, lightly beaten	half-and-half

✤ Preheat oven to 300°.

✤ In a small saucepan, heat milk just until it begins to boil. Pour the milk into an 8-inch square baking dish. Add bread and mix together until well coated. Add eggs, sugar, salt and vanilla and stir until well blended. You may be tempted to add more bread, but don't. Pour the butter on top. Bake until a knife is inserted into the pudding and comes out clean, about 1½ hours.

✤ Serve warm or cold with half-and-half.

Per serving: 200 calories; 7.43g protein; 29.1g carbohydrates; 6g fat (3.08g saturated fat); 70.2mg cholesterol.

I grew up in Mexico in a Catholic family. When I came to this country, it was a big change in language and culture—in everything. In addition, when we found St. Francis I had a different idea of what "Lutheran" meant. What I have found here is a unique way to be religious. We have different races, ethnic backgrounds, and cultures; we have straight people and gay people. But though we may be diverse, we're all just people.

Alejandro Cejudo, 36, is a financial services officer at Bank of America. He and his partner of almost ten years, Michael Utech, live in San Francisco's Potrero Hill neighborhood.

OSTAKAKA

This recipe has been served during the holidays for several generations by Michael Utech's Swedish ancestors and family in Kansas. Michael's mother and aunt insist on using whole unpasteurized milk for the best flavor. This delicious dessert was part of the baptism celebration for Michael's brand-new namesake and godson on November 20, 1994. Rennet is a key ingredient in this recipe, making the milk curdle and separating the curds from the whey. Rennet can be found in Scandinavian food shops, cheese stores or in the specialty section of some supermarkets.

4 quarts whole milk	¾ cup sugar
¾ cup flour	½ teaspoon salt
2-3 tablespoons water	1½ cups heavy (whipping)
½ cake Rennet (or 1 teaspoon Liquid Rennet)	cream
	1 teaspoon vanilla
3 eggs	Lingonberries (optional)

✤ In a large saucepan over medium heat, heat milk to lukewarm. Make a smooth paste with flour and water. Add paste to milk mixture and stir to blend. Dissolve rennet in a little water and add to mixture, stirring to combine. Remove milk mixture from heat and let stand until set, 1-2 hours. You should be able to cut the mixture with a knife once it is properly set.

✤ Preheat oven to 350°.

✤ Place a cheesecloth in a colander. Pour mixture into colander and drain milk curds of all excess water.

✤ In a separate bowl, beat eggs until light. Add sugar, salt, cream and vanilla, stirring until well blended. Add well-drained milk curds and mix thoroughly. Transfer to a 9x13-inch baking dish and bake until lightly browned, about 1 hour. Let rest at least 10 minutes. Serve slightly warm topped with Lingonberries, if desired.

Per serving: 373 calories; 8.48g protein; 35g carbohydrates; 22.6g fat (13.4g saturated fat); 157mg cholesterol.

and it is in dying that we are born to eternal life.

EPILOGUE

The Bible not only gives us food for thought but a lot of food stories. In the creation story, Adam and Even are given a garden where food is plentiful. Passover, one of the major religious events of Judaism, even provides recipes. A mysterious food called manna is provided for Israel's journey in the wilderness and the prophets offer metaphors about feasts that never end. Jesus fed 5,000 people, called himself the Bread of Life, and asked us to remember him with a meal of bread and wine.

Today, Christians all over the world gather regularly in their homes and in their churches to share food, tell stories of faith and, with bread and wine, remember Jesus who came from God, lived, died and rose again. St. Francis Lutheran Church is one of those gathering places.

We are an old church, but not just any old church. As these stories of food and faith tell, a number of people have gathered at St. Francis Lutheran who have been pushed aside by the church simply for being who they are. At St. Francis Lutheran, gay and lesbian children of God have reclaimed their faith and their rightful place in Christ's church. Others, like myself, have gathered here not only to walk with them, but to follow Christ on a journey of faith where God's grace is ever present. Together, we have learned and are learning what it means to be Christian in this generation. On this journey, we have had to deal with an epidemic called AIDS that has brought us untold suffering and many deaths, with disciplinary suspension by our denomination, and with a major earthquake. Along the way, we have met people who have thrown us flowers instead of brickbats and who have sent us their money as well as their prayers. Through it all, we have discovered God's gift of community to be quite precious and that the church is much larger than ourselves. We like to think we are different from other congregations, but we know we are not that different. Like churches everywhere, we gather to worship God, to study and pray, to do good work, and to enjoy each other's friends—and food.

We try to be what someone has called "the church that oughta be"—a church that makes a difference in the lives of individuals, in the whole church and in the world. I'm not sure we always succeed, but we keep on trying. However, we are not that only church that is trying. In many places, God gathers people to be "the church that oughta be." If you haven't found such a church, we hope you will look for one. It will cost you some time and you might have to suspend some disbelief, but I don't think you will leave hungry.

Several years ago, a young man, 22 years old, appeared on our doorstep with all of his possessions compressed into a very large backpack. His family had thrown him out when he told them he was gay. He had flown to San Francisco on a whim and heard about our church from a stranger while standing in a bank teller's line. Thus began a long story of coming out, of rage and of dangerous behavior. Through it all, he stayed connected with our church. Last year, this young man died. Still unreconciled with his parents, St. Francis Lutheran was the only family he had. We were honored to be here for him.

James De Lange

The Rev. James DeLange
Senior Pastor
November, 1994

COVER PORTRAITS:

Clockwise from upper left: John Brown; Peter Quam;
Airen, Jay and Claire Franz; Valerie Wagner and John Crimaldi;
Faye Robinson; Michael Hiller and Arthur Morris; Jack and
Barbara Kling; Betty Kretzmann; Jonathan Olow and Rand Allen;
Beverly Hines and David Cornuelle; Jeannine Janson and Joyce Soules;
Joy Noelle Hart.

BACK COVER PORTRAITS:

First row, left to right: Debbie Côté and Kerry Kelly; Matthew Bass
    and Rich Martin; Mari Irvin.
Second row, left to right: Wayne Strei; Jim Remer; Leland McCormick.
Third row, left to right: Erna Dennert, Michael Utech and Alejandro Cejudo;
    Barbara Genay.
Bottom row, left to right: Jim Kowalski and Bruce Jervis; Norman Chan;
    Marti and Jack Lundin; Meredith Karns.

To order additional copies of
*All Those People At That Church
Cookbook,* enclose check or money
order for:

$18.95 for each book
    ($23.95 Canadian)
$4.75 shipping and handling

California residents please add
applicable state sales tax.

Send to:

St. Francis Lutheran Church
152 Church Street
San Francisco, CA 94114-1111

To order by telephone with
MasterCard or Visa call:

415-621-1836 or 800-779-7179